Study Guide for
Modern Real Estate Practice

20th Edition

Fillmore W. Galaty, Wellington J. Allaway, and Robert C. Kyle

Martha R. Williams, JD, Contributing Editor

This publication is designed to provide accurate and authoritative information in regard to the subject matter covered. It is sold with the understanding that the publisher is not engaged in rendering legal, accounting, or other professional advice. If legal advice or other expert assistance is required, the services of a competent professional should be sought.

President: Dr. Andrew Temte
Executive Director, Real Estate Education: Melissa Kleeman-Moy
Development Editor: Jody Manderfeld

STUDY GUIDE FOR MODERN REAL ESTATE PRACTICE 20TH EDITION
©2018 Kaplan, Inc.
Published by DF Institute, Inc., d/b/a Dearborn Real Estate Education
332 Front St. S., Suite 501
La Crosse, WI 54601

Printed in the United States of America
Second revision, July 2019
ISBN: 978-1-4754-6374-3

CONTENTS

INTRODUCTION

Most students find their real estate principles class to be a challenging, rewarding, and traumatic experience, all at the same time. For some, mastering the jargon of the real estate industry can be as demanding as learning a foreign language. Students who have not attended classes or studied for exams for several years may find it difficult to get back into the habit—particularly when there are other demands on their time, and homework becomes another responsibility, among many. Because we are aware of the particular challenges facing today's real estate student, this *Study Guide* was written with your needs in mind.

ABOUT THIS BOOK

This *Study Guide* was developed as a companion to *Modern Real Estate Practice 20th Edition*. It can also be used with these textbooks (a chapter/unit correlation table is located on the inside front cover):

- *Mastering Real Estate Principles*
- *Real Estate Fundamentals*
- *Modern Real Estate Practice* (state-specific)
- *Practice & Law* (state-specific)

The *Study Guide* is designed to reinforce and elaborate on the basic information provided in your main textbook. Specifically, it is designed to help you master these three fundamental goals, which are vital to academic success:

1. **Recognize** important terms and concepts
2. **Evaluate** your understanding of basic real estate issues
3. **Apply** learned principles to real-world practice

These goals form the basis of the *Study Guide* learning objectives, which are to

- **define and explain** fundamental concepts and vocabulary terms of the real estate industry;
- **identify and discuss** the characteristics of various legal and financial relationships; and
- **perform and apply** basic financial and property-related calculations.

While the real estate examination is exclusively a multiple-choice format, this *Study Guide* uses several different learning strategies. These styles of self-testing have proven to be effective in helping students move from memorizing factual information, to retaining the material. By working through the components of each unit, you will reinforce your real estate knowledge, as well as improve your test-taking skills.

ACKNOWLEDGMENTS

We would like to specially acknowledge contributing editor Martha R. Williams for her work on this edition. Martha received her juris doctor from the University of Texas, is an author and educator, and has practiced law in Texas and California. She is author or coauthor of *Fundamentals of Real Estate Appraisal, The Art of Real Estate Appraisal, How to Use the Uniform Residential Appraisal Report, California Mortgage Loan Brokerage, California Real Estate Principles*, other textbooks, and numerous electronic courses.

HOW TO USE THIS *STUDY GUIDE*

Each unit consists of three primary sections: unit-specific learning objectives, a number of questions in varying formats, and an answer key.

LEARNING OBJECTIVES

Each unit begins with a series of learning objectives that are identical to the ones found in *Modern Real Estate Practice 20th Edition*. If you are familiar with the material in the learning objectives, then you are ready to move forward in that unit of the *Study Guide*.

QUESTIONS

Each unit includes some or all of these types of questions or problems:

Matching

Each unit lists the key terms found in *Modern Real Estate Practice, 20th Edition*. Test yourself to see how many of the key terms and other important real estate terms you can match to the correct definition. Note that some key terms might not be used.

True or false

You are presented with a series of statements based on material in the main text. It is important to read each statement closely and to clearly understand what you have read. Sometimes, just one word changes the statement from being true to false.

Multiple choice

This section prepares you for the format and structure of the licensing exam. It may help to recognize that each multiple-choice question is actually four true or false statements. The possible answers consist of three false statements and one true statement.

Fill-in-the-blank

This section format re-emphasizes key terms and concepts. Insert the term that best completes the sentence from the list provided. Note that some key terms will not be used.

Math practice

Before starting to work a math problem, carefully read the entire question. Separate the irrelevant facts or numbers from the information needed to perform the calculations. For example, if a question asks you to calculate a broker's commission on a sale, you can disregard information about the asking price or mortgage. You should be able to answer a question based only on the facts given; make sure that you know exactly what you are being asked to do.

Activity

Each activity is different; follow the instructions included with each activity to complete it.

ANSWER KEY

Each unit includes an answer key so that you can immediately check your comprehension of that unit's content. Many entries in the answer key include rationales, which are brief explanations of the answers. Multiple choice and true or false questions have page references to the source material in *Modern Real Estate Practice 20th Edition*.

UNIT 1

Introduction to the Real Estate Business

LEARNING OBJECTIVES

When you have completed this unit, you will be able to

> **list** the various careers available in the real estate industry;
> **describe** the different classifications and characteristics of real property and the types of housing available for purchase or rental;
> **explain** the factors of supply and demand in the real estate market; and
> **identify** the advantages and disadvantages of investing in real estate.

KEY TERMS

associate licensee	equity buildup	market
appreciation	exchanges	real estate licensee
broker	fair housing	sales associate
capital gain	leverage	salesperson
depreciation	liquidity	supply and demand

MATCHING

Write the letter of the matching term on the appropriate line.

A. home inspection

B. salesperson (sales associate)

C. appraisal

D. market

E. brokerage

F. immobility

G. leverage

H. uniqueness

I. condominium

J. property management

1. ___ When goods are bought and sold and a price for the goods is established there is this

2. ___ Even if two parcels appear identical, they are never exactly alike because of this quality

3. ___ Person who performs real estate activities while employed by, or associated with, a licensed real estate broker

4. ___ An owner of this type of housing owns an individual unit and also shares ownership of common facilities

5. ___ Maintaining and administering another's property for a fee

6. ___ Process of using established methods and good judgment to form an opinion of the value of a property

7. ___ The bringing together of parties interested in making a real estate transaction

8. ___ The property of real estate that refers to the fact that property cannot be relocated elsewhere

9. ___ Report based on visual survey of property structure, systems, and site conditions

10. ___ Use of a relatively small amount of initial capital to finance the purchase of real estate

TRUE OR FALSE

Circle the correct answer.

1. The six classes of real estate mentioned in the course are residential, commercial, rental, agricultural, mixed-use, and special purpose.
   A. True
   B. False

2. The real estate market is generally slow to adjust to the changing forces of supply and demand.
   A. True
   B. False

3. The supply of labor and the cost of construction generally have a direct effect on the demand for real estate in a market.
   A. True
   B. False

4. Real estate professionals generally tend to specialize in one activity or class of real estate.
   A. True
   B. False

5. Warehouses, factories, and power plants are examples of commercial property.
   A. True
   B. False

6. The amount invested in a property is the owner's debt.
   A. True
   B. False

7. In general, the most widely recognized real estate activity is brokerage.
   A. True
   B. False

8. Finding funds to put together real estate transactions is called appraising.
   A. True
   B. False

9. Market trends in supply and demand can be overturned by a natural disaster, such as a hurricane or earthquake.
   A. True
   B. False

10. Demand for real estate usually drops when jobs are scarce.
    A. True
    B. False

MULTIPLE CHOICE

Circle the correct answer.

1. Office buildings and retail space are examples of
    A. commercial real estate.
    B. special-use real estate.
    C. residential property.
    D. industrial property.

2. If payments on a real estate loan include payment of part of the principal owed, the property owner will benefit from
    A. supply and demand.
    B. liquidity.
    C. equity buildup.
    D. depreciation.

3. All of these factors will tend to affect demand for real estate *EXCEPT*
    A. construction and material costs.
    B. employment levels.
    C. wage rates.
    D. demographics.

4. When the population of a town suddenly increases, which of these is *MOST likely* to occur?
    A. Rental rates will fall due to increased competition
    B. Demand for housing will decrease
    C. New housing starts will decrease
    D. Real estate prices will increase

5. Property management, appraisal, financing, and development are all
    A. specializations directly linked to state and federal government financial policies.
    B. separate professions within the real estate industry.
    C. real estate brokerage professions.
    D. demographic factors that affect demand for real property in a commercial market.

6. The idea that no two parcels of land are exactly alike is called
    A. immobility.
    B. subdivision.
    C. uniqueness.
    D. location.

7. All of these factors can affect the supply of real estate *EXCEPT*
    A. demographics.
    B. labor force.
    C. construction costs.
    D. government controls.

8. A property owner who does not want to deal with the everyday tasks of managing a rental property can hire
    A. a property manager.
    B. an appraiser.
    C. a transactional broker.
    D. a property attorney.

9. When the supply of a certain commodity decreases while demand remains the same, the price of that commodity will tend to
    A. remain the same.
    B. increase.
    C. decrease slightly.
    D. decrease significantly.

10. All of these are examples of government policies that can affect the real estate market *EXCEPT*
    A. the Federal Reserve Board's discount rate.
    B. a shortage of skilled labor or building materials.
    C. land-use controls, such as zoning.
    D. federal environmental regulations.

FILL-IN-THE-BLANK

Select the word or words that best complete these statements:

appraiser

appreciation

continuing education

demographic

go down

go up

industrial

licensing

remain the same

residential

salesperson (sales associate)

subdivision

tax deduction

valuation

1. A person who conducts activities on behalf of a broker is called a(n) _____.

2. Appraisers must have detailed knowledge of the methods of property _____.

3. Real estate professionals keep their skills and knowledge current by obtaining _____.

4. A single-family home is a type of _____ property.

5. If the supply of single-family homes goes up and a major local employer lays off a large number of workers, the price of real estate tends to _____.

6. The splitting of a single piece of property into smaller parcels is called _____.

7. *Niche marketing* refers to the targeted marketing of specific _____ populations.

8. A _____ for mortgage interest payments is a benefit of home ownership.

9. A community implements land-use restrictions so that less vacant land is available for residential development. At the same time, demand for housing increases due to higher population. Prices for real estate will tend to _____.

10. Both homeowners and investors who own real estate hope to benefit from future property _____.

UNIT 1 ANSWERS

MATCHING

1. **D**
2. **H**
3. **B**
4. **I**
5. **J**
6. **C**
7. **E**
8. **F**
9. **A**
10. **G**

TRUE OR FALSE

1. **B** The answer is false. The six classes of real estate mentioned in the text are residential, commercial, mixed-use, industrial, agricultural, and special-purpose. Rental is *not* a class of real estate. (4)

2. **A** The answer is true. Because of real estate's uniqueness and immobility, the market generally adjusts slowly to the forces of supply and demand; development and construction are lengthy processes. (7)

3. **B** The answer is false. Supply of labor and the cost of construction generally have a direct effect on the supply of real estate in a market. (8–9)

4. **A** The answer is true. The real estate industry is complex, much more than brokers bringing together buyers and sellers, landlords and tenants. Other specialties include appraisal, property management, financing, education, and home inspection. (2–4)

5. **B** The answer is false. Warehouses, factories, and power plants are examples of *industrial* property. (4)

6. **B** The answer is false. The amount invested in a property is the owner's *equity*. (11)

7. **A** The answer is true. Although many people think that real estate is comprised of only brokers and their sales associates, many other specialties exist, including financing, appraising, education, and property management. (2–4)

8. **B** The answer is false. Finding funds involves *financing*; forming an opinion of the value of property is *appraising*. (2)

9. **A** The answer is true. Even when supply and demand can be forecast with some accuracy, natural disasters, such as hurricanes and earthquakes, can disrupt market trends; the market also can be affected by sudden changes in financial markets or business relocations. (7–9)

10. **A** The answer is true. When job opportunities are scarce or wage levels are low, demand for real estate usually drops; in fact, the market may be drastically affected by a single major employer moving in or shutting down. (7–9)

MULTIPLE CHOICE

1. **A** The answer is commercial real estate. Office buildings and retail space are examples of commercial real estate. Special use properties include churches and dormitories; industrial properties include warehouses and factories. (4)

2. **C** The answer is equity buildup. Equity buildup results from paying part of the principal of a loan each time the borrower makes a payment. Supply and demand establish the price of goods and services. Liquidity refers to the ease with which an asset can be converted to cash and depreciation is allowed to be taken in the form of tax deductions, to recover the cost of an income-producing investment. (11)

3. **A** The answer is construction and material costs. These affect the supply of real estate. Employment levels, wage rates, and demographics affect demand. (7–9)

4. **D** The answer is real estate prices will increase. With a sudden influx of residents, rental rates will increase, demand for housing will increase, and more new homes will be started to satisfy demand. (7–9)

5. **B** The answer is separate professions within the real estate industry. Property management, appraisal, financing, and development are not linked to the government; they are all linked to real estate business. (2–4)

6. **C** The answer is uniqueness. No matter how identical they may appear, no two parcels of real estate are ever exactly alike; each occupies its own unique geographic location. (7)

7. **A** The answer is demographics. Demographics affect the *demand* for real estate. The labor force, construction costs, and government controls affect the supply of real estate. (7–9)

8. **A** The answer is a property manager. A property manager handles the day-to-day tasks of managing property for an owner. An appraiser forms an opinion or property value, a home inspector examines the property and reports problems, and the developer improves the property. (2–4)

9. **B** The answer is increase. When consumers continue to demand a product for which there is limited supply, the price generally increases. (7–9)

10. **B** The answer is a shortage of skilled labor or building materials. A shortage of skilled labor will affect the supply of real estate, and this labor shortage is not generally associated with governmental policies. (7–9)

FILL-IN-THE BLANK

1. A person who conducts activities on behalf of a broker is called a *salesperson* or *sales associate*.

2. Appraisers must have detailed knowledge of the methods of property *valuation*.

3. Real estate professionals keep their skills and knowledge current by obtaining *continuing education*.

4. A single-family home is a type of *residential* property.

5. If the supply of single-family homes goes up and a major local employer lays off a large number of work-ers, the price of real estate tends to *go down*.

6. The splitting of a single piece of property into smaller parcels is called *subdivision*.

7. Niche marketing refers to the targeted marketing of specific *demographic* populations.

8. A *tax deduction* is a benefit of home ownership.

9. A community implements land-use restrictions so that less vacant land is available for residential development. At the same time, demand for housing increases due to higher population. Prices for real estate will tend to *go up*.

10. Both homeowners and investors who own real estate hope to benefit from future property *appreciation*.

UNIT 2

Real Property and the Law

LEARNING OBJECTIVES

When you have completed this unit, you will be able to

› **discuss** the concepts of land and ownership rights in real property;
› **distinguish** between real and personal property and the basic economic and physical characteristics of real property; and
› **discuss** the limitations of the real estate professional under the law.

KEY TERMS

accession	erosion	real property
accretion	fixture	riparian rights
air rights	improvement	severance
annexation	land	situs
appurtenance	littoral rights	subsurface rights
area preference	manufactured housing	surface rights
avulsion	nonhomogeneity	trade fixture
bundle of legal rights	personal property	water rights
chattel	prior appropriation	
emblements	real estate	

MATCHING

Write the letter of the matching term on the appropriate line.

A. accretion	
B. bundle of legal rights	
C. improvement	
D. surface rights	
E. emblements	
F. fixture	
G. subsurface rights	
H. riparian rights	
I. real property	
J. severance	
K. personal property	
L. water rights	
M. chattels	
N. trade fixture	
O. air rights	

1. ___ An article installed by a tenant under a commercial lease and removable before the lease expires

2. ___ Any property that is not real property

3. ___ Increases in the land resulting from the deposit of soil by the natural action of water

4. ___ Ownership of all legal rights to the land: control, possession, exclusion, enjoyment, and disposition

5. ___ The interests, benefits, and rights automatically included in the ownership of land and real estate

6. ___ The right to use the open space above the surface of a property

7. ___ Common law rights granted to owners of land along the course of a river, stream, or similar body of water

8. ___ Ownership rights in the water, minerals, gas, and oil that lie beneath a parcel of land

9. ___ Personal property that is converted to real property by being permanently attached to the real estate

10. ___ Any structure or modification erected or imposed on a site

11. ___ Changing an item of real estate to personal property by detaching it from the land

12. ___ Ownership rights excluding air or mineral rights

13. ___ Common law right of owners of land next to rivers, lakes, or oceans

14. ___ Another name for personal property

15. ___ Growing crops, such as corn or soybeans, that remain personal property

TRUE OR FALSE

Circle the correct answer.

1. The terms *land*, *real estate*, and *real property* are interchangeable and refer to the same thing.
   A. True
   B. False

2. Real property is defined as the earth's surface extending downward to the center of the earth and upward to infinity, including permanent natural objects, such as trees and water.
   A. True
   B. False

3. The term *real property* includes land, rights of ownership, and real estate.
   A. True
   B. False

4. The transfer of the right to use the surface of the earth always includes the right to the natural resources that lie beneath the surface of the earth.
   A. True
   B. False

5. Trees, perennial shrubbery, and grasses that do not require annual cultivation are considered personal property.
   A. True
   B. False

6. The process by which personal property becomes real property is called annexation.
   A. True
   B. False

7. A trade fixture is an article owned by a tenant and attached to a rented space or building used in conducting a business.
   A. True
   B. False

8. The economic characteristics of real estate are scarcity, improvements, permanence of investment, and uniqueness.
   A. True
   B. False

9. Immobility, indestructibility, and scarcity are physical characteristics of real property.
   A. True
   B. False

10. The image of a bundle of sticks is the traditional illustration of the set of legal rights of ownership.
    A. True
    B. False

11. When determining if an item is a fixture, you should consider the method of attachment to the property.
    A. True
    B. False

12. The economic characteristic of permanence of investment refers to the concept that the total supply of land is limited.
    A. True
    B. False

13. One of the rights of real property ownership is the right of enjoyment, or the right to use the property in any legal way.
    A. True
    B. False

14. A property's air rights extend upward into outer space.
    A. True
    B. False

15. Trade fixtures are typically excluded from a mortgage.
    A. True
    B. False

Unit 2

MULTIPLE CHOICE

Circle the correct answer.

1. Land rights, mineral rights, and air rights are included in the definition of
   A. attachments.
   B. real estate.
   C. littoral rights.
   D. improvements.

2. Which of these is an example of an economic characteristic of land?
   A. Immobility
   B. Indestructibility
   C. Uniqueness
   D. Scarcity

3. Another word for *uniqueness* is
   A. scarcity.
   B. nonhomogeneity.
   C. fructus industriales.
   D. immobility.

4. All of these are included in the bundle of rights *EXCEPT*
   A. possession.
   B. control.
   C. exclusion.
   D. expansion.

5. Owners with littoral rights enjoy
   A. unrestricted use of available waters, but they own the land adjacent to the water only up to the average high-water mark.
   B. the right of disposition.
   C. unrestricted use of the surface of the earth.
   D. unrestricted rights to the use of fixtures.

6. Growing trees, fences, and buildings are all considered
   A. chattels.
   B. land.
   C. fixtures.
   D. real estate.

7. The most important economic characteristic of land is
   A. permanence.
   B. location.
   C. uniqueness.
   D. possession.

8. The Law of the Sea identifies national territorial waters as those extending from a baseline up to
   A. 12 nautical miles.
   B. 15 nautical miles.
   C. 100 nautical miles.
   D. 200 nautical miles.

9. The developer added sewer lines and utilities and built two streets. What are these items called?
   A. Fixtures
   B. Additions
   C. Improvements
   D. Permanence of investment

10. The new owner of a condominium received the right to use a parking space in the multi-unit building. This right is an example of
    A. an improvement.
    B. a fixture.
    C. an appurtenance.
    D. a chattel.

11. Methods of annexation, adaptation of the item, and agreement of the parties are the legal tests for determining whether an item is
    A. a chattel or an emblement.
    B. real property or personal property.
    C. land or real estate.
    D. fructus naturales or fructus industriales.

12. An important distinction between real and personal property is that real property is transferred by
    A. a bill of sale.
    B. a purchase order.
    C. a receipt.
    D. a deed.

13. A seller asked a real estate professional to draw up several documents relating to seller financing. Under these circumstances, the real estate professional should
    A. ask the broker for assistance.
    B. draw up the documents.
    C. ignore the instructions.
    D. refer the seller to an attorney.

14. A buyer particularly liked the ornate brass lighting fixtures in a seller's house and immediately made an offer, which the seller accepted. On moving day, the buyer discovered that the seller had replaced all the ornate brass lighting fixtures with plain chrome ones. Which of these is *MOST* likely a correct assumption?
    A. Seller: "As long as I replaced the lighting fixtures with something of comparable value, I can take them with me."
    B. Buyer: "Lighting fixtures are normally considered to be real property."
    C. Seller: "The lighting fixtures were personal property when I bought them at the store, so they're personal property forever."
    D. Seller: "All the things that were in the house when I saw it should belong to me."

15. A rural landowner has posted a number of "No Trespassing" and "No Hunting" signs on his property. Which "stick" in the bundle of rights gives the landowner this authority?
    A. Exclusion
    B. Enjoyment
    C. Control
    D. Disposition

16. A right or privilege tied to real property, although not necessarily part of the property, is called
    A. an emblement.
    B. a trade fixture.
    C. an appurtenance.
    D. a deed.

17. An important characteristic of personal property is that it is
    A. small enough to be carried by a person.
    B. movable.
    C. alive.
    D. less than 100 years old.

18. *Manufactured housing* is the term used for a factory-built home as of
    A. 1976.
    B. 1980.
    C. 1987.
    D. 1990.

19. To determine whether an item is a fixture, the *MOST* important test is whether
    A. the effort needed to remove the item is significant.
    B. the item must be dismantled for removal.
    C. the value of the item is high.
    D. the person who installed it intended for it to be permanent.

20. A sales contract explicitly excludes some rose bushes from the sale. This provision is necessary because the rose bushes are ordinarily considered to be
    A. a trade fixture.
    B. personal property.
    C. an emblement.
    D. real estate.

ACTIVITY: REAL PROPERTY OR PERSONAL PROPERTY?

Mark the appropriate columns to indicate whether each item is real or personal property, and whether it is a fixture or a trade fixture (if applicable).

Property Description	Type of Property		Fixture	Trade Fixture
	Real	Personal		
1. Sidewalks and sewers in a subdivision				
2. Bushes surrounding a residence				
3. Wheat or corn crops on a farm				
4. Kitchen sink installed in a home				
5. Booths in a restaurant installed by tenant				
6. Curtains installed by a tenant				
7. Pumps installed by a gas station tenant				
8. Water well pump installed by the landowner				
9. Crystal chandelier hung from the ceiling				
10. An 80-gallon water heater with fiberglass insulating jacket				

UNIT 2 ANSWERS

MATCHING

1. **N**
2. **K**
3. **A**
4. **B**
5. **I**
6. **O**
7. **H**
8. **G**
9. **F**
10. **C**
11. **J**
12. **D**
13. **L**
14. **M**
15. **E**

TRUE OR FALSE

1. **B** The answer is false. Even though the terms *land*, *real estate*, and *real property* are used as if they are interchangeable, they refer to different aspects of ownership rights. (18)

2. **B** The answer is false. Land is defined as the earth's surface extending downward to the center of the earth and upward to infinity, including permanent natural objects, such as trees and water. Real property is defined as the interests, benefits, and rights that are considered part of the ownership of land and real estate. (18–19)

3. **A** The answer is true. The term *real property* is the broadest of all; it includes both land and real estate, as well as the interests, benefits, and rights that are automatically included in the ownership of land and real estate. (19)

4. **B** The answer is false. The transfer of the surface does not necessarily include subsurface rights, which are the natural resources that lie beneath the surface. An owner may transfer surface rights without transferring subsurface rights. (20–21)

5. **B** The answer is false. Trees, perennial shrubbery, and grasses that do not require annual cultivation are considered real estate. (25)

6. **A** The answer is true. It is possible to change personal property into real property through the process called annexation, such as mixing cement, stones, sand, and water (personal property) to create a sidewalk that is part of the real estate. (25)

7. **A** The answer is true. An article owned by a tenant and attached to a rented space and used in conducting a business is a trade fixture; it may be removed prior to the termination of the lease. (27)

8. **B** The answer is false. Economic characteristics of land include scarcity, improvements, permanence of investment, and *area preference*. (24)

9. **B** The answer is false. Physical characteristics of land include immobility, indestructibility, and *uniqueness*. (18–19)

10. **A** The answer is true. Because the rights of ownership (like sticks in a bundle) can be separated and individually transferred, the sticks are symbolic of those rights. (19–20)

11. **A** The answer is true. The same item may be treated as a fixture, and thus part of the real estate, depending on how it is attached. A window air conditioner that is easily removable is personal property, but the property's owner may still decide to include it in the property's sale. (26)

12. **B** The answer is false. *Permanence of investment* refers to the concept that the return on investment in real estate tends to be long-term and relatively stable. *Scarcity* refers to the concept that the total supply of land is limited. (24)

13. **A** The answer is true. Traditionally, ownership rights of real property include the right of possession, control, enjoyment, exclusion, and disposition. (19–20)

14. **B**   The answer is false. Property air rights began to be limited when air travel became common. Now, light and solar rights may limit air rights in certain areas. (21)

15. **A**   The answer is true. Because trade fixtures are considered personal property, they are not included in the sale or mortgage of real estate, except by special agreement. (27)

MULTIPLE CHOICE

1. **B**   The answer is real estate. Land, including subsurface and air rights, and improvements are included in the definition of real estate. (19)

2. **D**   The answer is scarcity. Immobility, indestructibility, and uniqueness are physical characteristics, while scarcity is an economic characteristic. (24)

3. **B**   The answer is nonhomogeneity. Uniqueness, or nonhomogeneity, indicates that no two parcels of land are alike. (19)

4. **D**   The answer is expansion. The bundle of rights includes possession, control, exclusion, enjoyment, and disposition. There is no right to expansion, except by acquiring another parcel. (19–20)

5. **A**   The answer is unrestricted use of available waters, but they own the land adjacent to the water only up to the average high-water mark. Owners of littoral rights enjoy unrestricted use of available waters, but own the land adjacent to the water only as far as the average high-water mark. (22–23)

6. **D**   The answer is real estate. The definition of real estate includes fences, buildings, and growing trees. Chattels are personal property. The definition of land would not include fences and buildings. (18–19)

7. **B**   The answer is location. Location is sometimes called *area preference* or *situs*. (24)

8. **A**   The answer is 12 nautical miles. The Law of the Sea identifies territorial waters as those extending up to 12 nautical miles from a baseline that is the mean low-water line of a coastal country. (23)

9. **C**   The answer is improvements. Permanent attachments are called *improvements*. (24)

10. **C**   The answer is an appurtenance. An *appurtenance* is a right or privilege associated with the property, although not necessarily a part of it; typical appurtenances include parking spaces in multiunit buildings, easements, water rights, and other improvements. (20)

11. **B**   The answer is real property or personal property. Whether an item is a fixture or personal property may be determined by method of annexation, adaptation to the real estate, or agreement of the parties. (26)

12. **D**   The answer is a deed. An important distinction between real and personal property is that real property is transferred by a deed and personal property is transferred by a bill of sale. (24)

13. **D**   The answer is refer the seller to an attorney. Real estate professionals should be careful not to practice law unless they are, in fact, licensed attorneys and are employed to act in that capacity. (27)

14. **B**   The answer is buyer: "Lighting fixtures are normally considered to be real property." The buyer is correct in assuming that lighting fixtures are normally part of the real property. If the seller had wanted to remove the fixtures, the seller should have done so before putting the house on the market, or specifically excluded them in the listing agreement. (26)

15. **A**   The answer is exclusion. A real estate owner has the inherent right to exclude others from the property, although this right is not absolute. An adjacent property owner may have an easement right to use the property. (19–20)

16. **C**   The answer is an appurtenance. An appurtenance is a right or privilege association with the property, although not necessarily a part of it. An *emblement* or trade fixture is a *tangible item* on the property. The *deed* is a document that transfers title. (20)

17. **B**   The answer is movable. Personal property is all the property than can be owned and that does not fit the definition of real property; the most important distinction between real and personal property is that personal property is moveable. (24)

18. **A**   The answer is 1976. With the passage of The National Manufactured Housing Construction and Safety Standards Act of 1976, manufactured homes became federally regulated. (25)

19. **D**   The answer is the person who installed it intended for it to be permanent. The intent of the person who installed the item is the most important test of whether the item is a fixture. (26)

20. **D**   The answer is real estate. Because the rose bushes are perennial shrubs, they are considered real estate. (25)

ACTIVITY: REAL PROPERTY OR PERSONAL PROPERTY?

Property Description	Type of Property			
	Real	Personal	Fixture	Trade Fixture
1. Sidewalks and sewers in a subdivision	✓			
2. Bushes surrounding a residence	✓			
3. Wheat or corn crops on a farm		✓		
4. Kitchen sink installed in a home	✓		✓	
5. Booths in a restaurant installed by tenant		✓		✓
6. Curtains installed by a tenant		✓		
7. Pumps installed by a gas station tenant		✓		✓
8. Water well pump installed by the landowner	✓		✓	
9. Crystal chandelier hung from the ceiling	✓		✓	
10. An 80-gallon water heater with fiberglass insulating jacket	✓		✓	

UNIT
3

Interests in Real Estate

LEARNING OBJECTIVES

When you have completed this unit, you will be able to

> **identify** the various types of estates;
> **explain** the difference between liens and other types of encumbrances; and
> **explain** the limitations on private property rights for the welfare of the public.

KEY TERMS

condemnation
covenants, conditions, and
    restrictions (CC&Rs)
deed restrictions
easement
easement appurtenant
easement by necessity
easement by prescription
easement in gross
eminent domain
encroachment
encumbrance

escheat
estate in land
fee simple
fee simple absolute
fee simple defeasible
fee simple determinable
fee simple subject to a
    condition subsequent
freehold estate
future interest
homestead
inverse condemnation

legal life estate
license
lien
life estate
police power
pur autre vie
remainder interest
reversionary interest
taking
taxation

MATCHING A

Write the letter of the matching term on the appropriate line.

A. condemnation	**1.** ___ A state's ability to enact legislation to preserve order, protect the public health and safety, and promote the general welfare
B. taxation	**2.** ___ The right of a government to acquire privately owned real estate for public use
C. fee simple defeasible	**3.** ___ The process by which the government exercises its right of eminent domain
D. eminent domain	**4.** ___ A charge imposed on real estate to raise funding for government services
E. escheat	**5.** ___ The automatic transfer of real property to the state when the owner dies without heirs or a will
F. estate in land	**6.** ___ The degree, quantity, nature, and extent of an owner's interest in real property
G. fee simple absolute	**7.** ___ A class of estates in land that lasts for an indeterminable period of time
H. freehold estates	**8.** ___ A class of estates in land for which the length of time can be determined
I. leasehold estates	**9.** ___ The highest interest in real estate recognized by law
J. police power	**10.** ___ An estate qualified by some action or activity that must or must not be performed

MATCHING B

Write the letter of the matching term on the appropriate line.

A. deed restriction	**1.** ___ A notice filed in the public record of pending litigation affecting the title to property or a claimed ownership interest in it
B. remainderman	**2.** ___ An estate based on the lifetime of a person other than the life tenant
C. license	**3.** ___ The person to whom property passes when a life estate ends
D. encroachment	**4.** ___ A legal life estate in which an individual's primary residence is protected, in whole or in part, against certain creditors
E. encumbrance	**5.** ___ An interest in real estate that does not rise to the level of ownership or possession yet still gives some degree of use or control of the property
F. homestead	**6.** ___ A charge against property that provides security for a debt or obligation of the property owner
G. easement	**7.** ___ A private agreement that affects the use of land
H. life estate pur autre vie	**8.** ___ The right to use another's land for a particular purpose
I. lien	**9.** ___ When a building, fence or driveway illegally extends beyond the boundaries of the land of its owner or legal building lines
J. lis pendens	**10.** ___ A personal privilege to enter the land of another for a specific purpose

TRUE OR FALSE

Circle the correct answer.

1. A state's power to enact legislation that preserves order, protects the public health and safety, and promotes the general welfare is called its police power.
   A. True
   B. False

2. The four governmental rights that affect real estate are taxation, eminent domain, escheat, and police power.
   A. True
   B. False

3. The process by which the government exercises its right to acquire privately owned real estate for public use through either judicial or administrative proceedings is called *condemnation*.
   A. True
   B. False

4. The purpose of escheat is to expand governmental property holdings.
   A. True
   B. False

5. A freehold estate is the highest interest in real estate recognized by law.
   A. True
   B. False

6. While it does not have a physical effect on property, a lis pendens creates a "cloud on the title" to the property.
   A. True
   B. False

7. If the grantor is silent about what happens to property after a life estate ends, the grantor has a remainder interest in the property.
   A. True
   B. False

8. A homestead is a legal life estate in real estate occupied as a family home.
   A. True
   B. False

9. An easement appurtenant is attached to the ownership of real estate and allows the owner of that property the use of a neighbor's land.
   A. True
   B. False

10. An easement that arises when an owner sells property that has no access to a street or public way except across the seller's remaining land is an easement by prescription.
    A. True
    B. False

11. The concept of tacking provides that successive periods of occupation by different parties may be combined to reach the required total number of years necessary to establish a class for an easement in gross.
    A. True
    B. False

12. A license may be terminated or canceled by the owner of the property, and a license ends on the death of either party or the sale of the affected property by the licensor.
    A. True
    B. False

13. Dower and curtesy are types of legal life estates.
    A. True
    B. False

14. Real estate taxes, mortgages, judgments, and mechanics' liens all represent possible liens against an owner's real estate.
    A. True
    B. False

15. Covenants, conditions, and restrictions (CC&Rs) are used by a subdivision developer to maintain specific standards in a subdivision.
    A. True
    B. False

MULTIPLE CHOICE

Circle the correct answer.

1. A spouse dies, leaving real estate owned as separate property to the surviving spouse, but with the provision that when the surviving spouse dies, the real estate goes to a specified charity. The surviving spouse owns a bundle of rights but does not own the right to
   A. will the property.
   B. sell the property.
   C. lease the property.
   D. decorate the property.

2. Every workday for the past 20 years, an accountant has paid to park in a specific place in a nearby parking garage. Today, the accountant receives a notice that the garage will be replaced by an office building. Can the property owners do this after all the years the accountant parked there?
   A. No, because the accountant has been parking there for more than 20 years and now has an easement by prescription.
   B. No, because the accountant paid for the parking space regularly and on time.
   C. Yes, because the accountant only had a license.
   D. Yes, because the accountant has nothing in writing.

3. A property owner conveyed a one-acre parcel of land to a preschool. The deed stated that the property was to be used only as a playground; the property owner reserved a right of reentry. What kind of estate has been granted?
   A. Leasehold
   B. Fee simple subject to a condition subsequent
   C. Fee simple absolute
   D. Curtesy

4. There is notice in the public record of pending litigation affecting the title to a property. The notice reflects which of the following?
   A. Fee simple determinable
   B. Police power
   C. An encroachment
   D. A lis pendens

5. A property owner gave land to a school "so long as the land is used for only academic and recreational purposes." The ownership interest granted here is called
   A. an easement by prescription.
   B. an encumbrance.
   C. a bundle of rights.
   D. a fee simple determinable.

6. If the government acquires privately owned real estate through a condemnation suit, it is exercising its power of
   A. escheat.
   B. reverter.
   C. eminent domain.
   D. defeasance.

7. A resident of Sunny Oaks owned two acres of land, sold one acre, and reserved an easement appurtenant for entrance and exit over that acre to reach the public road. The acre that was sold is
   A. capable of being cleared of the easement if the woman sells to a third party.
   B. the servient tenement.
   C. the dominant tenement.
   D. subject to an easement in gross.

8. A large undeveloped parcel of land on the side of a hill borders a road on its lower edge. The owner of the parcel sells the lower portion of the property to a buyer who builds a home on it. Several years later, the upper portion of the property is sold to someone else. The upper portion of the property does not border any road. To gain access to the road, the owner of that property has a legally implied right to an easement
   A. by necessity.
   B. in gross.
   C. by prescription.
   D. by restriction.

9. If the dominant estate merges with the servient estate, which of these is *TRUE*?
   A. The easement remains in effect for the entire parcel.
   B. The easement is suspended but cannot be terminated.
   C. The easement is terminated.
   D. The new owner must bring a suit seeking severance of the easement from the combined properties.

10. The homestead exemption in a town is $15,000. Four years ago, a resident purchased a home for $58,000 and then experienced hard times. At a court-ordered sale, the property is purchased for $60,000. If the resident has an outstanding mortgage balance of $35,000 and credit card debts amounting to $24,360, how much is protected by the homestead exemption?
    A. $640
    B. $2,140
    C. $15,000
    D. $16,500

11. In some states, a husband could not sell his property unless his wife also signed the deed. The wife's interest was called
    A. personal property.
    B. homestead.
    C. curtesy.
    D. dower.

12. The state's authority to enact legislation to protect the public is passed through to municipalities and counties by
    A. police power.
    B. enabling acts.
    C. licensing laws.
    D. processing papers.

13. The state requires enough land to build a four-lane highway. For the state to acquire the needed land from a property owner, the state must do all of these *EXCEPT*
    A. demonstrate that the taking of the land is for the public good.
    B. pay a fair and just compensation to the owner.
    C. allow the property owner the right to appeal any decision.
    D. reimburse the property owner for the amount that the property owner paid for the land.

14. A patient died in a nursing home. The deceased left no will and had no heirs. What happens to the deceased's $250,000 estate?
    A. It escheats to the state or county.
    B. The nursing home gets to keep it.
    C. It will be split between the nursing home and the county.
    D. It can be paid over to the deceased's church.

15. Which of these is defined as any claim, charge, or liability that attaches to real estate?
    A. Lien
    B. Easement
    C. Deed restriction
    D. Encumbrance

16. Which of these *must* exist for an appurtenant easement to exist?
    A. Two adjacent parcels, different owners
    B. Two adjacent parcels, one owner
    C. Landlocked property that requires passage to the street
    D. Long-time unauthorized usage

17. What are deed restrictions?
    A. Public land restrictions
    B. Illegal land restrictions
    C. Private agreements affecting the use of the land
    D. Informal agreements between neighbors

18. The electric company has the right to extend its wires over 50 parcels of land. What right does the electric company have?
    A. Appurtenant easement
    B. Easement by necessity
    C. Easement by prescription
    D. Easement in gross

19. For as long as anyone can remember, neighbor families have used a footpath to get to the river. Recently, the current owner of the footpath erected a fence across the path. Which of these easements might the neighbors claim would require the owner of the footpath to remove the fence?
    A. Easement by necessity
    B. Easement by prescription
    C. Easement in gross
    D. Appurtenant easement

20. The holder of a life estate is called
    A. an encumbrance.
    B. a life tenant.
    C. a remainderman.
    D. a successor.

FILL-IN-THE-BLANK

Select the word or words that best complete these statements:

appurtenant

by necessity

by prescription

conventional life estate

deed restriction

freehold estate

future interest

in gross

legal life estate

lis pendens

public use

special limitation

reversionary interest

1. Due to a court decision in 2005, many states are drafting legislation to establish a narrow meaning to the term _____ in eminent domain proceedings to stop condemnations justified solely for economic reasons.

2. A type of life estate established by state law rather than voluntarily by an owner is a(n) _____.

3. A fee simple determinable is qualified by a(n) _____ that ends the estate automatically on the current owner's failure to comply with this element.

4. A life estate is a type of _____ that is limited in duration to the life of the owner or some other specified person or persons.

5. In a fee simple subject to a condition subsequent estate, the right of re-entry may never take effect. Therefore, this right is considered to be a(n) _____.

6. A railroad right of way is an example of an easement _____.

7. If the creator of a life estate does not name a remainderman, the original owner retains a(an) _____ upon the end of the life estate.

8. A _____ cannot violate any law, such as a fair housing law, by attempting to prohibit certain property transfers.

9. When a claimant has used another person's land for a certain period of time and in a manner defined by state law, the claimant can claim an easement _____.

10. When two properties share a party wall that straddles the boundary line between the two lots, each lot owner owns the half of the wall on each lot and has a(n) _____ easement in the other half of the wall.

ACTIVITY: COMPOUND INTERESTS IN SPINDLEY ACRES

Based on the narrative below, enter the name of each player in the Spindley Acres scenario into the appropriate box. Also label his or her interest in the estate and how it is conveyed from one to another.

Ben conveys a life estate in Spindley Acres to Carol, with a remainder to Bob, "so long as Spindley Acres continues to be a working farm." If it ceases to be a farm, the property will go back to Ben (or his estate).

Meanwhile, Carol conveys a life estate in Spindley Acres to Sally "for as long as my Cousin Tom shall live." When Tom dies, the estate will return to Carol for the remainder of her life.

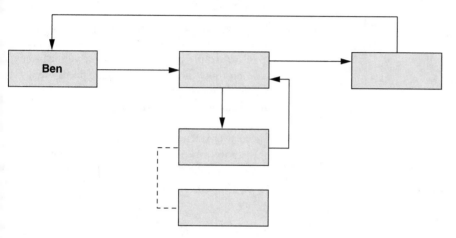

UNIT 3 ANSWERS

MATCHING A

1. J
2. D
3. A
4. B
5. E
6. F
7. H
8. I
9. G
10. C

MATCHING B

1. J
2. H
3. B
4. F
5. E
6. I
7. A
8. G
9. D
10. C

TRUE OR FALSE

1. **A** The answer is true. Police power is the state's right to enact legislation to preserve order, protect the public health, and promote the general welfare of its citizens. (42)

2. **A** The answer is true. Government rights include police power (building codes), eminent domain (right to acquire private property for public use), taxation (raise funds to meet public needs), and escheat (acquires private property for which no owner can be found). (42)

3. **A** The answer is true. Eminent domain is the right of the government to acquire privately owned real estate for public use; condemnation is the process by which the government exercises this right. (42–43)

4. **B** The answer is false. Escheat is a process by which the state acquires privately owned property when no owner can be found. For example, when an owner dies and leaves no heirs and there is no will. (44)

5. **B** The answer is false. A freehold estate lasts for an indeterminable length of time; a *fee simple absolute estate* is the highest interest in real estate recognized by law. (34)

6. **A** The answer is true. A lis pendens is a notice filed in the public record of pending litigation affecting title to the property. This "cloud on the title" may prevent the property from being sold or further encumbered. (42)

7. **B** The answer is false. When the creator of a life estate chooses not to name a remainderman, ownership returns to the original owner upon the end of the life estate. (36–37)

8. **A** The answer is true. A legal life estate is a form of life estate established by state law and becomes effective automatically when certain events occur. Homestead is a legal life estate in real estate occupied as the family home. (37)

9. **A** The answer is true. An *appurtenant easement* is said to run with the land and transfers with the deed of the *dominant* tenement. (39)

10. **B** The answer is false. An easement that arises when an owner sells property that has no access to a street or public way except across the seller's remaining land is an *easement by necessity*. (40)

11. **B** The answer is false. The concept of *tacking* provides that successive periods of continuous occupation by different parties may be combined to reach the required total number of years necessary to establish a claim for an *easement by prescription*. (40)

12. **A** The answer is true. A license is a personal privilege to enter the land of another for a specific purpose; it can be terminated or canceled and ends with the death of either party or with the sale of the land. (41)

13. **A** The answer is true. A legal life estate is a form of life estate established by state law and becomes effective automatically when certain events occur. Dower and curtesy provide that the nonowning spouse has a lifetime right to an interest in the real estate, even if the owning spouse wills the estate to others. (37)

14. **A** The answer is true. A lien is a charge against property that provides security for a debt or an obligation of the property owner. (38)

15. **A** The answer is true. CC&Rs might apply to certain architectural or design specifications. CC&Rs are detailed in the original development plans and referenced in the deeds to individual properties in the subdivision. (38)

MULTIPLE CHOICE

1. **A** The answer is will the property. The surviving spouse owns a life estate, and has the entire bundle of rights except the right to will the property. (36–37)

2. **C** The answer is yes, because the accountant only had a license. A license is a personal right to enter a property for a specific purpose. There is no *buildup* of rights. (41)

3. **B** The answer is fee simple subject to a condition subsequent. The property owner has granted a fee simple subject to a condition subsequent. If, at some point in the future, the land is not used as a playground, the former owner or the former owner's heirs may exercise the right of reentry by retaking physical possession of the land. (35–36)

4. **D** The answer is a lis pendens. A lis pendens is a notice filed in the public record affecting the title to property or a claimed ownership interest in it. (42)

5. **D** The answer is a fee simple determinable. The terms *so long as*, *while*, and *during* generally indicate creation of a fee simple determinable interest. The school obtains the full bundle of rights of a property owner, but one of the "sticks" in that bundle has a special feature. (35)

6. **C** The answer is eminent domain. The right of the state to acquire private property for public use is *eminent domain*. The court action is called *condemnation*. Property *escheats* back to the state when it becomes ownerless; that is, the owner dies leaving no heirs and no will. (42–43)

7. **B** The answer is the servient tenement. The man's parcel is the dominant tenement and benefits from the easement. The easement runs over the property that was sold, the servient tenement. (39)

8. **A** The answer is by necessity. An *easement by necessity* could be created by court order to permit legal access to the second property. (40)

9. **C** The answer is the easement is terminated. If the owner of the dominant tenement also becomes owner of the servient tenement (or vice versa), the easement terminates. Because the same person owns both properties, there is no need for the easement to exist. (41)

10. **C** The answer is $15,000. The homestead exemption is $15,000. So, when the property is sold for $60,000, the mortgage of $35,000 is paid and $15,000 is reserved, leaving $10,000 for the credit card debt. (37)

11. **D** The answer is dower. Historically, a wife's interest in her deceased husband's property was *dower*, a husband's interest was *curtesy*. Protection of some part of the family home is called *homestead*. (37)

12. **B** The answer is enabling acts. The state passes police power to local counties and municipalities by enabling acts. Licensing laws are an example of police power. (42)

13. **D** The answer is reimburse the property owner for the amount that the property owner paid for the land. To acquire private property through eminent domain, the state must prove that the purchase is for the public good, pay a fair price, and allow the property owner full rights to appeal. The price may or may not reflect what the owner paid for the property. (42–43)

14. **A**   The answer is it escheats to the state or county. Because the patient died without a will and there are no heirs, the $250,000 becomes the property of the state or county. (44)

15. **D**   The answer is encumbrance. An encumbrance is any claim, charge, or liability that attaches to real estate. Liens, easements, and deed restrictions are all types of encumbrances. (38)

16. **A**   The answer is two adjacent parcels, different owners. An easement appurtenant must have two owners and two parcels of land. A landlocked parcel would require an easement by necessity; long-time unauthorized usage would lead to an easement by prescription. (39)

17. **C**   The answer is private agreements affecting the use of the land. *Deed restrictions* are private agreements written into a deed and are privately enforced. Examples of public restrictions include zoning and building codes. (38)

18. **D**   The answer is easement in gross. Commercial easements such as this are called easements in gross. They are not attached or appurtenant to a property right. (39–40)

19. **B**   The answer is easement by prescription. Long-time unauthorized usage may create legal rights leading to an easement by prescription. An easement in gross is a personal right, often used by utility companies. An easement by necessity could be imposed by court order to provide access to a landlocked property. (40)

20. **B**   The answer is a life tenant. A life tenant is not a renter like a tenant associated with a lease. A life tenant is entitled to the rights of ownership and can benefit from both possession and ordinary use, just as if the individual were a fee simple owner, but only while the life tenant is still living. (36)

FILL-IN-THE BLANK

1.   Due to a court decision in 2005, many states are drafting legislation to establish a narrow meaning to the term *public use* in eminent domain proceedings to stop condemnations justified solely for economic reasons.

2.   A type of life estate established by state law rather than voluntarily by an owner is a *legal life estate.*

3.   A fee simple determinable is qualified by a *special limitation* that ends the estate automatically on the current owner's failure to comply with this element.

4.   A life estate is a type of *freehold estate* that is limited in duration to the life of the owner or some other specified person or persons.

5.   The right of re-entry may never take effect. Therefore, this right is considered to be a *future interest.*

6.   A railroad right of way is an example of an *easement in gross.*

7.   If the creator of a life estate does not name a remainderman, the original owner retains a *reversionary interest* upon the end of the life estate.

8.   A *deed restriction* cannot violate any law, such as a fair housing law, by attempting to prohibit certain property transfers. A deed restriction that attempts to do so would be void and thus unenforceable.

9.   When a claimant has used another person's land for a certain period of time defined by state law, the claimant can claim an easement *by prescription.*

10.   When two properties share a party wall that straddles the boundary line between the two lots, each lot owner owns the half of the wall on each lot and has an *appurtenant* easement in the other half of the wall.

ACTIVITY: COMPOUND INTERESTS IN SPINDLEY ACRES

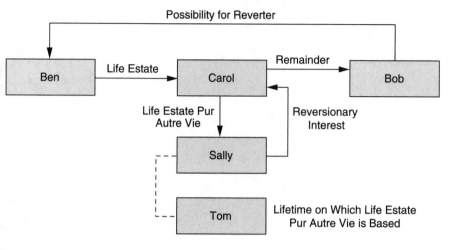

UNIT 4

Forms of Real Estate Ownership

LEARNING OBJECTIVES

When you have completed this unit, you will be able to

> **distinguish** between ownership in severalty and co-ownership;
> **describe** the various forms of co-ownership in real estate;
> **describe** the key elements of trusts, partnerships, corporations, and LLCs; and
> **identify** the types of property ownership for common-interest properties.

KEY TERMS

common elements	joint tenancy	separate property
community property	limited liability company (LLC)	severalty
condominium	limited partnership	tenancy by the entirety
cooperative	partition	tenancy in common (TIC)
co-ownership	partnership	time-share
corporation	PITT	town house
general partnership	right of survivorship	trust

MATCHING A

Write the letter of the matching term on the appropriate line.

A. tenancy in common	**1.** ___ The ownership of real estate by one individual
B. joint tenancy	**2.** ___ A form of property ownership in which owners hold undivided fractional interests that are inheritable by their heirs
C. partition	**3.** ___ A form of ownership in which multiple owners hold property with a right of survivorship
D. partnership	
E. proprietary lease	**4.** ___ A legal method for dissolving a co-ownership
F. severalty	**5.** ___ A special form of co-ownership for married couples
G. tenancy by the entirety	**6.** ___ A device by which one person transfers ownership of property to someone else to hold or manage for the benefit of a third party
H. bylaws	**7.** ___ A form of trust established by will after the owner's death
I. trust	**8.** ___ An association of two or more persons who carry on a business for profit as co-owners
J. testamentary trust	**9.** ___ The evidence of the right to occupy a unit in a cooperative
	10. ___ The rules determining the operation and management of a cooperative

MATCHING B

Write the letter of the matching term on the appropriate line.

A. assessments

B. homeowners association (HOA) fees

C. condominium

D. corporation

E. general partnership

F. right of survivorship

G. limited liability company

H. separate property

I. time-share estate

J. time-share use

1. ___ A business organization in which all members participate in the operation and management of the business and share full liability for business losses and obligations

2. ___ A business organization that is a legal entity managed and operated by a board of directors

3. ___ On the death of a joint tenant, the deceased's interest transfers directly to the remaining joint tenants

4. ___ A business organization that combines the tax advantages of limited partnerships and the limited liability of corporations

5. ___ In a community property state, real or personal property that was owned solely by either spouse prior to marriage, or acquired by inheritance or gift during the marriage

6. ___ A form of property ownership in which each owner holds an undivided interest in certain common elements in addition to holding individual property in fee simple

7. ___ Special payments required of condominium unit owners to address specific expenses

8. ___ Recurring fees required of condominium unit owners to cover basic maintenance and operations

9. ___ A real property interest in a specified unit for a particular period of the year

10. ___ A contract right under which a developer retains ownership of property and the purchaser receives the right to occupy and use the facilities for a certain period

TRUE OR FALSE

Circle the correct answer.

1. The three basic ways in which a fee simple estate may be held are in severalty, in co-ownership, and in trust.
   A. True
   B. False

2. The term *severalty* means that there is only one owner of a property.
   A. True
   B. False

3. In a tenancy in common, property is owned by two or more owners with the right of survivorship.
   A. True
   B. False

4. The ownership of an undivided fractional interest in a property is characteristic of a tenancy in common.
   A. True
   B. False

5. When all of the other owners' interests in a joint tenancy have passed to the sole surviving owner, that owner then holds title in entirety.
   A. True
   B. False

6. When title to a single parcel of real estate is held by two or more individuals, the parties may be called concurrent owners.
   A. True
   B. False

7. The four unities characteristic of a tenancy in common are possession, interest, title, and time.
   A. True
   B. False

8. When a joint tenant conveys interest in the jointly held property to a new owner, the new owner becomes a joint tenant.
   A. True
   B. False

9. Co-tenants may terminate their co-ownership by asking a court to partition the property.
   A. True
   B. False

10. In a tenancy by the entirety, neither spouse can convey a half-interest to a third party, and neither spouse may take court action to partition or divide the property.
    A. True
    B. False

11. In a community property state, community property includes all property, both real and personal, acquired by either party prior to or during the marriage.
    A. True
    B. False

12. The person who creates a trust is called the trustor.
    A. True
    B. False

13. In a general partnership, the death of one of the partners automatically bankrupts the remaining partners.
    A. True
    B. False

14. Condominium owners hold their own units in fee simple and the common elements under proprietary leases.
    A. True
    B. False

15. The management and operation of a cooperative are determined by the bylaws of the corporation that owns the property.
    A. True
    B. False

16. Ownership of a cooperative interest is personal property.
    A. True
    B. False

17. A time-share estate includes the right to use the property for a certain specified period of time.
    A. True
    B. False

18. An owner can transfer or sell a condominium unit to anyone, unless the condominium association provides for a right of first refusal.
    A. True
    B. False

19. A major advantage of living trusts is that they reduce the time and costs of probate.
    A. True
    B. False

20. A limited liability company (LLC) combines the most attractive features of land trusts and testamentary trusts.
    A. True
    B. False

MULTIPLE CHOICE

Circle the correct answer.

1. Which of these cannot take title as a joint tenant with right of survivorship?
   A. Wife and husband
   B. Two female business partners
   C. Two brothers in partnership
   D. A corporation

2. When two or more individuals decide to buy a property together, it results in
   A. a cooperation.
   B. a co-ownership.
   C. a community effort.
   D. a joint venture.

3. Three siblings bought a farm together. The deed listed all of their names, but failed to designate any form of concurrent ownership. What form of ownership are they presumed to have taken?
   A. Tenancy by the entireties
   B. Joint tenancy with right of survivorship
   C. Tenancy in common
   D. In severalty

4. What form of ownership is employed when one person transfers ownership to someone else to hold and manage for a third person?
   A. Joint venture
   B. Joint tenancy
   C. Trust
   D. Severalty

5. Two people, each of whom has two children, are getting married, and they are buying a house together. They ask the real estate professional for advice about how to take title. What advice should the real estate professional offer?
   A. Advise they take title as tenants in common, so that each one-half in interest would go to the appropriate children
   B. Advise they take title as joint tenants to protect each other, so that if one dies, the other gets the house
   C. Suggest that they consult the real estate professional's employing broker
   D. Suggest that they consult an attorney

6. A will provided that the local banker take care of the deceased's estate until the deceased's children reach age 25. What kind of trust is this?
   A. Testamentary trust
   B. Living trust
   C. Land trust
   D. Trust deed

7. What kind of ownership do the horizontal property acts regulate?
   A. Cooperatives
   B. Condominiums
   C. Time-shares
   D. Planned unit developments

8. Shareholders in a cooperative receive shares of stock that entitle them to
   A. a common element lease.
   B. a trust deed.
   C. a proprietary lease.
   D. a corporate deed.

9. Membership camping is similar to
   A. cooperative ownership.
   B. condominium ownership.
   C. planned use development.
   D. time-share use.

10. In a large highrise condominium, each unit is owned by individual owners. The elevators, parking garage, and swimming pool are called
    A. community property.
    B. separate property.
    C. common elements.
    D. proprietary elements.

11. Two people own an apartment building together as joint tenants. They share equally in the expenses and profits. One day, one of the owners decides to end the relationship. If that owner signs and delivers a deed to the buyer, which of these statements is *TRUE*?
    A. The buyer will become a joint tenant with the other owner.
    B. The buyer and the other owner will be tenants in common.
    C. The buyer will be a tenant in common with the other owner and a joint tenant with the seller.
    D. The conveyance will be invalid; the two original owners will remain joint tenants.

12. In February, a seller conveyed an undivided one-half interest in a parcel of land to buyer A. In March, the seller conveyed the remaining one-half interest to buyer B. The deed to buyer B included the statement: "Buyer B is to be a joint tenant with buyer A." Both deeds were recorded. Based on these facts, which of these statements is *TRUE*?
    A. Buyer A and buyer B hold title to the land as joint tenants under the terms of the two conveyances from the seller.
    B. Buyer A and buyer B own the land by partition.
    C. Buyer A and buyer B are tenants in common.
    D. Buyer B owns the land as a joint tenant; buyer A owns the land as a tenant in common.

13. Three people own a large parcel of undeveloped land in joint tenancy. One of them wants to build a shopping center on the property, while the other two want to use it as an organic farm. The individual who wants to build on the land tries to buy the other tenants' interests, but they refuse to sell. Which of these is the individual's *BEST* option?
    A. File a suit for partition
    B. Begin building a shopping center on one-third of the property
    C. Wait for the other two to die
    D. File a suit to quiet title

14. A resident owns and lives year-round in a cottage in a lakefront community. The resident's ownership of the cottage is in fee simple. The resident also owns an undivided percentage interest in a parking lot, a golf course, and a swimming pool, all located in the development. Based on these facts alone, the resident's ownership is probably *BEST* described as
    A. a time-share estate.
    B. a time-share use.
    C. a condominium.
    D. a cooperative.

15. Three friends agree to purchase and operate a property as a permanent investment. Two friends each contribute $50,000. The third contributes $30,000 and agrees to manage the day-to-day operations of the business, which the friends call "Property Group Partners." Only the third friend has any right to participate in the operation of the venture. Based on these facts, what type of business organization have these friends established?
    A. Joint venture
    B. Limited partnership
    C. General partnership
    D. Limited liability company

16. Three friends agree to purchase and operate a property as a permanent investment. Two friends each contribute $50,000. The third contributes $30,000 and agrees to manage the day-to-day operations of the business, which the friends call "Property Group Partners." Only the third friend has any right to participate in the operation of the venture. If a structure on the property collapses, resulting in injury and property damage worth $275,000, what will be the liability of the friend who contributed $50,000?
    A. None
    B. $50,000
    C. $91,667
    D. $100,000

17. All of these unities are required for a joint tenancy *EXCEPT*
    A. unity of title.
    B. unity of ownership.
    C. unity of time.
    D. unity of possession.

18. All of these are characteristics of a tenancy by the entirety *EXCEPT*
    A. title may be conveyed only by a deed signed by both parties.
    B. the surviving spouse automatically becomes sole owner of the property upon the death of the other spouse.
    C. each spouse owns an equal, undivided interest in the property as a single, indivisible unit.
    D. the surviving spouse automatically owns one-half of the property acquired during the marriage.

19. A grandparent creates a trust to pay for a grandchild's education. The trust is operated by an attorney who makes payments directly to the school. Based on these facts, which of these statements *BEST* characterizes the relationships among these parties?
    A. The attorney is the trustor, the grandchild is the beneficiary, and the grandparent is the trustee.
    B. The grandparent is the trustor, the school is the beneficiary, and the attorney is the trustee.
    C. The grandparent is the trustor, the grandchild is the beneficiary, and the attorney is the trustee.
    D. The grandparent is the trustor, the grandchild is the beneficiary, the attorney is the trustee, and the school is the fiduciary.

20. A company is a legal entity, created by charter under the laws of the state. The company is managed and operated by a board and is permitted to buy and sell real estate. When one of its directors dies, the company continues to operate. Because of its structure, the company's income is subject to double taxation (first by the company, and then by its shareholders). The company is *BEST* described as
    A. a partnership.
    B. a condominium trust.
    C. a corporation.
    D. a limited liability company.

21. When a corporation takes complete ownership of a property, it is considered to be ownership in
    A. joint tenancy.
    B. tenancy in common.
    C. partnership.
    D. severalty.

22. In a tenancy in common, if the fractions of ownership are *NOT* stated in the deed, how are they determined?
    A. The tenants need a judicial decision to determine the fractional shares.
    B. The tenants are presumed to hold equal shares.
    C. The tenants settle the issue through binding arbitration.
    D. The tenants must terminate the tenancy in common through partition.

23. In a land trust, the beneficiary is usually also
    A. the trustor.
    B. the trustee.
    C. the fiduciary.
    D. the attorney in fact.

ACTIVITY: TYPES OF OWNERSHIP

Mark the characteristics that apply to ownership for each type of property.

Condominium	Cooperative	Time-Share
☐ Corporate ownership	☐ Corporate ownership	☐ Corporate ownership
☐ Undivided interest in common elements	☐ Undivided interest in common elements	☐ Undivided interest in common elements
☐ Occupancy and use for limited periods	☐ Occupancy and use for limited periods	☐ Occupancy and use for limited periods
☐ Proprietary lease	☐ Proprietary lease	☐ Proprietary lease
☐ Fee simple ownership of units	☐ Fee simple ownership of units	☐ Relatively small interest in real estate

UNIT 4 ANSWERS

MATCHING A

1. **F**
2. **A**
3. **B**
4. **C**
5. **G**
6. **I**
7. **J**
8. **D**
9. **E**
10. **H**

MATCHING B

1. **E**
2. **D**
3. **F**
4. **G**
5. **H**
6. **C**
7. **A**
8. **B**
9. **I**
10. **J**

TRUE OR FALSE

1. **A** The answer is true. Although the forms of ownership available are controlled by state law, a fee simple estate may be held in three basic ways: in sole ownership, in co-ownership with others, and in trust. (49)

2. **A** The answer is true. Ownership in severalty occurs when property is owned by one individual or corporation. (50)

3. **B** The answer is false. In a *joint tenancy*, property is owned by two or more owners with the right of survivorship. (51–52)

4. **A** The answer is true. In a tenancy in common, each tenant holds an undivided fractional interest in the property; the co-owners have unity of possession, meaning that each is entitled to possession of the whole property. It is the ownership interest, not the property, that is divided. (50)

5. **B** The answer is false. A joint tenancy continues indefinitely, until there is only one remaining owner, who then holds title in *severalty*. (53–54)

6. **A** The answer is true. When title to one parcel of real estate is held by two or more individuals, those parties are called co-owners or concurrent owners. (50)

7. **B** The answer is false. The four unities characteristic of a *joint tenancy* are possession, interest, title, and time. (52)

8. **B** The answer is false. A joint tenant may freely convey interest in the jointly held property to a new owner; however, doing so will destroy the unities of time and title, and the new owner *cannot* become a joint tenant. (53–54)

9. **A** The answer is true. Partition is a legal way to dissolve the relationship when the parties do not voluntarily agree to its termination. (53)

10. **A** The answer is true. During their lives, under tenancy by the entirety, the spouses can convey title only by a deed signed by both parties. (54)

11. **B** The answer is false. In a community property state, *community property* includes all property, both real and personal, acquired by either party during the marriage, except by gift or inheritance or with the proceeds of separately owned property. (54)

12. **A** The answer is true. A trust is a device by which one person, called the trustor, transfers property to the trustee, who is entrusted to carry out the trustor's instruction regarding the property held in the trust. The party who benefits from the trust is called the beneficiary. (55)

13. **B** The answer is false. If a partner in a general partnership dies, withdraws, or goes bankrupt, the traditional common law result would be to dissolve the partnership, which could be reorganized as a partnership of the surviving partners in order to conduct business. Nearly every state has now adopted the Uniform Partnership Act, which provides for the continuation of the existing business even under these circumstances. (57)

14. **B** The answer is false. Condominium owners hold their own units in fee simple and the common elements as *tenants in common.* (59–60)

15. **A** The answer is true. The bylaws of the corporation that owns the property determine the management and operation of a cooperative. (60–61)

16. **A** The answer is true. When buying into a cooperative, the purchaser becomes a shareholder in the corporation by virtue of stock ownership and receives a proprietary lease to the apartment for the life of the corporation. (60–61)

17. **A** The answer is true. Time-share ownership permits multiple purchasers to buy interest in real estate; each purchaser receives the right to use the facilities for a certain period. (62)

18. **A** The answer is true. Under condominium ownership, each unit becomes a separate parcel of real estate that is owned in fee simple and may be transferred to whomever the owner chooses, unless the condominium association provides for a right of first refusal. (59–60)

19. **A** The answer is true. Living trusts have become a major estate planning tool used to minimize the time and costs of probate. (56)

20. **B** The answer is false. An LLC combines the most attractive features of limited partnerships and corporations. The members of an LLC enjoy the limited liability offered by a corporate form of ownership. In addition, the LLC offers the tax advantages of a partnership—income flows directly to the member of the LLC, instead of being subject to the double taxation of a corporation. (57–58)

MULTIPLE CHOICE

1. **D** The answer is a corporation. Because a corporation continues indefinitely until terminated by legal action, a corporation may never take title as a joint tenant. (57–58)

2. **B** The answer is a co-ownership. When two or more people buy property together, it is called *co-ownership.* A *joint venture* is a form of partnership in which two or more people carry out a single business project with no intention of establishing an ongoing relationship. (50)

3. **C** The answer is tenancy in common. The siblings are presumed to be tenants in common because the deed did not specify they would take title as joint tenants with right of survivorship. Joint must be specified if that is the desired form of taking title. Severalty ownership cannot be taken by more than one person. (50–51)

4. **C** The answer is trust. A trust is a device by which one person transfers ownership of property to someone else to hold or manage for the benefit of a third party. Severalty indicates one owner. Joint tenancy is a form of ownership whereby, as joint owners die, the surviving owners acquire the deceased tenant's interest. (55)

5. **D** The answer is suggest that they consult an attorney. Because the choice of ownership affects the ability to transfer the real estate, has tax implications, and affects rights to future claims, real estate professionals should tell their clients to discuss the issue with an attorney. Real estate professionals and their brokers are not permitted to give legal advice. (49)

6. **A** The answer is a testamentary trust. A testamentary trust is established by will after the trustor's death. A living trust is established during the trustor's lifetime. Real estate is the only asset in a land trust. A deed of trust (also called a trust deed) is a financing instrument. (56)

7. **B** The answer is condominiums. Condominiums are regulated by the horizontal property acts enacted in most states. (58–59)

8. **C** The answer is a proprietary lease. The proprietary lease is part of the ownership of the cooperative stock and gives the owner the right to occupy a specific dwelling unit. Common elements are owned by condominium owners as tenants in common. (60)

9. **D** The answer is time-share use. The owner of a membership interest in a campground purchases the right to use the developer's facilities, which is similar to time-sharing; however, the owner may not be limited to a specific time as in the case of a typical time-share arrangement. (61)

10. **C**   The answer is common elements. The parts of the property that condominium owners own together are the common elements. Community property is a system of property ownership based on the theory that each spouse has an equal interest in property acquired during the marriage, which is distinct from property acquired before marriage, considered separate property. (58)

11. **B**   The answer is the buyer and the other owner will be tenants in common. A co-owner can sell whatever the co-owner owns; however, once the unities of time, title, and interest are destroyed, as they are if one joint tenant sells that interest, there can no longer be a joint tenancy. (53)

12. **C**   The answer is buyer A and buyer B are tenants in common. Because there are two deeds made at different times, the four unities of joint tenancy have not been met; therefore, buyer A and buyer B are tenants in common. (50–51)

13. **A**   The answer is file a suit for partition. When co-owners cannot come to an agreement, they must file for partition in court. The property will not physically be divided, unless the nature of the property allows for an equal division and the parties agree to it; rather, each owner (or a group of owners) will be given the opportunity to buy the others out. If this is not possible, then the property will be sold, and the proceeds will be divided appropriately. (53–54)

14. **C**   The answer is a condominium. It appears that the resident has condominium ownership, because the resident owns the cottage as well as the interest in the common elements. Cooperative ownership is ruled out, because the resident does not have a proprietary lease. It is not a time-share, because the resident clearly owns more than the right to use the property only at specific times. (58–61)

15. **B**   The answer is limited partnership. A limited partnership limits the participation of the silent partners, and also limits their liability. A general partnership would require that all are equally involved in running the operation, which would mean that all are exposed to liability. (57)

16. **B**   The answer is $50,000. A limited partner is limited in liability to the amount of the original investment. (57)

17. **B**   The answer is unity of ownership. To create joint tenancy ownership, four unities are required: possession, interest, time, and title. (52)

18. **D**   The answer is the surviving spouse automatically owns one-half of the property acquired during the marriage. Under tenancy by the entirety, title may be conveyed only by a deed signed by both parties, each spouse owns an equal, undivided interest in the property, and the surviving spouse automatically becomes the owner of the entire property upon the death of the other. (54)

19. **C**   The answer is the grandparent is the trustor, the grandchild is the beneficiary, and the attorney is the trustee. The grandparent is the owner-trustor, the grandchild is the beneficiary, and the attorney is the person who manages the trust—that is, the trustee. (55)

20. **C**   The answer is a corporation. The corporation would not be affected if one of the directors dies. The company's income is subject to double taxation, which defines the company as a corporation. (57)

21. **D**   The answer is severalty. A corporation is an artificial person, which means that it can hold ownership in severalty. (57)

22. **B**   The answer is the tenants are presumed to hold equal shares. The deed creating a tenancy in common may or may not state the fractional interest held by each co-owner; if no fractions are stated, the tenants are presumed to hold equal shares. (50–51)

23. **A**   The answer is the trustor. In a land trust, the beneficiary is usually also the trustor. The beneficiary retains management and control of the real property and has the right of possession as well as the right to any income. (56)

ACTIVITY: TYPES OF OWNERSHIP

Condominium
- Undivided interest in common elements
- Fee simple ownership of units

Cooperative
- Corporate ownership
- Proprietary lease

Time-Share
- Undivided interest in common elements
- Occupancy and use for limited periods
- Relatively small interest in real estate

UNIT
5

Land Description

LEARNING OBJECTIVES

When you have completed this unit, you will be able to

> **identify** the methods used for describing real estate; and
> **explain** the process involved in identifying and measuring property rights including those above and below the surface.

KEY TERMS

air lots	metes-and-bounds method	rectangular (government)
base lines	monuments	survey system
benchmarks	plat map	sections
datum	point of beginning (POB)	survey
legal description	principal meridians	tiers
lot-and-block (recorded plat)	ranges	township lines
method		townships

MATCHING

Write the letter of the matching term on the appropriate line.

A. metes and bounds

B. rectangular survey system

C. sections

D. monuments

E. lot and block

F. benchmarks

G. datum

H. POB

I. township lines

J. ranges

1. ____ The type of legal description that relies on a property's physical features to determine and to describe the boundaries and measurements of the parcel

2. ____ The designated starting point for a metes-and-bounds description

3. ____ Fixed objects used to identify significant points of measurement in a metes-and-bounds description

4. ____ A land description system based on principal meridians and base lines

5. ____ Lines running 6 miles apart and parallel to the base line

6. ____ Strips of land running parallel to the meridian

7. ____ Numbered squares of land within a township square

8. ____ A system of description that uses numbered areas referred to in a plat map

9. ____ A point, line, or surface from which elevations are measured

10. ____ Permanent reference markers, usually found on embossed brass markers set in concrete or asphalt

TRUE OR FALSE

Circle the correct answer.

1. The metes-and-bounds method established by Congress in 1785 to standardize the description of land.
   A. True
   B. False

2. In the metes-and-bounds method, a monument may be either a natural object or an artificial marker.
   A. True
   B. False

3. For a parcel described under the lot-and-block method, the lot refers to the numerical designation of any particular parcel.
   A. True
   B. False

4. Principal meridians run east and west.
   A. True
   B. False

5. Township lines and base lines are parallel.
   A. True
   B. False

6. Ranges are strips of land six miles wide that are parallel to the base line.
   A. True
   B. False

7. When the horizontal township lines and the vertical range lines intersect, they form townships.
   A. True
   B. False

8. Every township contains 36 sections of 640 acres each.
   A. True
   B. False

9. A datum is a permanent reference point, which is usually found on an embossed brass marker set into a solid concrete or asphalt base.
   A. True
   B. False

10. Section 6 is always in the northeast, or upper-left, corner.
    A. True
    B. False

11. Air lots are composed of the airspace within specific boundaries located over a parcel of land.
    A. True
    B. False

12. When preparing a plat map of a new condominium, the surveyor shows the elevations of floor and ceiling surfaces.
    A. True
    B. False

MULTIPLE CHOICE

Circle the correct answer.

1. All of these systems are used to express a legal description *EXCEPT*
    A. lot and block.
    B. metes and bounds.
    C. rectangular survey.
    D. benchmarks.

2. Air lots, condominium descriptions, and other vertical measurements may be computed from the U.S. Geological Survey
    A. datum.
    B. benchmark.
    C. principal meridian.
    D. base line.

3. Six acres of prime undeveloped property are sold for $2.25 per square foot. How much did the buyer pay?
    A. $466,560
    B. $588,060
    C. $612,360
    D. $733,860

4. Which township section number is directly north of Section 7?
    A. Section 1
    B. Section 5
    C. Section 6
    D. Section 8

5. Which of these *MOST* accurately describes the dimensions of a quarter-section?
    A. ⅛ mile by ⅛ mile
    B. ¼ mile by ¼ mile
    C. ½ mile by ½ mile
    D. ½ mile by 1 mile

6. A buyer is willing to pay $1,200 per acre for the SE ¼ of the SE ¼ of the SE ¼ of Section 11. How much will the buyer pay for the land?
    A. $3,000
    B. $6,000
    C. $12,000
    D. $24,000

7. A farm that is a quarter-section is
    A. 20 acres.
    B. 80 acres.
    C. 160 acres.
    D. 320 acres.

8. How many acres are contained in a parcel described as follows: The NE ¼ of the NW ¼, and the S ½ of the NW ¼, and the NE ¼, of Section 10?
    A. 140 acres
    B. 280 acres
    C. 380 acres
    D. 640 acres

9. The basic units of the rectangular survey system are
    A. the base lines.
    B. the principal meridians.
    C. the ranges.
    D. the townships.

10. A metes-and-bounds description is required in a rectangular survey system description when
    A. a tract is too small to be described by quarter-sections.
    B. describing a regular tract.
    C. a tract is too large to be described by quarter-sections.
    D. a tract follows the lot or block lines of a recorded subdivision.

11. What is the square footage for this property described by the metes-and-bounds method?

    Beginning at a point on the southerly side of Smith Street, 200 feet easterly from the corner formed by the intersection of the southerly side of Smith Street and the easterly side of Johnson Street; then east 200 feet; then south 100 feet; then west 200 feet; then north 100 feet to the POB.

    A. 5,000 square feet
    B. 10,000 square feet
    C. 15,000 square feet
    D. 20,000 square feet

12. The end of a metes-and-bounds land description is always
    A. a monument.
    B. a benchmark.
    C. a point of beginning.
    D. a base line.

13. The lot-and-block system starts with the preparation of
    A. a subdivision plat.
    B. a range map.
    C. a survey.
    D. an air lot.

Refer to the example plat for Honeysuckle Hills Subdivision when answering Questions 14 through 20.

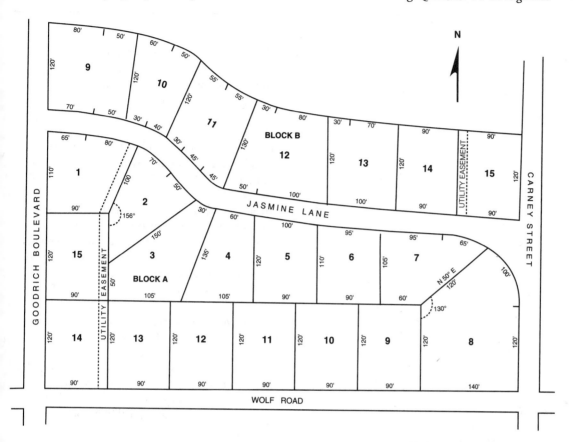

14. Which lot in Block A has the *MOST* frontage on Jasmine Lane?
    A. 1
    B. 2
    C. 7
    D. 11

15. How many lots have easements?
    A. 1
    B. 3
    C. 4
    D. 6

16. Which road or roads run east and west?
    A. Wolf and Jasmine
    B. Carney and Goodrich
    C. Wolf only
    D. Goodrich only

17. Which of these lots has the *LEAST* street exposure?
    A. Lot 3, Block A
    B. Lot 15, Block B
    C. Lot 9, Block A
    D. Lot 10, Block B

18. Beginning at the intersection of the west line of Carney Street and the north line of Wolf Road, running west 140 feet, then north 120 feet, then north 50 degrees east 120 feet, then following the southeasterly curvature of the south line of Jasmine Lane for 100 feet, then south 120 feet to POB. To which lot does this description refer?
    A. Lot 15, Block B
    B. Lot 8, Block A
    C. Lot 7, 8, and 9, Block A
    D. Lot 8 and 9, Block A

19. If lot 13 and lot 14, Block A were combined into one parcel, how many square feet would it contain?
    A. 1,020
    B. 19,800
    C. 21,600
    D. 22,800

20. If a buyer is willing to pay $3 per square foot for lot 10, Block A, how much would the buyer pay for the land?
    A. $20,600
    B. $24,000
    C. $28,000
    D. $32,400

UNIT 5 ANSWERS

MATCHING

1. **A**

2. **H**

3. **D**

4. **B**

5. **I**

6. **J**

7. **C**

8. **E**

9. **G**

10. **F**

TRUE OR FALSE

1. **B** The answer is false. The rectangular survey system was established by Congress in 1785 to standardize the description of land. (70)

2. **A** The answer is true. The oldest type of legal description is metes and bounds, which relies on a property's physical features to determine the boundaries and measurements of the parcel. It may include natural and artificial landmarks called monuments. (68)

3. **A** The answer is true. The lot-and-block (recorded plat) method of land description, which uses lot and block numbers referred to in a plat map and that indicates the location and boundaries of individual properties, is filed in the public records of the county where the land is located. (74)

4. **B** The answer is false. A principal meridian runs north and south; base lines run east and west. (71)

5. **A** The answer is true. Lines running east and west, parallel to the base line, and 6 miles apart, are called township lines. (71)

6. **B** The answer is false. Ranges are strips of land six miles wide that are parallel to the principal meridian. (71)

7. **A** The answer is true. When the horizontal township lines and the vertical range lines intersect, they form townships, which are the basic units of the rectangular survey system. (71)

8. **A** The answer is true. Townships are 6 miles square and contain 36 square miles. They are further subdivided into 36 sections, each 1 square mile, and each containing 640 acres. (71–72)

9. **B** The answer is false. A *benchmark* is a permanent reference point that is usually found on an embossed brass marker set into a solid concrete or asphalt base. It is used for marking the datum—the point, line, or surface from which elevations are measured or indicated. (77)

10. **B** The answer is false. Section 6 is always in the northwest, or upper-left, corner. (72)

11. **A** The answer is true. In the same way land may be measured and divided into parcels, the air space above land may also be divided; air lots are composed of the airspace within specific boundaries located over a parcel of land. (76)

12. **A** The answer is true. The condominium laws passed in all states require that a registered land surveyor prepare a plat map that shows the elevations of floor and ceiling surfaces, and the vertical boundaries of each unit with reference to an official datum. (76)

MULTIPLE CHOICE

1. **D** The answer is benchmarks. A benchmark is a permanent reference point used as a reference for marking data, not for expressing a legal description. (77)

2. **A** The answer is datum. The U.S. Geological Survey datum is defined as the mean sea level at New York Harbor. A surveyor uses the datum to determine the height of a structure or to establish the grade of a street. (77)

3. **B** The answer is $588,060. The buyer paid $588,060:

   square feet × 6 = 261,360 square feet

   261,360 square feet × $2.25 = $588,060

   (77)

4. **C** The answer is Section 6. Township sections are numbered in an S fashion: 1 through 6, right to left, then 7 to 12, left to right. Section 7 is directly south of Section 6. (72)

5. **C** The answer is ½ mile by ½ mile. A *section* is 1 square mile. (72)

6. **C** The answer is $12,000. The buyer will pay $12,000:

   ¼ × 640 = 160

   160 × ¼ = 40

   40 × ¼ = 10 acres

   10 acres × $1,200 = $12,000

   (77)

7. **C** The answer is 160 acres. A quarter (¼) of 640 acres is 160 acres. (77)

8. **B** The answer is 280 acres. There are three parcels in this description.

   The first: ¼ × 640 = 160, and ¼ × 160 = 40 acres

   The second: ¼ × 640 = 160, and ½ × 160= 80 acres

   The third: 640 × ¼ = 16040 + 80 + 160 = 280 acres

   (77)

9. **D** The answer is the townships. Townships are the basic units of the rectangular survey system. Principal meridians and base lines are the two sets of intersecting lines in the system. Ranges are the 6-mile strips of land on either side of a principal meridian. (71)

10. **A** The answer is a tract is too small to be described by quarter-sections. Metes-and-bounds descriptions within the rectangular survey system usually occur when describing an irregular tract, when a tract is too small to be described by quarter-sections, or when a tract does not follow the lot or block lines of a recorded subdivision, quarter-section lines, or other fractional section lines. (74)

11. **D** The answer is 20,000 square feet. The property is 200 × 100 = 20,000 square feet. (77)

12. **C** The answer is a point of beginning. A metes-and-bounds description must always begin and end at the point of beginning, thus enclosing the described property. (68)

13. **A** The answer is a subdivision plat. The lot-and-block system starts with the preparation of a subdivision plat by a licensed surveyor or an engineer. (74)

14. **C** The answer is 7. In Block A, Lot 7 has the longest frontage with 160 feet. (75)

15. **C** The answer is 4. Four lots have easements: Lots 1, 14, and 15 on Block A, and Lot 15 on Block B. (75)

16. **A** The answer is Wolf and Jasmine. Wolf and Jasmine run east and west. (75)

17. **A** The answer is Lot 3, Block A. Lot 3, Block A with 30 feet on a roadway has the least street exposure. (75)

18. **B** The answer is Lot 8, Block A. The description refers to Lot 8, Block A. (75)

19. **C** The answer is 21, 600. The combined parcel would have 21,600 square feet. The parcel would be 180 × 120 = 21,600. (77)

20. **D** The answer is $32,400. The buyer would pay $32,400:

   90 × 120 = 10,800 square feet

   10,800 square feet × $3 = $32,400

   (77)

UNIT 6

Transfer of Title

LEARNING OBJECTIVES

When you have completed this unit, you will be able to

> **describe** the fundamental concepts of title as it relates to the ownership of land, and the processes and instruments used to apply these concepts;
> **describe** the circumstances and conditions which may provide for the involuntary transfer of title; and
> **explain** testate, intestate, wills, and the probate process.

KEY TERMS

acknowledgment	granting clause	special warranty deed
adverse possession	grantor	testate
bargain and sale deed	habendum clause	testator
deed	intestate	title
deed of trust	involuntary alienation	transfer tax
devise	probate	trustee's deed
general warranty deed	quitclaim deed	voluntary alienation
grantee	reconveyance deed	will

MATCHING A

Write the letter of the matching term on the appropriate line.

A. acknowledgment	**1.** ___ The right to, and evidence of, ownership of land
B. deed	**2.** ___ The transfer of title by gift or sale
C. deed of trust	**3.** ___ A written instrument by which an owner intentionally conveys the right, title, or interest in a parcel of real estate to someone else
D. grantee	
E. quiet enjoyment	**4.** ___ The person who transfers title
F. grantor	**5.** ___ The person who acquires title by gift or sale
G. granting clause	**6.** ___ A statement of the intention to convey property by deed
H. seisin	**7.** ___ A formal declaration, made before a notary public, that the person who is signing the deed is doing so voluntarily and that the signature is genuine
I. title	
J. voluntary alienation	**8.** ___ A covenant in a deed that warrants that the grantor is the owner of the property and has the right to convey it
	9. ___ A guarantee in a deed that the grantee's title will be good against any third party who might bring legal action to establish superior title
	10. ___ A conveyance by deed from a trustor to a trustee for the benefit of a beneficiary

MATCHING B

Write the letter of the matching term on the appropriate line.

A. reconveyance deed	**1.** ___ A type of deed that warrants only that the grantor received title and that the property has not been encumbered during the grantor's ownership
B. devise	
C. involuntary alienation	**2.** ___ A deed that contains no express warranties against encumbrances, but implies that the grantor holds title and possession of the property
D. probate	**3.** ___ A deed that contains no covenants, warranties, or implications, and that provides the least amount of protection of any deed
E. quitclaim	
F. special warranty	**4.** ___ A conveyance by deed from a trustee to anyone other than the trustor
G. bargain and sale	**5.** ___ A conveyance by deed from a trustee to the trustor
H. testate	**6.** ___ The transfer of title without the owner's consent
I. testator	**7.** ___ Having prepared a will indicating how property is to be disposed of after death
J. trustee's deed	
	8. ___ The gift of real property by will
	9. ___ The person who makes a will
	10. ___ A formal judicial process to confirm a will's validity and to see that assets are distributed correctly

TRUE OR FALSE

Circle the correct answer.

1. A title to real estate is a printed document signed by the secretary of state.
   A. True
   B. False

2. A deed is the written instrument by which an owner of real estate intentionally conveys the right, title, or interest in the real estate to someone else.
   A. True
   B. False

3. To be valid, a deed must include a recital of consideration, an identifiable grantee, and a recital of exceptions and reservations.
   A. True
   B. False

4. Title is considered transferred when the deed is actually signed and acknowledged by the grantor.
   A. True
   B. False

5. To be valid, a deed must be signed by both the grantor and the grantee.
   A. True
   B. False

6. In a special warranty deed, the covenant of seisin warrants that the grantor's title will be good against third parties.
   A. True
   B. False

7. In a general warranty deed, the covenant of further assurances represents a promise by the grantor that the grantor will obtain and deliver any instrument needed to ensure good title.
   A. True
   B. False

8. A bargain and sale deed does not contain any express warranties against encumbrances.
   A. True
   B. False

9. If a trustee wants to convey real estate back to the trustor, the trustee uses a trustee's deed.
   A. True
   B. False

10. In a deed executed under a court order, the full amount of consideration is stated in the deed.
    A. True
    B. False

11. Adverse possession is an example of involuntary alienation of property.
    A. True
    B. False

12. When a property owner dies, the owner's heirs by descent or by will may immediately take possession of any real estate.
    A. True
    B. False

13. While a deed must be delivered during the grantor's lifetime, a will takes effect only after the owner's death.
    A. True
    B. False

14. A person who receives real property through a testamentary transfer is called the devisee.
    A. True
    B. False

15. Real property of an owner who dies intestate is distributed according to the laws of the state in which the owner resided at the time of death.
    A. True
    B. False

16. The type of property ownership the grantees will receive is stated in the deed.
    A. True
    B. False

17. Encumbrances that run with the land, such as an easement, are stated in the sale disclosures rather than the deed.
    A. True
    B. False

18. One of the functions of probate is to determine the precise assets of the deceased person.
    A. True
    B. False

19. Many states have laws establishing a transfer tax that must be paid on conveyances of real estate.
    A. True
    B. False

20. When an estate is probated, the court usually selects the executor to distribute the assets to the heirs.
    A. True
    B. False

MULTIPLE CHOICE

Circle the correct answer.

1. The grantor is conveying an interest that is less than fee simple absolute. This explanation of the extent of ownership will be found in
   A. the seisin clause.
   B. the granting clause.
   C. the habendum clause.
   D. the exceptions and reservations.

2. A seller conveys property to a buyer by a written document that contains five covenants protecting the buyer's title. What is the seller's role in the transaction?
   A. Grantee
   B. Grantor
   C. Devisor
   D. Devisee

3. The verification that the grantor's signature is both genuine and voluntary is
   A. a judgment.
   B. an attachment.
   C. a consideration.
   D. an acknowledgment.

4. Which of these is an example of involuntary alienation?
   A. Sale
   B. Gift
   C. Foreclosure
   D. Will

5. The transfer of an interest in a parcel of real estate is typically in a document called
   A. the title.
   B. the deed.
   C. the attachment.
   D. the mortgage.

6. All of these are necessary to a valid deed *EXCEPT*
   A. recital of consideration.
   B. words of conveyance.
   C. the grantee's signature.
   D. delivery.

7. "I do hereby convey to my nearest relative all my interest in the property called 123 Main Street, Bismarck, North Dakota, to have and to hold, in consideration of receipt of the amount of $10 and other good and valuable consideration." When signed, this document is
   A. a valid conveyance by deed.
   B. an invalid conveyance by deed, because the property conveyed is inadequately described.
   C. an invalid conveyance by deed, because there is no recital of exceptions and reservations.
   D. an invalid conveyance by deed, because the grantee is inadequately identified.

8. The type of deed that imposes the least liability on the grantor is
   A. a special warranty deed.
   B. a bargain and sale deed.
   C. a quitclaim deed.
   D. a general warranty deed.

9. Title is *NOT* considered transferred until the deed is
   A. signed by the grantor.
   B. delivered to and accepted by the grantee.
   C. delivered to the grantee.
   D. released from escrow.

10. Which of these is a guarantee that the grantor has the right to convey the property?
    A. Covenant of seisin
    B. Covenant of further assurance
    C. Covenant of quiet enjoyment
    D. Covenant against encumbrances

11. A bargain and sale deed contains how many express warranties?
    A. 0
    B. 2
    C. 3
    D. 5

12. Which type of deed is used by a grantor whose interest in the real estate may be unknown?
    A. Bargain-and-sale deed
    B. Special warranty deed
    C. General warranty deed
    D. Quitclaim deed

13. Under state law, one-half of an intestate decedent's property goes to the decedent's spouse, one- fourth is divided equally among the decedent's children, and one-fourth goes to the state. If there is no spouse, the children divide three-fourths equally. A citizen of this state dies intestate, survived by an ex-spouse and seven adult children. If the estate is $865,550, how much will each child receive under state law?
    A. $0
    B. $61,825.25
    C. $92,737.50
    D. $123,650.00

14. In one state, transfer tax is $1.20 for each $300 (or fraction of $300) of the sales price of any parcel of real estate. If a seller's property sold for $250,000, what will be the amount of the transfer tax due?
    A. $97.00
    B. $999.99
    C. $1,000.80
    D. $1,250.50

15. In front of witnesses, a property owner says to a friend, "I never made a will, but I want you to have my property when I die." If the friend becomes the owner of the property, it is because the state recognizes what kind of will?
    A. Holographic
    B. Testamentary
    C. Nuncupative
    D. Probated

16. In one state, the transfer tax is $0.80 per $500 or fraction thereof. There is no tax charged on the first $500 of the price. What tax must the seller pay if the property sells for $329,650?
    A. $525.60
    B. $526.40
    C. $527.20
    D. $528.00

17. A modification to a will is called
    A. an addendum.
    B. an amendment.
    C. a probate.
    D. a codicil.

18. All of these are reasons for probate *EXCEPT*
    A. to ensure that the heirs do not fight among themselves.
    B. to confirm that the will is valid.
    C. to determine the exact assets of the deceased person.
    D. to identify which persons get any of the estate.

19. When a corporation transfers ownership of property, the deed must be signed by
    A. an authorized officer.
    B. a shareholder.
    C. a broker.
    D. a grantee.

20. The granting clause in a special warranty deed generally contains the words
    A. "grantor conveys and warrants."
    B. "grantor grants, bargains, and sells."
    C. "grantor remises, releases, and quitclaims."
    D. "grantor remises, releases, alienates, and conveys."

21. A general power of attorney
    A. is illegal in most states.
    B. requires delivery and acceptance by the grantee.
    C. provides general legal authority for intestate succession.
    D. provides authority to carry out all of the business dealings of the person giving it.

22. What limits are set by the covenants in a general warranty deed?
    A. No limits are set.
    B. The covenants are limited to matters that occurred during the time the grantor owned the property.
    C. The covenants are limited to the matters that occurred within the last 10 years.
    D. The covenants are limited to the matters that occurred before the grantor owned the property.

ACTIVITY: DEED CHARACTERISTICS

Identify the characteristics of deeds by marking the appropriate columns.

Characteristics	Types of Deeds			
	General Warranty	**Special Warranty**	**Bargain and Sale**	**Quitclaim**
Covenant of warranty forever				
Covenant of further assurances				
Covenant of quiet enjoyment				
Covenant against encumbrances				
Covenant of seisin				
Express warranties				
Implied warranties				
Delivery and acceptance				
Legal description				
Habendum clause				
Granting clause				
Identifiable grantee				
Signature of grantor				
Consideration				
Grantor of sound mind				
Grantor of lawful age				

UNIT 6 ANSWERS

MATCHING A

1. **I**
2. **J**
3. **B**
4. **F**
5. **D**
6. **G**
7. **A**
8. **H**
9. **E**
10. **C**

MATCHING B

1. **F**
2. **G**
3. **E**
4. **J**
5. **A**
6. **C**
7. **H**
8. **B**
9. **I**
10. **D**

TRUE OR FALSE

1. **B** The answer is false. Title to real estate is a way of referring to ownership; it is not an actual printed document. (84)

2. **A** The answer is true. A *deed* is the written instrument by which an owner of real estate intentionally conveys the right, title, or interest in the real estate to someone else. (84)

3. **B** The answer is false. To be valid, a deed must include a recital of consideration and an identifiable grantee; a deed *may* contain a recital of exceptions and reservations. (84–85)

4. **B** The answer is false. Title is considered transferred when the deed is actually delivered to the grantee by the grantor. (85)

5. **B** The answer is false. To be valid, a deed must be signed by all grantors named in the deed. Grantees are not required to sign the deed, but must be willing to accept it for title to transfer. (84–85)

6. **B** The answer is false. In a general warranty deed, the covenant of seisin warrants that the grantor is the owner of the property and has the right to convey it. (89)

7. **A** The answer is true. The covenant of further assurances represents a promise by the grantor that the grantor will obtain and deliver any instrument needed to ensure good title. (89)

8. **A** The answer is true. Although a bargain and sale deed does not contain any express warranties against encumbrances, it does imply that the grantor holds title and possession of the property. (89–90)

9. **B** The answer is false. A trustee uses a reconveyance deed to return title to the trustor. (91)

10. **A** The answer is true. One common characteristic of deeds executed pursuant to court order is that the full consideration is usually stated in the deed, instead of "$10 and other valuable consideration." (91)

11. **A** The answer is true. Adverse possession is a means of involuntary transfer; it will take title away from an owner who fails to use or inspect the property for a number of years. (93)

12. **B** The answer is false. When a property owner dies, the owner's heirs by descent or will immediately take title to the property, but they may take possession *only after probate*. (96–97)

13. **A** The answer is true. A will is made by an owner to convey title to real or personal property after the owner's death. A deed must be delivered during the lifetime of the grantor to convey a present interest in property. (94–95)

14. **A** The answer is true. The gift of real property by will is called a devise, and a person who receives real property by will is called a devisee. (95)

15. **B** The answer is false. Real property of an owner who dies intestate is distributed according to the laws of the state in which the property is located. (96)

16. **A** The answer is true. When it is necessary to define or explain the ownership to be enjoyed by the grantee, a habendum clause may follow the granting clause. (86)

17. **B** The answer is false. A deed may note any encumbrances that affect the title being conveyed. (86)

18. **A** The answer is true. Probate is a formal judicial process that proves or confirms the validity of a will, determines the precise assets of the deceased person, and identifies the people to whom the assets are to pass. (96)

19. **A** The answer is true. Many states have enacted laws providing for a state transfer tax on a conveyance of real estate; the tax is usually payable when the deed is recorded. (91)

20. **B** The answer is false. The executor is named in the will; if no executor is named in the will or the named executor refuses or is unable to perform that function, the court will appoint an administrator for the estate. (96)

MULTIPLE CHOICE

1. **C** The answer is the habendum clause. The habendum clause defines the extent of ownership that is being conveyed. (86)

2. **B** The answer is grantor. Because the seller is conveying the property interest, the seller is the *grantor*. The person who receives the interest is the *grantee*. (85)

3. **D** The answer is an acknowledgement. An acknowledgment is a formal declaration under oath that the person who signs a written document does so voluntarily, and that the signature is genuine. (87)

4. **C** The answer is a foreclosure. When a property owner defaults on a loan secured by the property, the lender may force the sale of the property by the process called foreclosure. (92–93)

5. **B** The answer is the deed. A deed is the written document that transfers a real estate interest. Evidence of ownership (title) is written in the deed. An attachment is the process of taking a person's property into legal custody by a court order. A mortgage provides the security for a loan. (84)

6. **C** The answer is the grantee's signature. The grantee does not need to sign the deed, because the grantee receives the property. (85)

7. **D** The answer is an invalid conveyance by deed, because the grantee is inadequately identified. Although the property may be adequately described, the grantee is not sufficiently identified, making the deed insufficient to serve as an instrument of transfer. (85–86)

8. **C** The answer is a quitclaim deed. A quitclaim deed carries no covenants or warranties and generally only conveys whatever interest the grantor has when the deed is delivered. (90)

9. **B** The answer is delivered to and accepted by the grantee. The most complete answer is delivered to and accepted by the grantee during the grantor's lifetime. (88)

10. **A** The answer is covenant of seisin. The covenant against encumbrances is a warranty that the property is free from encumbrances, except as so noted. The grantor further assures that everything will be done to make the title good. Quiet enjoyment guarantees that the title will be good against third parties who might try to bring legal action to gain the property. (89)

11. **A** The answer is 0. A bargain and sale deed contains no express warranties against encumbrances; however, it does imply that the grantor holds title and possession of the property. (89–90)

12. **D** The answer is a quitclaim deed. A quitclaim deed transfers whatever interest the grantor may have. If the grantor has no interest, the grantee will acquire nothing and have no right of warranty claim against the grantor. (90)

13. **C** The answer is $92,737.50. The ex-spouse gets nothing. The state gets one-fourth and the remaining three-fourths will be divided equally among the seven children: $865,550 ÷ 4 = $216,387.50 to the state. The remaining amount, $649,162.50, is divided seven ways, leaving $92,737.50 per child. (95–96)

14. **C** The answer is $1,000.80. The transfer tax due is $1,000.80:

    $250,000 ÷ $300 = 833.33, rounded up to 834

    834 × $1.20 = $1,000.80

    (91–92)

15. **C** The answer is nuncupative. A nuncupative will is an oral will. A holographic will is completely handwritten. A testamentary trust is established by will after the owner's death. *Probate* is the process of determining the validity of the will and distributing the assets of the estate. (95)

16. **C** The answer is $527.20. The seller must pay $527.20:

    $329,650 – the $500 = $329,150

    $329,150 ÷ $500 = 658.3, rounded up to 659 659 × $0.80 = $527.20

    (91–92)

17. **D** The answer is a codicil. Any modification to a previously executed will is contained in a separate document called a codicil. Additional agreements attached to an agreement of sale are addenda; an amendment is a change to the existing content of a contract. Probate is the process of determining the validity of a will. (95)

18. **A** The answer is to ensure that the heirs do not fight among themselves. Preventing fights among heirs is not the reason for probate. (96–97)

19. **A** The answer is an authorized officer. Proper authority for the sale must be given by bylaws or by a resolution passed by the board of directors. Shareholders are not necessarily officers, nor are brokers. A grantee does not sign a deed. (88)

20. **D** The answer is "grantor remises, releases, alienates, and conveys." The granting clause in a special warranty deed generally contains the words *grantor remises, releases, alienates,* and *conveys.* (89)

21. **D** The answer is provides authority to carry out all of the business dealings of the person giving it. A general power of attorney provides authority to carry out all of the business dealings of the person giving it. A special power of attorney permits the execution of only certain acts. (87)

22. **A** The answer is no limits are set. No limits are set by the covenants in a general warranty deed; the grantor defends the title against the grantor and all those who previously held title. (88–89)

ACTIVITY: DEED CHARACTERISTICS

Characteristics	Types of Deeds			
	General Warranty	Special Warranty	Bargain and Sale	Quitclaim
Covenant of warranty forever	✓	✓		
Covenant of further assurances	✓	✓		
Covenant of quiet enjoyment	✓	✓		
Covenant against encumbrances	✓	✓		
Covenant of seisin	✓	✓		
Express warranties	✓	✓		
Implied warranties	✓	✓	✓	
Delivery and acceptance	✓	✓	✓	✓
Legal description	✓	✓	✓	✓
Habendum clause	✓	✓	✓	✓
Granting clause	✓	✓	✓	✓
Identifiable grantee	✓	✓	✓	✓
Signature of grantor	✓	✓	✓	✓
Consideration	✓	✓	✓	✓
Grantor of sound mind	✓	✓	✓	✓
Grantor of lawful age	✓	✓	✓	✓

Note that the check marks for the Special Warranty Deed column show that its basic warranties are similar to the general warranty's. Remember that a special warranty deed only warrants the covenants for the period of time the property was owned by the grantor.

UNIT 7

Title Records

LEARNING OBJECTIVES

When you have completed this unit, you will be able to

> **explain** the public recordation system and its importance to the title insurer; and
> **explain** the benefits of title insurance and the difference between an owner's policy and a lender's policy.

KEY TERMS

abstract of title
action to quiet title
actual notice
attorney's opinion of title
certificate of title

chain of title
constructive notice
marketable title
priority
recording

subrogation
title insurance
title search
Torrens system

MATCHING

Write the letter of the matching term on the appropriate line.

A. abstractor	**1.** ___ The act of placing documents in the public record
B. actual notice	**2.** ___ The legal presumption that information may be obtained through diligent inquiry
C. chain of title	
D. constructive notice	**3.** ___ When an individual is actually aware of a fact, they are said to have this type of notice
E. title insurance	
F. recording	**4.** ___ The order of rights in time, such as who recorded first, which party was in possession first, et cetera
G. cloud on the title	
H. priority	**5.** ___ The record of a property's ownership
I. action to quiet title	**6.** ___ A legal action to remove a cloud on the title and establish legal ownership
J. title search	

A. abstractor
B. actual notice
C. chain of title
D. constructive notice
E. title insurance
F. recording
G. cloud on the title
H. priority
I. action to quiet title
J. title search

1. ___ The act of placing documents in the public record

2. ___ The legal presumption that information may be obtained through diligent inquiry

3. ___ When an individual is actually aware of a fact, they are said to have this type of notice

4. ___ The order of rights in time, such as who recorded first, which party was in possession first, et cetera

5. ___ The record of a property's ownership

6. ___ A legal action to remove a cloud on the title and establish legal ownership

7. ___ An examination of all the public records to determine if any defects exist in a property's history of ownership

8. ___ The individual who prepares a summary report of the results of a title search

9. ___ A contract under which a policyholder is protected from losses arising from defects in title

10. ___ Title problem that is created by a gap in the chain of title or other dispute of ownership

TRUE OR FALSE

Circle the correct answer.

1. Any individual who is interested in a particular property may review the public records to learn about the documents, claims, and other issues that affect its ownership.
    A. True
    B. False

2. A written document that affects any estate, right, title, or interest in land must be recorded in the county in which the property owner resides.
    A. True
    B. False

3. To be eligible for recording, a document pertaining to real estate must be drawn and executed in accordance with the requirements of the federal government.
    A. True
    B. False

4. Constructive notice means that information about a property is not only available, but that someone has been made aware of that information.
    A. True
    B. False

5. A search of the public records will disclose all liens that exist against a property.
    A. True
    B. False

6. The term *chain of title* refers to the record of a property's ownership.
    A. True
    B. False

7. In a typical title search, the chain of title is examined, beginning with the earliest records of ownership and proceeding forward up to the present owner.
    A. True
    B. False

8. An extended coverage title insurance policy protects a homeowner against rights of parties in possession and unrecorded liens.
    A. True
    B. False

9. One of the requirements of marketable title is that it could convince a reasonably well-informed and prudent purchaser, acting on business principles and with full knowledge of the significant facts, that the property could be resold or mortgaged at a later time.
    A. True
    B. False

10. A certificate of title is a guarantee of legal ownership.
    A. True
    B. False

MULTIPLE CHOICE

Circle the correct answer.

1. All of these are acceptable evidence of an owner's title *EXCEPT*
   A. a recorded deed.
   B. an abstract of title and attorney's opinion.
   C. a title insurance policy.
   D. a certificate of title.

2. To serve as public notice, a deed is recorded in
   A. the city where the owner lives.
   B. the county (or counties) or, in some states, the town where the property is located.
   C. the state capital.
   D. the largest city in the state.

3. Five years ago, a lien was recorded against a parcel of property by a construction company. When the lien was recorded, X was the owner of the property and Z was an active partner in the construction company. The property is in county A, but the lien was recorded in county B. Now, Z is trying to buy the property from X. A title search in county A disclosed no liens against the property. Which of these is *TRUE*?
   A. Z has constructive notice of the lien but not actual notice, because of the mistake in recording.
   B. Z has actual notice of the lien but not constructive notice, because of the mistake in recording.
   C. Z has both actual and constructive notice of the lien, because of Z's association with the construction company and the recorded lien.
   D. Z has no notice of the lien.

4. Shortly after closing on the purchase of a parcel of real estate, the buyer discovered that there were serious flaws in the title that made it unlikely that the property could be resold in the future. What can the buyer do now?
   A. Because the title was flawed, the buyer can legally void the sale, and the seller must return any consideration.
   B. The buyer has no recourse.
   C. Because the seller conveyed unmarketable title, the buyer is entitled to a new title report.
   D. Because the buyer has accepted the deed, the only recourse is to sue the seller under any covenants contained in the deed.

5. The reason that deeds and liens and other claims are recorded is to give
   A. constructive notice.
   B. actual notice.
   C. direct notice.
   D. nominal notice.

6. A history of all recorded liens and encumbrances is revealed in
   A. the title insurance policy.
   B. the unrecorded documents.
   C. the chain of title.
   D. the abstract.

7. The person who prepares a certificate of title is
   A. the broker.
   B. the abstractor.
   C. the buyer.
   D. the seller.

8. Which of these would be covered in a standard title insurance policy?
   A. Defects discoverable by physical inspection
   B. Unrecorded liens
   C. Forged documents
   D. Easements and restrictive covenants

9. A title insurance policy that protects the interests of a mortgagee is called
   A. a leasehold policy.
   B. a lender's policy.
   C. a certificate of sale policy.
   D. an ALTA policy.

10. In the states in which it has been adopted, the Marketable Title Act
    A. establishes standardized forms for abstracts of title.
    B. disqualifies use of an attorney's opinion of title as acceptable evidence of title.
    C. limits the time beyond which title records must be searched.
    D. provides a certification system for qualifying title insurance companies.

FILL-IN-THE-BLANK

Select the word or words that best complete these statements:

abstract of title

actual notice

opinion of title

constructive notice

exclusions

improperly delivered deeds

marketable title

once, at closing

preliminary title search

rights of parties in possession

action to quiet title

Torrens system

twice, at purchase and resale

1. To protect the buyer, in some states, a(n) _____ is conducted as soon as an offer to purchase has been accepted.

2. The type of notice that means the information is not only available but that someone has been given the information and is aware of it is called _____.

3. If a title has no serious defects, does not expose a purchaser to litigation, and does not cause the property to have a poor likelihood of resale, it is called _____.

4. Rather than a certificate of title, in some parts of the country an attorney's _____ is used as evidence of title.

5. The premium for a title insurance policy is paid _____.

6. Uninsurable losses, such as zoning ordinances, named in a title insurance policy are called _____.

7. A summary report of what a title search found in the public record is called a(an) _____.

8. The standard coverage title policy insures against hidden defects, such as _____.

9. Registration in the _____ provides evidence of title without needing to make an additional search of public records.

10. The legal presumption that information about rights in a property may be obtained by a person through diligent questioning and research is called _____.

ACTIVITY: TRACING THE CHAIN OF TITLE

This abstract illustrates the complete title record for Lot 27, Block 6 of a subdivision. Mark the point at which the chain of title is broken.

Grantor	Grantee	By Instrument	Conveyance Date
Ferris-Bumper Builders, Inc.	Barton Doyle and Jane Doyle	Warranty Deed	January 19, 1909
Barton Doyle and Jane Doyle	Market Title & Trust Company	Trust Deed	January 20, 1909
Market Title & Trust Company	Barton Doyle and Jane Doyle	Reconveyance Deed	June 10, 1935
Barton Doyle and Jane Doyle	Anton Feldspar	Bargain and Sale Deed	March 7, 1940
Peter Parker and Mary Parker	Lamont Cranston and Gloria Reeve	Warranty Deed	November 16, 1958
Lamont Cranston and Gloria Reeve	Brookfield Bank and Trust Company	Mortgage	November 8, 1958
Lamont Cranston and Gloria Reeve	Gerald Carlos and Lydia Carlos	Warranty Deed	September 4, 1979
Brookfield Bank and Trust Co.	Lamont Cranston and Gloria Reeve	Release	May 2, 1995

UNIT 7 ANSWERS

MATCHING

1. **F**

2. **D**

3. **B**

4. **H**

5. **C**

6. **I**

7. **J**

8. **A**

9. **E**

10. **G**

TRUE OR FALSE

1. **A** The answer is true. Public records are open to anyone interested in a particular property. A review of the records will reveal the documents, claims, and other details that affect its ownership. (103)

2. **B** The answer is false. A written document that affects any estate, right, title, or interest in land must be recorded in the county (or counties) or, in some states, town in which the property is located. (104–105)

3. **B** The answer is false. To be eligible for recording, a document pertaining to real estate must be drawn and executed in accordance with the requirements of the recording acts of the state in which the property is located. (104–105)

4. **B** The answer is false. Actual notice means that not only is the information about property available, but someone has been made aware of that information. (104)

5. **B** The answer is false. A search of the public records will disclose all recorded liens that exist against a property. (106)

6. **A** The answer is true. The chain of title is the record of a property's ownership, beginning with the earliest owner. (105–106)

7. **B** The answer is false. In a typical title search, the chain of title is examined beginning with the present owner and tracing backwards to the earliest records of ownership or a definite period of years, depending on state law. (106)

8. **A** The answer is true. Extended coverage as provided by an American Land Title Association (ALTA) policy includes the protections of a standard policy plus additional protections. (109)

9. **A** The answer is true. A marketable title should disclose no serious defects, should not depend on doubtful questions of law, and should convince a reasonably well-informed and prudent purchaser, acting on business principles and with full knowledge of the significant facts, that the property could be resold or mortgaged at a later time. (107)

10. **B** The answer is false. A certificate of title is evidence but not a guarantee of ownership. A certificate of title is a statement of opinion of the title's status on the date the certificate is issued. (107)

MULTIPLE CHOICE

1. **A** The answer is a recorded deed. A recorded deed is nothing more than that. Through examination of recorded documents can either bolster or reveal defects in the title. (104–105)

2. **B** The answer is the county (or counties) or, in some states, the town where the property is located. Because land is immobile, it makes sense to record all information about title to the property in the county or counties in which it is located. Some owners frequently relocate, and they would be hard to find. (104)

3. **B** The answer is Z has actual notice of the lien but not constructive notice, because of the mistake in recording. Because Z was a partner, Z knew that the lien was filed. Constructive notice is not given because the lien was not filed in the county where the property is located, which is where it would be expected to be filed. (104)

4. **D**   The answer is because the buyer has accepted the deed, the only recourse is to sue the seller under any covenants contained in the deed. Professionals should look at the evidence of ownership before closing. There is more leverage to get problems corrected before closing than after closing. (107)

5. **A**   The answer is constructive notice. The recorder's office is a central place to deposit and discover information. If a document is recorded, a buyer or other interested party cannot claim ignorance of it; its presence would have been revealed by a search of the records. (104)

6. **D**   The answer is the abstract. The title insurance policy lists coverage and exceptions to the policy. Unrecorded documents have not been examined. The chain of title traces ownership. The abstract is the most complete documentation of recorded liens and encumbrances. (106)

7. **B**   The answer is the abstractor. The abstractor searches all of the public records, and then summarizes the various events that affected the title throughout its history. (106)

8. **C**   The answer is forged documents. Title insurance protects against forged documents, but does not protect against claims of parties in possession because the grantee should have visited the property; nor does it cover unrecorded liens. Easements and restrictive covenants are found in the deed and should be known to the grantee. (108–109)

9. **B**   The answer is a lender's policy. The mortgagee is the lender. The mortgagee's policy is transferable. (109)

10. **C**   The answer is limits the time beyond which title records must be searched. The law extinguishes certain interests and cures certain defects arising before the root of the title. (106)

FILL-IN-THE-BLANK

1.   To protect the buyer, in some states, a *preliminary title search* is conducted as soon as an offer to purchase has been accepted.

2.   The type of notice that means the information is not only available but that someone has been given the information and is aware of it is called *actual notice*.

3.   If a title has no serious defects, does not expose a purchaser to litigation, and does not cause the proper-ty to have a poor likelihood of resale, it is called *marketable title*.

4.   Rather than a certificate of title, in some parts of the country an attorney's *opinion of title* is used as evidence of title.

5.   The premium for a title insurance policy is paid *once, at closing*.

6.   Uninsurable losses, such as zoning ordinances, named in a title insurance policy are called *exclusions*.

7.   A summary report of what a title search found in the public record is called an *abstract of title*.

8.   The standard coverage title policy insures against hidden defects, such as *improperly delivered deeds*.

9.   Registration in the *Torrens system* provides evidence of title without needing to make an additional search of public records.

10.   The legal presumption that information about rights in a property may be obtained by a person through diligent questioning and research is called *constructive notice*.

ACTIVITY: TRACING THE CHAIN OF TITLE

In November 1958, Peter and Mary Parker conveyed title as grantors, but there is no indication that they ever received title as grantees from Anton Feldspar.

Grantor	Grantee	By Instrument	Conveyance Date
Ferris-Bumper Builders, Inc.	Barton Doyle and Jane Doyle	Warranty Deed	January 19, 1909
Barton Doyle and Jane Doyle	Market Title & Trust Company	Trust Deed	January 20, 1909
Market Title & Trust Company	Barton Doyle and Jane Doyle	Reconveyance Deed	June 10, 1935
Barton Doyle and Jane Doyle	Anton Feldspar	Bargain and Sale Deed	March 7, 1940
Peter Parker and Mary Parker	Lamont Cranston and Gloria Reeve	Warranty Deed	November 16, 1958
Lamont Cranston and Gloria Reeve	Brookfield Bank and Trust Company	Mortgage	November 8, 1958
Lamont Cranston and Gloria Reeve	Gerald Carlos and Lydia Carlos	Warranty Deed	September 4, 1979
Brookfield Bank and Trust Co.	Lamont Cranston and Gloria Reeve	Release	May 2, 1995

UNIT
8

Real Estate Brokerage

LEARNING OBJECTIVES

When you have completed this unit, you will be able to

> **describe** the fundamentals of real estate brokerage and licensing laws;
> **describe** the purpose and basic elements of antitrust laws including price fixing, boycotts, and allocation of markets;
> **discuss** the services provided to real estate practitioners by professional organizations, including the creation and enforcement of ethical codes; and
> **explain** how real estate professionals should use technology in real estate practice to comply with laws and ethical standards.

KEY TERMS

antitrust laws	Electronic Signatures in	minimum level of services
boycott	Global and National	multiple listing service (MLS)
brokerage	Commerce Act (E-Sign)	National Do Not Call Registry
code of ethics	employee	price-fixing
commission	independent contractor	procuring cause
disclaimers	Internet Data Exchange (IDX)	ready, willing, and able buyer
electronic contracting	policy	Uniform Electronic
	managing broker	Transactions Act (UETA)

MATCHING

Write the letter of the matching term on the appropriate line.

A. allocation of markets	**1.** ___ Membership in this service provides an opportunity for the marketing of property
B. antitrust laws	**2.** ___ Statutes enacted by state legislatures to protect the public and ensure a standard of competence in the real estate industry
C. multiple listing service (MLS)	**3.** ___ The device by which a state licensing authority administers and enforces the statutory law
D. commission	**4.** ___ The business of bringing parties together
E. sales associate	**5.** ___ An individual who is licensed to buy, sell, exchange, or lease property for others, and to charge a fee for those services
F. brokerage	**6.** ___ When two or more businesses conspire against another business to withhold patronage to reduce competition
G. independent contractor	**7.** ___ A person who is licensed only to perform real estate activities on behalf of a broker
H. administrative regulations	**8.** ___ A sales associate whose activities are closely controlled, and who is entitled to benefits, unemployment compensation, and income tax withholding
I. employee	
J. ready, willing, and able buyer	**9.** ___ A sales associate who works under the terms of a written contract and receives a substantial portion of her income from sales production rather than hours worked
K. real estate broker	**10.** ___ A form of compensation computed as a percentage of the total sales price of a property
L. procuring cause	**11.** ___ The broker who starts an uninterrupted chain of events that results in the sale of a property
M. comparative market analysis (CMA)	**12.** ___ A person who is prepared to buy on the seller's terms and is ready to take positive steps toward consummation of the transaction
N. real estate license laws	**13.** ___ An analysis performed to assist a seller in pricing a property
O. group boycott	**14.** ___ An illegal division of territories to avoid competition
	15. ___ Laws that prohibit price fixing and tie-in agreements

TRUE OR FALSE

Circle the correct answer.

1. Only a few states regulate the activities of real estate licensees.
   A. True
   B. False

2. Real estate license laws set up a disciplinary system to enforce the acceptable standards of conduct and practice for licensees.
   A. True
   B. False

3. A real estate sales associate is licensed to buy, sell, exchange, or lease real property for others, and to charge a fee for those services.
   A. True
   B. False

4. The Internal Revenue Service has established criteria for determining whether a sales associate is classified as an employee or a nonemployee for income tax purposes.
   A. True
   B. False

5. The amount of a broker's compensation is always negotiable.
   A. True
   B. False

6. A real estate sales associate is an individual who is licensed to perform real estate activities on behalf of a licensed broker.
   A. True
   B. False

7. If present at the time the transaction closes, a broker is considered to be the procuring cause of a sale.
   A. True
   B. False

8. Price-fixing, group boycotting, and allocation of markets are three examples of antitrust violations.
   A. True
   B. False

9. The practice of illegally setting standard prices for products or services is called a tie-in agreement.
   A. True
   B. False

10. Real estate trade associations offer professional training to members, who must follow a code of ethics.
    A. True
    B. False

MULTIPLE CHOICE

Circle the correct answer.

1. Why have real estate license laws been put into effect?
   A. To protect licensees from lawsuits
   B. To protect the public and establish standards of professionalism
   C. To prevent licensees from engaging in profit-making activities
   D. To establish maximum levels of competency and a moral marketplace

2. In real estate, a sales associate is always
   A. an independent contractor.
   B. an employee of a licensed broker.
   C. a licensee who performs real estate activities on behalf of a broker.
   D. a combination office manager, marketer, and organizer with a fundamental understanding of the real estate industry, who may or may not be licensed.

3. All of these are requirements for independent contractor status used by the Internal Revenue Service *EXCEPT*
   A. a current real estate license.
   B. specific hours stated in a written agreement.
   C. a written agreement that specifies that the individual will not be treated as an employee for tax purposes.
   D. a substantial portion of the individual's income is based on sales production rather than hours worked.

4. A broker who owns a realty agency does not permit his sales associates to agree to more than a 5% commission in any transaction. After reading a newspaper article about this realty agency's policies, the broker of another realty agency decides to also adopt the 5% maximum. Based on these facts, which of these statements is *TRUE*?
   A. The first realty agency's policy is price-fixing and violates the antitrust law.
   B. Although the first realty agency's policy is legal, the second realty agency's adoption of the same maximum commission may constitute an antitrust violation if both brokers are in the same real estate market.
   C. Both brokers engaged in illegal price-fixing.
   D. Neither broker has committed an antitrust violation.

5. A real estate broker had a listing agreement with a seller that specified a 6% commission. The broker showed the home to a prospective buyer. The next day, the buyer called the seller directly and offered to buy the house for 5% less than the asking price. The seller agreed to the price and informed the broker in writing that no further brokerage services would be required. The sale went to closing six weeks later. Based on these facts, which of these statements is *TRUE*?
   A. While the broker was the procuring cause of the sale, the seller properly canceled the contract; without a valid employment agreement in force at the time of closing, the broker is not entitled to a commission.
   B. The broker is entitled to a partial commission, and the buyer is obligated to pay it.
   C. Under the facts stated, the broker is not the procuring cause of this sale but is still entitled to a commission.
   D. The broker was the procuring cause of the sale and is entitled to the full 6% commission.

6. A qualified buyer makes a written offer on a property on March 6 by filling out and signing a purchase offer. Later that day, the seller accepts and signs the offer, keeping one copy. The broker gives a copy of the signed agreement to the buyer on March 8. The seller's deed is delivered on May 1. The deed is recorded on May 7, and the buyer takes possession on May 15. When is the broker's commission payable if this is a *usual* transaction?
   A. March 8
   B. May 1
   C. May 7
   D. May 15

7. All of these are violations of federal antitrust law *EXCEPT*
   A. group boycotting.
   B. allocation of customers.
   C. commission splitting.
   D. tie-in agreements.

8. All of these are ways for a broker to charge for services *EXCEPT*
   A. standard community rate.
   B. flat fee.
   C. hourly rate.
   D. commission based on a percentage of the selling price.

9. What is the main value of a multiple listing service (MLS) for sellers?
   A. Real estate professionals do not have to work as hard to secure property listings.
   B. It simplifies closing procedures.
   C. It reduces cooperation among brokers.
   D. It exposes the property to a greater number of prospective buyers.

10. After license laws are enacted by the legislature, who is responsible for adopting administrative regulations?
    A. A subcommittee that reports to the legislature
    B. A local association of REALTORS®
    C. Licensing authority (division, Commission, etc.)
    D. Brokers and sales associates appointed by the governor

11. When communicating with clients or consumers via email, all of these are examples of professional email etiquette *EXCEPT*
    A. using spell check.
    B. providing useful information in the subject line.
    C. avoiding sending large attachments.
    D. responding to emails within one week.

12. Although state laws vary regarding internet advertising, which of these is a typical element of state policy or law?
    A. Email sent by a real estate professional needs to include the professional's name, phone number, and real estate license number.
    B. Ads must contain true, current information and avoid misleading the potential client or customer.
    C. On a website containing their ads, real estate professionals only need to identify themselves as a broker or sales associate on the site's home page.
    D. It is acceptable for only the sales associate's name (without the broker's name) to be shown in an ad.

13. The broker may still be entitled to a commission in which of these situations where a pending property sale did *NOT* close?
    A. The buyer wanted to add the kitchen appliances to the sale, but the seller refused.
    B. The buyer decided not to buy the property.
    C. The seller decided not to sell.
    D. Financing fell through for the buyer.

14. An arrangement to sell one product only if the buyer purchases another product as well is called
    A. a tie-in agreement.
    B. a fee-for-services.
    C. a buydown provision.
    D. an allocation of customers.

15. The primary purpose of the Uniform Electronic Transactions Act (UETA) is to
    A. facilitate the use of social media.
    B. protect consumers against unwanted email.
    C. remove barriers in electronic commerce that would otherwise prevent enforceability of contracts.
    D. allow brokers to close more deals.

16. Even if a consumer has requested placement on the National Do Not Call Registry, a real estate professional may call the consumer up to how many months after the consumer's last purchase, delivery, or payment?
    A. 3 months
    B. 6 months
    C. 12 months
    D. 18 months

17. The name for the current policy of the National Association of REALTORS® that allows all multiple listing service (MLS) members equal rights to display MLS data is
    A. the virtual office website.
    B. the Internet Listing Display Policy.
    C. the Internet Data Exchange.
    D. the Open Listing Data Service.

18. An important purpose of the E-Sign Act is to
    A. give contracts created using email the same legal standing as those on paper.
    B. require stringent security measures for email communication.
    C. prevent notarization of electronically transmitted agreements.
    D. require all parties to use electronic contracting if the seller prefers it.

19. What is the compensation plan called if a sales associate's commission split increases depending on whether the sales associate achieves higher production goals?
    A. Procuring cause commission
    B. Cooperating broker commission
    C. Graduated commission split
    D. 100% commission plan

20. What is the practice called when a consumer selects specific services to use and only pays the real estate professional for those services?
    A. Unbundling services
    B. Tie-in agreement
    C. Discounted services
    D. Allocation of markets

MATH PRACTICE

Circle the correct answer.

1. A seller listed and sold property for $325,000. The seller agreed to pay the listing broker a 7% commission. The listing broker offered a listing 40/60 selling split to any cooperating broker who sold the property. How much did the seller have to pay in commission fees?
    A. $9,100
    B. $11,375
    C. $13,650
    D. $22,750

2. The sales associate's agreement with the broker was a 40/60 split with the broker keeping 40% of the commission. The seller was charged 5.5%. How much did the sales associate receive for obtaining the listing and then selling a house for $279,500?
    A. $6,149.00
    B. $7,686.25
    C. $9,223.50
    D. $15,372.50

3. A broker listed a seller's home for $425,000 with a 4% commission, plus $3,000 for advertising costs. The buyer offered $380,000, and after several counteroffers, finally agreed to $400,000. What was the total cost to the seller?
    A. $16,000
    B. $18,000
    C. $19,000
    D. $20,000

4. Sales associates in a realty agency are compensated based on a formula: 35% of the commission earned on any sale, less a $200 per-transaction desk rental. Sales associates are responsible for paying 75% of all marketing and sales expenses for any property they list, and a $75 per-transaction fee to cover the monthly expenses of advertising and marketing the agency's services. If a sales associate sold a house for $500,000, with a 6% commission, how much would the sales associate be paid if the sale incurred $800 in marketing and advertising costs?
    A. $9,625
    B. $9,700
    C. $10,225
    D. $10,500

5. At a realty agency, sales associates pay a monthly desk rent of 15% of their monthly income. In May, one sales associate receives 5% on a $560,000 sale; 6% on a $348,000 sale; and 6.75% on an $89,500 sale. The only other sales associate at the agency who received a commission in May got 6% on a $410,000 sale. How much did the agency receive in May?
    A. $7,095.97
    B. $11,928.19
    C. $12,251.53
    D. $14,945.00

ACTIVITY: WHO'S WHO?

Based on their statements below, place each speaker's name in the appropriate box of Open Door Realty's organizational chart.

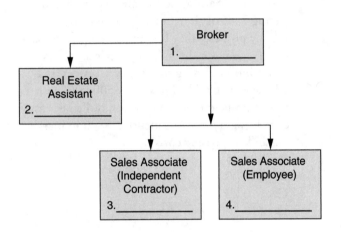

Open Door Realty

Broker
1._____

Real Estate
Assistant
2._____

Sales Associate
(Independent
Contractor)
3._____

Sales Associate
(Employee)
4._____

A: "I'm a licensed real estate salesperson. I set my own hours and pay my own taxes."

B: "I am a broker licensed to buy, sell, exchange, or lease real property for a fee. I'm responsible for the actions performed in the course of the real estate business by all persons licensed under my name."

C: "I am licensed to perform real estate activities on behalf of a broker. I have health insurance and a retirement plan through the company."

D: "Although I don't have a real estate license, I work closely with the licensed real estate professionals in the office to ensure that the office runs smoothly and transactions go to closing."

ACTIVITY: STATE LICENSE REQUIREMENTS

Fill in the license requirements in this table based on your state's license laws, rules, and regulations.

Requirements	Sales License	Broker License
Age		
Education		
Experience		
Bond		
Credit Report		
Recommendations		
Photograph		
Fingerprints		
Continuing Education		
Licensure Period		
Expiration Date		

UNIT 8 ANSWERS

MATCHING

1. **C**

2. **N**

3. **H**

4. **F**

5. **K**

6. **O**

7. **E**

8. **I**

9. **G**

10. **D**

11. **L**

12. **J**

13. **M**

14. **A**

15. **B**

TRUE OR FALSE

1. **B** The answer is false. All 50 states, the District of Columbia, and all Canadian provinces license and regulate the activities of real estate professionals. (116)

2. **A** The answer is true. The real estate license laws not only set standards for conduct and practice, but they also enforce those standards. (116)

3. **B** The answer is false. A real estate *broker* is licensed to buy, sell, exchange, or lease real property for others and to charge a fee for those services. (117)

4. **A** The answer is true. The Internal Revenue Service (IRS) has established three requirements needed to establish a nonemployee status for tax purposes: (1) the individual must have a current real estate license, (2) the individual must have a written contract with the broker specifying that the individual will not be treated as an employee for federal tax purposes, and (3) a substantial portion of the individual's income as a real estate professional must be based on sales production and not on the number of hours worked. (118–119)

5. **A** The answer is true. Because the real estate industry is subject to antitrust laws, the amount of a broker's compensation is always negotiable and may not be set or determined by a multiple listing association or any professional organization. (120)

6. **A** The answer is true. A real estate sales associate is any person licensed to perform real estate activities on behalf of a licensed real estate broker; the broker is fully responsible for the actions performed in the course of the real estate business performed on behalf of the broker. (117–118)

7. **B** The answer is false. A broker is considered the *procuring* cause of a sale if the broker started an uninterrupted chain of events that resulted in the sale. (121)

8. **A** The answer is true. Antitrust laws prohibit monopolies and any contracts, combinations, and conspiracies that unreasonably restrain trade, such as price-fixing, group boycotting, allocation of customers or markets, and tie-in agreements. (124–125)

9. **B** The answer is false. *Price-fixing* is the practice of competitors setting prices for products or services. A tie-in agreement is an agreement to sell one product only if the buyer also purchases another product. (124)

10. **A** The answer is true. Real estate trade associations have a long history of advancing the real estate profession, particularly by establishing a code of ethics to which members must comply. (125–126)

MULTIPLE CHOICE

1. **B** The answer is to protect the public and establish standards of professionalism. Real estate license laws protect the public by ensuring a standard of competence and professionalism in the real estate industry. (116)

2. **C**   The answer is a licensee who performs real estate activities on behalf of a broker. While the sales associate may be treated as an independent contractor for income tax purposes, the sales associate must still work directly under the broker. (117–118)

3. **B**   The answer is specific hours stated in a written agreement. The real estate broker may require an employee to follow rules, such as working a certain number of hours, but the broker may not do so if treating the affiliated sales associate as an independent contractor. (118–119)

4. **D**   The answer is neither broker has committed an antitrust violation. Brokers must independently determine commission rates or fees for their own firms. Because the second agency's broker learned about the first agency's policies from a public source, the newspaper, and did not discuss the policy with the first agency, neither broker has committed an antitrust violation. (124–125)

5. **D**   The answer is the broker was the procuring cause of the sale and is entitled to the full 6% commission. Because the broker introduced a ready, willing, and able buyer to the seller prior to the seller's cancellation of the listing agreement, the broker is entitled to the commission. (121)

6. **B**   The answer is May 1. Although the commission was earned when the buyer was notified of the seller's acceptance (March 8), the commission is typically paid at the time the transaction is closed; that is, the purchase price is paid by the buyer and the buyer receives the deed. (121)

7. **C**   The answer is commission splitting. Brokers may legally share and split commissions. Price fixing, allocation of customers, and group boycotting are illegal under federal antitrust law. (124–125)

8. **A**   The answer is standard community rate. Under antitrust laws, brokers may not collaborate and agree to charge the same rates to customers. Brokers may charge for services using a flat fee, an hourly rate, or a commission based on a percentage of the selling price. (124–125)

9. **D**   The answer is it exposes the property to a greater number of prospective buyers. The MLS exposes the property to many different real estate professionals, encouraging cooperation among brokers and expediting sales. (127)

10. **C**   The answer is licensing authority (division, Commission, etc.). Administrative regulations are written and adopted by the licensing authorities in each state. They have the force and effect of law, but they are easier to change because they do not require legislative action. (116–117)

11. **D**   The answer is responding to emails within one week. Examples of email etiquette include using the subject line in a useful and helpful manner; avoiding spelling errors; responding promptly to all email messages; and being specific, to the point, and brief. Do not send unsolicited emails. (128)

12. **B**   The answer is ads must contain true, current information and avoid misleading the potential client or customer. A phone number and license number are not usually required in an email. Status as a broker or sales associate should be disclosed on every page of a website with ads. Both the sales associate's name and the broker's name should be shown in the ads. (128–129)

13. **C**   The answer is the seller decided not to sell. If the sale is not completed due to the seller's default (deciding not to sell), then the broker is generally due a commission. Courts may prevent a real estate broker from receiving a commission if the broker knew that the buyer was unable to perform. (120–122)

14. **A**   The answer is a tie-in agreement. A tie-in arrangement is an agreement to sell one product only if the buyer purchases another product. *Fee-for-services* refers to splitting apart the collection of services that a broker offers. A *buydown provision* is a financing option. *Allocation of customers* refers to dividing a market and refraining from competing. (124–125)

15. **C**   The answer is remove barriers in electronic commerce that would otherwise prevent enforceability of contracts. The primary purpose of the Uniform Electronic Transactions Act (UETA) is to remove barriers in electronic commerce that would otherwise prevent enforceability of contracts. UETA sets forth basic rules for entering an enforceable contract using electronic means. (129)

16. **D**   The answer is 18 months. Real estate professionals may call consumers with whom they have an established business relationship for up to 18 months after the consumer's last purchase, delivery, or payment, even if the consumer is listed on the National Do Not Call Registry. However, if the consumer specifically asks the company not to call, then the company must stop calling. (130)

17. **C**   The answer is the Internet Data Exchange. NAR has adopted the Internet Data Exchange (IDX). The policy allows all MLS members to have equal rights to display MLS data, while also respecting the rights of the property owners and the brokers who represent them to market the property as they wish. (127)

18. **A**   The answer is give contracts created using email the same legal standing as those on paper. The E-Sign Act diminishes legal barriers in electronic contracting, but it does not specify required security measures. Notarization is allowed. Parties are not required to use electronic contracting. (129)

19. **C**   The answer is graduated commission split. A graduated commission split is based on a sales associate's achieving specified production goals. A 100% commission plan provides for a sales associate to pay a monthly service charge to the broker so that the sales associate can keep 100% of the commissions earned. (121)

20. **A**   The answer is unbundling services. Unbundling services means offering services as the consumer desires them. With discounted services, the consumer receives the full package of services but pays a discounted price. Allocation of markets involves an agreement between brokers to divide their markets and stop competition, and it is illegal. (124)

MATH PRACTICE

1. **D**   The answer is $22,750. What the brokers agree to regarding splitting the commission is not relevant to the total cost to the seller. The seller paid $22,750 in commission fees: $325,000 × 7% = $22,750.

2. **C**   The answer is $9,223.50. The sales associate received $9,223.50: $279,500 × 5.5% × 60% = $9,223.50.

3. **C**   The answer is $19,000. The seller's total cost is $19,000: $400,000 × 4% + $3,000 = $19,000.

4. **A**   The answer is $9,625. The sales associate is paid $9,625:

$500,000 × 6% = $30,000

$30,000 × 35% = $10,500

$10,500 − $200 − $75 − $600 ($800 × 75%) = $9,625

5. **B**   The answer is $11,928.19. In May, the realty agency received $11,928.19:

$560,000 × 5% = $28,000

$348,000 × 6% = $20,880

$89,500 × 6.75% = $6,041.25

$410,000 × 6% = $24,600

$28,000 + $20,880 + $6,041.25 + $24,600 = $79,521.25

$79,521.25 × 15% = $11,928.19

ACTIVITY: WHO'S WHO

1. Broker   **B**

2. Real Estate Assistant   **D**

3. Sales associate (Independent Contractor)   **A**

4. Sales associate (Employee)   **C**

ACTIVITY: STATE LICENSE REQUIREMENTS

Each state will have different answers. Students should work together, when possible.

UNIT
9

Real Estate Agency

LEARNING OBJECTIVES

When you have completed this unit, you will be able to

> **explain** agency concepts and terminology;
> **explain** express and implied agency and an agent's fiduciary duties;
> **define** the types of agency and **identify** which, if any, are involved in real estate practice; and
> **describe** an agent's duties to third-party customers, especially regarding misstatements, misrepresentation, and potential fraud.

KEY TERMS

agency
agent
buyer representation
  agreement
buyer's agent
client
customer
designated agency
designated agent
dual agency

express agency
express agreement
fiduciary
fiduciary relationship
fraud
general agent
implied agency
implied agreement
latent defect
law of agency

listing agreement
negligent misrepresentation
nonagent
principal
puffing
single agency
special agent
transaction broker
universal agent

MATCHING A

Write the letter of the matching term on the appropriate line.

A. nonagent

B. customer

C. fiduciary relationship

D. special agent

E. agent

F. general agent

G. implied agency

H. law of agency

I. puffing

J. principal

1. ___ The basic framework that governs the legal responsibilities of an agent to a principal

2. ___ An agent who is authorized to represent the principal in one specific act or business transaction, under detailed instructions

3. ___ The individual who is authorized and consents to represent the interests of another person

4. ___ The establishment of an agency relationship as the result of the actions of the parties that indicate mutual consent

5. ___ The individual who hires and delegates to the agent the responsibility of representing the individual's interests

6. ___ An affiliation of trust and confidence as between a principal and an agent

7. ___ Nonfraudulent exaggeration of a property's benefits or features

8. ___ An agent authorized to represent the principal in a broad range of matters related to a specific business or activity

9. ___ In a real estate agency relationship, the third party (or nonrepresented consumer) who receives some level of service and who is entitled to honesty and fair dealing

10. ___ An intermediary between a buyer and seller who assists both parties with a transaction but who represents neither party

MATCHING B

Write the letter of the matching term on the appropriate line.

A. disclosed dual agency

B. common law agent duties

C. Megan's Law

D. client

E. undisclosed dual agency

F. latent defect

G. stigmatized property

H. universal agent

I. express agreement

J. errors and omissions insurance

1. ___ An agency relationship in which the agent represents two principals simultaneously, without their knowledge or permission

2. ___ A contract in which the parties formally state their intention to establish an agency relationship

3. ___ Registry of sex offenders that affects a real estate professional's duty of disclosure

4. ___ Type of insurance that covers liability for mistakes and negligence in the usual activities of a real estate office

5. ___ A property that has been branded as undesirable because of the events that occurred in or near it

6. ___ The principal in a real estate agency relationship

7. ___ An agency relationship in which the agent represents two principals simultaneously, with their knowledge or permission

8. ___ The responsibilities of care, obedience, accounting, loyalty, and disclosure

9. ___ A person who is empowered to do anything the principal could do personally; this person has unlimited authority

10. ___ A hidden structural problem that would not be discovered by ordinary inspection

TRUE OR FALSE

Circle the correct answer.

1. The fiduciary is the individual who hires and delegates to the agent the responsibility of representing the fiduciary's other interests.
   A. True
   B. False

2. Examples of nonagents are facilitators, transactional brokers, transactional coordinators, and contract brokers.
   A. True
   B. False

3. An agent works with a client and for the customer.
   A. True
   B. False

4. Under the common law of agency, the agent owes the principal these six duties: care, obedience, loyalty, disclosure, accounting, and confidentiality.
   A. True
   B. False

5. The common law fiduciary duty of obedience obligates the agent to obey all the principal's instructions.
   A. True
   B. False

6. The common law duty of loyalty requires that an agent avoid disclosing material facts about the condition of the property.
   A. True
   B. False

7. The source of compensation is the key determining factor in whether an agency relationship exists.
   A. True
   B. False

8. A buyer's agent helps the buyer prepare the strongest offer.
   A. True
   B. False

9. A real estate broker is usually the general agent of a buyer or seller.
   A. True
   B. False

10. Real estate professionals can sell property in which they have a personal interest, but only if the real estate professional informs the buyer of that interest.
    A. True
    B. False

11. In a dual agency relationship, the agent represents two principals in the same transaction.
    A. True
    B. False

12. A dual agency relationship is legal if either the buyer or the seller consents to the dual representation.
    A. True
    B. False

13. An agent owes a customer the duties of reasonable care and skill, honest and fair dealing, and disclosure of known facts.
    A. True
    B. False

14. A negligent misrepresentation occurs when the broker makes a statement such as "This is the prettiest house I've ever seen."
    A. True
    B. False

15. When a property has a hidden structural defect that could not be discovered by ordinary inspection, it is called a stigmatized property.
    A. True
    B. False

MULTIPLE CHOICE

Circle the correct answer.

1. An individual who is authorized and consents to represent the interests of another person is
    A. a customer.
    B. a principal.
    C. an agent.
    D. a facilitator.

2. A broker represents G but is currently working with K to find a home. Assuming that no statute has replaced the traditional common law, which of these correctly identifies the parties in this relationship?
    A. The broker is K's agent; G is the broker's client.
    B. K is the broker's client; G is the broker's principal.
    C. G is the broker's customer; K is the broker's client.
    D. The broker is G's agent; K is the broker's customer.

3. An agent's obligation to use skill and expertise on behalf of the principal arises under which of these common-law duties?
    A. Care
    B. Obedience
    C. Loyalty
    D. Disclosure

4. An agent representing the seller has a duty to disclose to the principal all of these *EXCEPT*
    A. the offers that are ridiculously low.
    B. the buyer's financial ability to offer a higher price.
    C. the agent's advertising budget.
    D. the buyer's intention to resell the property for a profit.

5. A broker has an agency agreement to represent a seller in the sale of a house. The agreement's expiration date is June 10. On May 5, the house is struck by lightning and burns to the ground. The seller, overwhelmed by grief, dies. Based on these facts, which of these is *TRUE*?
    A. The agency agreement was terminated by the fire, although the seller's death also would have done so.
    B. The agency agreement was not terminated until the seller's death.
    C. If the house had not been destroyed by the fire, the seller's death would not have terminated the agreement; the broker would become the broker for the seller's estate.
    D. Only the mutual agreement of the parties can terminate a valid agency agreement before its expiration date.

6. A person who is designated by the principal in a broad range of matters related to a particular transaction or activity is
    A. a facilitator.
    B. a special agent.
    C. a designated agent.
    D. a general agent.

7. A real estate broker signed an agency agreement with a seller. The asking price for the seller's house was $499,000. A few days later, the broker met a prospective buyer who was interested in buying a home in the $480,000 to $510,000 price range. The broker agreed to help the buyer locate such a property and to represent the buyer in negotiating a favorable purchase price. Based on these facts, which of these statements is *TRUE*?
    A. The broker's relationships with the buyer and seller are separate issues, and no dual agency question arises.
    B. The seller is the broker's client, and the buyer is the broker's customer; there is no dual agency problem.
    C. The broker has created a potential undisclosed dual agency problem and should disclose the relationships to both parties before showing the seller's home to the buyer.
    D. The broker has created a dual agency problem and should immediately terminate the agreement with either the buyer or seller.

8. A broker is showing a house to a prospective buyer. The broker points out the rustic charm of the sagging front porch and refers to a weed-choked backyard as a delightful garden. The broker is engaging in
   A. intentional misrepresentation.
   B. negligent misrepresentations.
   C. puffing.
   D. fraud.

9. A house built years ago over a ditch covered with decaying timber or a house with ceilings that were improperly attached to the support beams are examples of
   A. stigmatized properties.
   B. environmental hazards.
   C. latent defects.
   D. conditions that need not be disclosed.

10. The seller's agent has certain duties to the client-principal. All of these are duties of the principal *EXCEPT*
    A. cooperating with the agent.
    B. compensating the agent.
    C. suggesting marketing strategies to the agent.
    D. dealing with the agent in good faith.

11. Every state has mandatory agency disclosure laws that stipulate
    A. how an implied agency may occur.
    B. when, how, and to whom agents must reveal for whom they provide client-based services.
    C. restrictions on disclosure of confidential information.
    D. how a customer is differentiated from a client.

12. Who is the agent's principal?
    A. Seller
    B. Buyer
    C. Person who pays the commission
    D. Whoever hired the agent

13. A broker was hired to represent the seller, to market the seller's property, and to solicit offers to purchase. The broker is called
    A. a general agent.
    B. a special agent.
    C. a facilitator.
    D. a nonagent.

14. A house was the scene of a drug arrest and a violent murder last year. When it was listed on the market, many people considered it to be
    A. a latent property.
    B. a stigmatized property.
    C. a damaged property.
    D. a property with a material defect.

15. All of these will terminate an agency relationship *EXCEPT*
    A. the death of either party.
    B. the destruction of the property.
    C. an offer made on the property.
    D. an expiration of the agreement.

16. What is a seller's agent required to disclose to prospective buyers about material defects in the property?
    A. Only information about material defects the seller has provided the agent
    B. Only information about material defects that the agent has personally observed
    C. Both information the seller has provided the agent, and material defects that the agent has personally observed
    D. All information about material defects that the agent knows or should know

17. Which of these statements could be negligent misrepresentation?
    A. "The uneven floors just mean that the building dates to colonial times."
    B. "I think these low doorways are a charming part of the Cape Cod style."
    C. "The simple design is uncluttered and offers many possibilities for decorating."
    D. "The size of the bedrooms makes them wonderfully cozy and perfect for your children."

18. The seller's agent is aware that a new landfill has been approved for development on an adjacent property but does not disclose this information to a buyer. This could be an example of
    A. negligent misrepresentation.
    B. a latent defect.
    C. fraudulent misrepresentation.
    D. unnecessary disclosure.

19. A key element of an agent's fiduciary responsibility of loyalty is to
    A. report the status of all funds received from or on behalf of the principal.
    B. avoid conflicts of interest.
    C. obey the principal's instructions in accordance with the contract.
    D. reveal relevant information or material facts.

20. When a broker places trust funds of others into the company's operating account and then withdraws funds for the firm's use, what illegal practice has taken place?
    A. Escrowing
    B. DBA accounting
    C. Commingling and conversion
    D. Asset-liability management

Unit 9

FILL-IN-THE-BLANK

Select the word or words that best complete these statements:

accounting

compensation

designated agent

fraud

implied agreement

listing agreement

confidentiality

negligent
misrepresentation

obedience

operation of law

seller disclaimer

stigmatized property

1. The written employment contract that establishes the agency relationship between the seller and the broker is called a(n) _____.

2. The requirement that brokers promptly deposit funds entrusted to the broker into an escrow account is an example of how brokers fulfill the fiduciary duty of _____.

3. Even when a property is sold as is or with a(n) _____, the seller must still disclose known problems with the property if they will affect the health and well-being of the occupants.

4. Although not available in all states, when a person is authorized by the broker to act as the agent of a specific principal-seller (in an in-house sale by two agents), this agent is called a(n) _____.

5. The intentional misrepresentation of a material fact in such a way as to harm or take advantage of another person is called _____.

6. Discovery of a methamphetamine lab on a property can result in the property being regarded as a(n) _____

7. A man tells a real estate broker that he has been thinking about selling his condominium. The broker contacts several buyers that she knows are looking for a condominium, and one makes an offer for the property. The broker presents the offer to the man, who accepts it. Although no documents were signed by the man, an agency may have been created by _____.

8. If a buyer's agent reveals to the seller that the buyer must move within one month, this action would violate the agent's fiduciary duty of _____ to the buyer.

9. The source of _____ does not determine agency.

10. An agency is terminated by _____ when a principal declares bankruptcy and property title transfers to a court-appointed receiver.

UNIT 9 ANSWERS

MATCHING A

1. H
2. D
3. E
4. G
5. J
6. C
7. I
8. F
9. B
10. A

MATCHING B

1. E
2. I
3. C
4. J
5. G
6. D
7. A
8. B
9. H
10. F

TRUE OR FALSE

1. **B** The answer is false. The *principal* is the individual who hires and delegates to the agent the responsibility of representing the *principal's* other interests. (139)

2. **A** The answer is true. A nonagent (facilitator, transactional broker, transaction coordinator, or contract broker) is a middleman between a buyer and a seller (or a landlord and a tenant), who assists one or both parties with the transaction without representing either party's interest. (139)

3. **B** The answer is false. An agent works *for* the client and *with* the customer. The client is the principal. (139)

4. **A** The answer is true. The six common-law fiduciary duties are care, obedience of lawful instructions, loyalty, disclosure of material facts, accounting, and confidentiality (remember the acronym COLD AC). (142)

5. **B** The answer is false. The common law fiduciary duty of *obedience* obligates the agent to obey all of the principal's *lawful and ethical* instructions. (142–143)

6. **B** The answer is false. The common law duty of *loyalty* requires that an agent place the principal's interests above all others; however, the law of most states requires that the agent disclose material facts about the condition of the property. (143)

7. **B** The answer is false. The source of compensation is not the key determining factor in whether an agency relationship exists. An agent's commission may be paid, in whole or in part, by someone other than the agent's client-principal. Moreover, an agency can exist even when no fee is involved. (141)

8. **A** The answer is true. A buyer's agent represents the buyer in the transaction and is strictly accountable to the buyer; a buyer agency relationship is established in the same way as any other agency relationship: by contract or agreement. (146)

9. **B** The answer is false. A real estate broker is usually the *special agent* of a buyer or seller, with limited responsibilities; for example, the real estate broker may not bind the principal to any contract. (145)

10. **A** The answer is true. The duty of loyalty requires that the agent place the principal's interests above those of all others, including the agent's own self-interest. Real estate professionals may not sell property in which they have a personal interest without disclosing that interest to the purchaser. (143)

11. **A**   The answer is true. In a dual agency, the agent represents two principals in the same transaction, thus requiring equal loyalty to two different principals at the same time. While practical methods of ensuring fairness and equal representation may exist, it should be noted that a dual agent can never fully represent either party's interests. (147)

12. **B**   The answer is false. The states that permit dual agency require that the both the seller and the buyer consent to the dual representation. (147)

13. **A**   The answer is true. Even though an agent's primary responsibility is to the principal, the agent also has duties to third parties; such duties include reasonable care and skill in performance, honest and fair dealing, and disclosure of all facts that materially affect the value or desirability of the property. (150)

14. **B**   The answer is false. *Puffing* occurs when the broker engages in exaggeration of a property's benefits or features. Brokers need to be careful about statements of fact or opinion. In this case, the broker is expressing what is clearly an opinion and is not concealing any defects. (150)

15. **B**   The answer is false. A hidden structural defect in a property that could not be discovered by ordinary inspection, it is called a *latent defect*. A stigmatized property is one that is considered undesirable because of events that occurred there. (151)

MULTIPLE CHOICE

1. **C**   The answer is an agent. The agent is hired by the principal. The customer is a third party. A facilitator works in a nonagency capacity. (139)

2. **D**   The answer is the broker is G's agent; K is the broker's customer. Watch the terminology: the broker is working *for* (representing) G and is working *with* K (a customer) to find a home. (139)

3. **A**   The answer is care. *Care* requires skill and expertise; *obedience* requires following lawful instructions; *loyalty* is putting the client's interests above the agent's; and *disclosure* refers to material defects of the property. (142)

4. **C**   The answer is the agent's advertising budget. The seller's (special) agent must present all offers and any facts about the buyers that would assist the seller in making a decision, including the fact that the buyer intends to resell the property. There is no requirement that the agent disclose an advertising budget. (143)

5. **A**   The answer is the agency agreement was terminated by the fire, although the seller's death also would have done so. An agency agreement may be terminated by either destruction of the property or death of either party. In this case, destruction of the property occurred first. (149)

6. **D**   The answer is a general agent. A *special agent* is given limited authority for a limited time. A *general agent* is given broad authority in a specific circumstance; a property manager is typically a general agent for the owner as are most real estate sales associates representing their broker. (145)

7. **C**   The answer is the broker has created a potential undisclosed dual agency problem and should disclose the relationships to both parties before showing the seller's home to the buyer. The broker is representing the seller and now is at least implying representation of the buyer in locating a property; hence, there are two clients. If the broker intends to show the seller's property, the broker must disclose the relationship to both clients, gain their agreement to a dual agency, and only then proceed. (147–148)

8. **C**   The answer is puffing. Because any prudent buyer can see the sagging porch and weed-choked garden, these are *puffing* statements. An agent must take care not to make statements in such a way as to harm the buyer or take advantage of the buyer's ignorance, which would constitute *fraud*. (150)

9. **C**   The answer is latent defects. A latent defect is a hidden structural defect that would not be discovered by ordinary inspection. (151)

10. **C**   The answer is suggesting marketing strategies to the agent. Marketing is the agent's responsibility. The principal who hired the agent is responsible for cooperating with the agent, disclosing material defects, and compensating the agent. (139–140)

11. **B**   The answer is when, how, and to whom agents must reveal for whom they provide client-based services. Mandatory agency disclosure laws now exist in every state. In addition, state laws may require a particular type of written form be used and may require that all agency alternatives be explained. (145)

12. **D**   The answer is whoever hired the agent. The most complete answer is *whoever hired the agent*. That could be either the buyer or the seller, but the source of the agent's compensation is not the determining factor. (139)

13. **B**   The answer is a special agent. A *special agent* is one who is hired for a limited time and given limited authority. A broker taking a listing is generally a special agent. (145)

14. **B**   The answer is a stigmatized property. Presuming that the property is physically intact, the drug arrest and violent murder may create psychological reactions to the property, rendering it *stigmatized*. (152)

15. **C**   The answer is an offer made on the property. An offer on the property does not terminate the agency relationship; however, the death of either party, destruction of the property, or expiration of the term of the agreement will terminate the relationship. (149)

16. **D**   The answer is all information about material defects that the agent knows or should know. Agents are responsible for disclosing information they are told or that they discover on their own, plus information they should have known. (143–144)

17. **A**   The answer is "The uneven floors just mean that the building dates to colonial times." Presenting an opinion is acceptable as long as it is not presented as a fact. Uneven floors could mean a latent defect, such as rotten supports. (143–144)

18. **C**   The answer is fraudulent misrepresentation. This is an example of misleading a party by withholding a material fact. It is deliberate misrepresentation by silence. The proposed landfill adjacent to the property is not a latent defect, because it does not threaten structural soundness or personal safety. (150)

19. **B**   The answer is avoid conflicts of interest. As a fiduciary, an agent should hold the client's interests above those of all others and avoid even the appearance of a conflict of interest. Reporting the status of funds is an accounting responsibility. Obeying the principal's instructions relates to obedience. Revealing relevant information relates to the responsibility of disclosure. (142–144)

20. **C**   The answer is commingling and conversion. Both commingling the funds (placing them in an account that contains the business's funds) and the practice of conversion (making business use of client funds) are illegal. (144)

FILL-IN-THE-BLANK

1. The written employment contract that establishes the agency relationship between the seller and the broker is called a *listing agreement*.

2. The requirement that brokers promptly deposit funds entrusted to the broker into an escrow account is an example of how brokers fulfill the fiduciary duty of *accounting*.

3. Even when a property is sold as is or with a *seller disclaimer*, agents should still disclose known problems with the property if they could affect the health and well-being of the occupants.

4. Although not available in all states, when a person is authorized by the broker to act as the agent of a specific principal-seller (in an in-house sale by two agents), this agent is called a *designated agent*.

5. The intentional misrepresentation of a material fact in such a way as to harm or take advantage of another person is called *fraud*.

6. Discovery of a methamphetamine lab on a property can result in the property being regarded as a *stigmatized property*.

7. A man tells a real estate broker that he has been thinking about selling his condominium. The broker contacts several buyers that she knows are looking for a condominium, and one makes an offer for the property. The broker presents the offer to the man, who accepts it. Although no documents were signed by the man, an agency may have been created by *implied agreement*.

8. If a buyer's agent reveals to the seller that the buyer must move within one month, this action would violate the agent's fiduciary duty of *confidentiality* to the buyer.

9. The source of *compensation* does not determine agency. An agent does not necessarily represent the person who pays the agent's commission.

10. An agency is terminated by *operation of law* when a principal declares bankruptcy and property title transfers to a court-appointed receiver.

UNIT
10

Client Representation Agreements

LEARNING OBJECTIVES

When you have completed this unit, you will be able to

> **describe** the different types of listing agreements and how they may be terminated;
> **describe** the listing presentation and the information needed for a listing agreement;
> **identify** the listing agreement terms and the responsibilities of both parties; and
> **describe** the types of buyer representation agreements and how they may be terminated.

KEY TERMS

buyer representation
  agreement
comparative market analysis
  (CMA)

exclusive agency listing
exclusive buyer representation
  agreement
exclusive right-to-sell listing

multiple listing service (MLS)
net listing
open listing

MATCHING

Write the letter of the matching term on the appropriate line.

A. buyer representation agreement

B. broker protection clause

C. exclusive-agency listing

D. home warranty program

E. exclusive-right-to-sell listing

F. listing agreement

G. multiple listing service (MLS)

H. listing presentation

I. indemnification (hold harmless) clause

J. open listing

1. ___ An employment contract for a broker's services for a property seller

2. ___ A listing agreement under which the seller must pay the broker a commission regardless of who sells the property

3. ___ A listing agreement with a single broker, under which the seller retains the right to sell the property independently without being obligated to pay a commission

4. ___ A listing agreement in which the seller may employ multiple brokers, retain the right to market the property independently, and is obligated to compensate only the broker who produces a buyer, if any

5. ___ A marketing organization whose broker members make their own exclusive listings available to other brokers

6. ___ A meeting with a property owner where a sales associate describes the marketing efforts that the brokerage will make to bring about a sale of the property as quickly as possible

7. ___ An employment contract where the broker is employed as a purchaser's agent to find a suitable property

8. ___ Language in a listing agreement that states the broker and seller agree not to sue one another for any incorrect information supplied by one to the other

9. ___ An optional item in the listing contract that protects the buyer against the expense of certain types of repairs (such as plumbing, electrical, and heating systems) after the sale is completed

10. ___ A part of a listing agreement that stipulates that the property owner will pay the listing broker a commission if the broker was the procuring cause of a sale that is completed after the listing expired

TRUE OR FALSE

Circle the correct answer.

1. The listing price is always identical to the actual sales price.
   A. True
   B. False

2. A listing agreement is a contract for the sale of real estate.
   A. True
   B. False

3. The parties to a listing agreement are a broker and a seller.
   A. True
   B. False

4. A listing agreement in which the seller retains the right to employ any number of brokers as agents is called a multiple listing.
   A. True
   B. False

5. In an exclusive agency listing, one broker is authorized to act as the exclusive agent of the principal, who retains the right to sell the property without obligation to the broker.
   A. True
   B. False

6. A buyer representation agreement is not an employment contract.
   A. True
   B. False

7. In an exclusive right-to-sell listing, the seller must pay the broker's commission even if the seller finds a buyer without the broker's assistance.
   A. True
   B. False

8. Because a listing agreement is a personal service contract between a broker and seller, the broker may transfer the listing to another broker with or without the seller's consent.
   A. True
   B. False

9. Verbal agreement by the seller is adequate for a broker to list the property in a multiple listing service (MLS).
   A. True
   B. False

10. A broker protection clause in a listing contract provides for payment of a commission to the listing broker if the owner sells the property within a certain number of days after the listing expires and to a broker-introduced buyer.
    A. True
    B. False

11. Seller disclosures of property conditions usually cover structural, mechanical, and other conditions that the buyer needs to know to make an informed decision.
    A. True
    B. False

12. Automatic extension clauses in exclusive listing agreements are generally prohibited or discouraged.
    A. True
    B. False

MULTIPLE CHOICE

Circle the correct answer.

1. In a buyer representation agreement, the broker acts as the agent of the buyer and must protect the buyer's interests
   A. at all points in the transaction.
   B. only during property showings.
   C. until the representation agreement is signed.
   D. only when negotiating on behalf of the buyer.

2. An owner listed a home for sale with a broker. When the owner sold the home without the broker's assistance, she did not owe anyone a commission. Which of the following is the type of listing that the broker and the owner most likely signed?
   A. Exclusive right-to-sell listing
   B. Net listing
   C. Multiple listing
   D. Open listing

3. All of this information is generally included in a listing agreement *EXCEPT*
   A. lot size.
   B. termination clause.
   C. client's specific requirements for a suitable property to buy.
   D. property condition disclosures.

4. When may a broker's agreement to represent a property buyer be terminated?
   A. The property buyer dislikes all of the properties shown by the broker.
   B. Only agreements between brokers and sellers can be terminated.
   C. The broker and buyer mutually agree to cancel the agreement.
   D. None of these are correct.

5. A listing agreement is
   A. a contract between the buyer and the seller.
   B. a contract to purchase real property.
   C. an employment agreement between the broker and the sales associate.
   D. an employment contract between the seller and the broker.

6. Who are the parties to a listing agreement?
   A. Buyer and seller
   B. Seller and broker
   C. Seller and sales associate
   D. Buyer and sales associate

7. There are five different brokerage signs in the front yard. Evidently, the seller has signed
   A. an exclusive-agency listing.
   B. an exclusive-right-to-sell listing.
   C. a net listing.
   D. an open listing.

8. A broker just explained the value of signing an exclusive agency listing with a broker who is a member of the multiple listing service. The broker is trying to overcome the misconceptions of the seller who asked about
   A. an open listing.
   B. an option listing.
   C. an exclusive right-to-sell listing.
   D. a net listing.

9. What kind of listing agreement is illegal in many states because of the potential for conflict of interest between a broker's fiduciary responsibility to the seller and the broker's profit motive?
   A. Open listing
   B. Net listing
   C. Exclusive right-to-sell
   D. Exclusive agency listing

10. Buyer agents may be compensated in any of these ways *EXCEPT*
    A. flat fee for service.
    B. percentage of selling price.
    C. hourly rate.
    D. percentage of list price.

11. Any of these will terminate a listing agreement *EXCEPT*
    A. performance.
    B. expiration.
    C. an offer to purchase.
    D. abandonment by broker.

12. A broker is retiring and wants to submit the firm's listings to another broker. How can the broker do this?
    A. The broker must sign over the listings to the new broker.
    B. The new broker has to sign an acceptance agreement.
    C. Each sales associate must sign over the listings to the new broker.
    D. Each seller must agree to a new listing with the new broker.

13. In which of these types of listing agreements is the broker appointed as the seller's only agent?
    A. Exclusive right-to-sell and exclusive agency listings
    B. Open listing
    C. Net listing
    D. Option listing

14. In most states, a broker's license can be suspended or revoked if the broker
    A. breaches the terms of the listing agreement.
    B. cancels the listing agreement without cause.
    C. takes a listing that does not include a date on which the listing expires.
    D. does not include an automatic extension clause in the listing agreement.

15. What information is *NOT* needed for a listing agreement?
    A. The dimensions of the lot
    B. The possibility of seller financing
    C. The age of the seller
    D. The most recent property taxes

16. An example of personal property that a seller may take away from the property and, therefore, *MUST* be identified on the listing agreement is
    A. a built-in dishwasher.
    B. the door key.
    C. stacked firewood.
    D. a ceiling light fixture.

MATH PRACTICE

Circle the correct answer.

1. A brokerage charged the seller $1,000 as an
    advertising fee and 4% of the selling price.
    The house was listed for $439,500 and sold for
    $429,350. What was the total amount the seller
    paid the brokerage?
    A. $15,174
    B. $15,580
    C. $16,580
    D. None of these

2. A seller agreed to a 5% commission on a sale
    price of $175,000. The brokerage split with the
    sales associate involved in the sale is 30/70, with
    30% remaining with the company. How much is
    the sales associate's share if the sales associate both
    lists and sells the property?
    A. $2,625
    B. $6,125
    C. $8,750
    D. None of these

3. It is the broker's office policy that salespeople
    keep 60% of the firm's share of any commission
    earned from any property they list. The salesper-
    son listed a property that was later sold by a co-
    operating broker for $285,000. If the two brokers
    agree to split the 6.5% commission equally, what
    will the sales person receive?
    A. $5,557.50
    B. $6,092.00
    C. $7,235.25
    D. $7,654.00

4. The commission on the sale of a house was
    $16,500, which was based on a 7.5% commission
    rate. What was the final selling price of the house?
    A. $127,000
    B. $145,000
    C. $199,000
    D. $220,000

5. The broker listed a home for $360,000 under
    a 90-day exclusive right-to-sell listing agree-
    ment with a 6% commission. The next week,
    the broker began advertising the home in a local
    paper and showed the property to two prospective
    buyers. Later that week, the seller announced that
    he had decided to sell his home to a relative for
    $340,000. The seller is liable to the broker for
    A. $1,200.
    B. $20,400.
    C. $21,600.
    D. none of these.

ACTIVITY: LISTING CONTRACTS

Label each of these three diagrams to indicate the type of listing contract it represents.

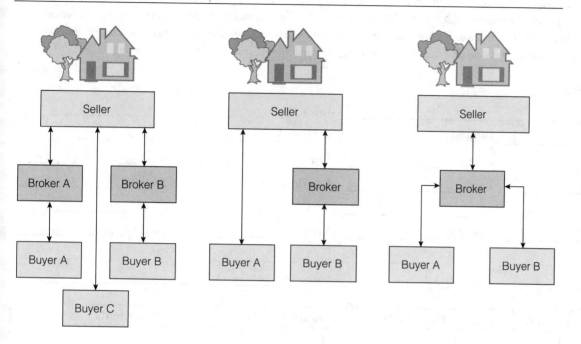

Seller retains any number of brokers; seller does not pay a commission to broker if seller finds the buyer.

1. _____

Broker is the exclusive agent of the buyer; seller does not pay a commission to broker if seller finds the buyer.

2. _____

One broker is the seller's only agent; seller pays broker a commission no matter who sells the property.

3. _____

ACTIVITY: LISTING WORKSHEET

Complete the following practice listing worksheet using the floor plan of seller K's property (128 Winding Way). The scale is 1 inch = 12 feet (approximate dimensions are acceptable). The property is a 20-year-old, stuccoed, ranch-style house with terra cotta roof and no basement. Last year's taxes were $1,875. The original carpeting throughout is quite worn, but the tile baths are in excellent condition. Six years ago, a security system and TV cabling were installed. The kitchen was remodeled three years ago with a new dishwasher, range, refrigerator, disposal, and ceramic floor covering.

Property Address: _____   Lot Size: _____

Owners: _____   Taxes: _____

Style: _____   **Utilities:**   Softener: _____   Sunroom: _____

Sq. Ft.: _____   Electric: _____   Sewer: _____   Pool: _____

Bedrooms: _____   Heat: _____   **Exterior:**   Shed: _____

Age: _____   A/C: _____   Roof: _____   Fence: _____

Stories: _____   Humidifier: _____   Siding: _____   Landscaping: _____

Basement: _____   Air Filter: _____   Deck: _____   Other: _____

Garage: _____   Water: _____   Patio: _____   _____

Rooms	Level	Size	Floor Cover	Features	Comments
Living Room					
Dining Room					
Family Room					
Kitchen					
Rec. Room					
Master BR					
Bedroom 1					
Bedroom 2					
Bedroom 3					
Bath (full)					
Bath (¾)					
Bath (½)					
Other (Den)					
Utility Room					

Property of Seller K

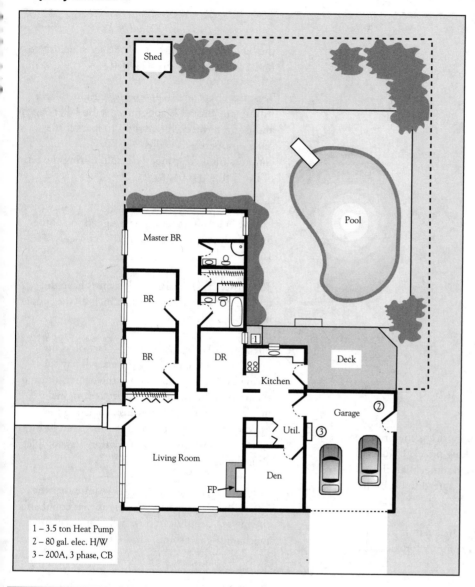

1 – 3.5 ton Heat Pump
2 – 80 gal. elec. H/W
3 – 200A, 3 phase, CB

UNIT 10 ANSWERS

MATCHING

1. **F**
2. **E**
3. **C**
4. **J**
5. **G**
6. **H**
7. **A**
8. **I**
9. **D**
10. **B**

TRUE OR FALSE

1. **B** The answer is false. The listing price is the proposed sales price (also called the asking price). It's usually a starting point for negotiation rather than the amount which will actually be agreed upon in the eventual purchase contract. (172)

2. **B** The answer is false. A listing agreement is an employment contract, not a contract for the sale of real estate. (160)

3. **A** The answer is true. A listing agreement is an employment contract between a broker and a seller; it is a contract for the real estate professional services of the broker, not for the transfer of real estate. (160)

4. **B** The answer is false. A listing agreement in which the seller retains the right to employ any number of brokers as agents is called an open listing. (161)

5. **A** The answer is true. Under an exclusive agency listing, the seller retains the right to sell the property without the obligation to pay the broker. (160–161)

6. **B** The answer is false. Like a listing agreement, a buyer representation agreement is an employment contract. In this case, the broker is employed by the buyer and the purpose of the agreement is to find a suitable property. (175)

7. **A** The answer is true. In an exclusive right-to-sell listing, one broker is appointed as the seller's agent and is given the exclusive right to market the seller's property; the seller must pay the broker a commission if the property is sold during the term of the listing. (160)

8. **B** The answer is false. Because the broker's services are unique, a listing may not be assigned to another broker without the seller's written consent. (162–163)

9. **B** The answer is false. The broker must have the written consent of the seller to include the property in an MLS. (161)

10. **A** The answer is true. A broker protection clause provides that the property owner will pay the listing broker a commission if the owner transfers the property to someone the broker originally introduced to the owner, thus protecting the broker who was the procuring cause from losing a commission because the transaction was completed after the listing expired. (163)

11. **A** The answer is true. Most states require that the seller disclose property conditions that could affect the buyer's decision to buy, including structural, mechanical, and so on. (164–165)

12. **A** The answer is true. Legislatures and courts have prohibited or discouraged the use of automatic extension clauses in exclusive listings. (163)

MULTIPLE CHOICE

1. **A** The answer is at all points in the transaction. In a buyer representation agreement, the broker acts as the agent of the buyer and must protect the buyer's interests at all points in the transaction. (175)

2. **D** The answer is open listing. Under the open listing, the seller is permitted to sell the house and is not obligated to pay a commission. (161)

3. **C** The answer is client's specific requirements for a suitable property to buy. When obtaining the listing, the agent should gather as much information as possible, including the lot size and

property conditions. The listing should also include a termination clause; however, when taking the listing from the seller, the agent is not concerned about the seller's future housing needs. (164)

4. **C** The answer is the broker and buyer mutually agree to cancel the agreement. A broker's agreement to represent a property buyer may be terminated for various reasons, one of which is mutual agreement between the broker and buyer. (180)

5. **D** The answer is an employment contract between the seller and the broker. Although the broker can subcontract the work to sales associates, the listing agreement is an employment contract between the seller and the broker. (165)

6. **B** The answer is seller and broker. The seller and broker are parties to the listing agreement. Listings remain the property of the broker even if the sales associate leaves the company. (165)

7. **D** The answer is an open listing. In an open listing, the seller retains the right to sell the property and may employ more than one broker to perform agency duties. (161)

8. **A** The answer is an open listing. Sellers are often confused, thinking that the only way to find buyers from a number of brokers is to enter into an open listing. Explaining the advantages of a multiple listing service can overcome the misconception. (161)

9. **B** The answer is net listing. Because a broker is free to offer the property at any price greater than the net amount to be paid to the seller, a net listing can create a conflict of interest between the broker's fiduciary responsibility to the seller and the broker's profit motive. Net listings are illegal in many states and discouraged in others. (161)

10. **D** The answer is percentage of list price. Buyer agents are most likely compensated by sharing the commission paid by the seller, or by receiving a flat fee, percentage of the selling price, or hourly rate from the buyer. (172)

11. **C** The answer is an offer to purchase. Because an offer to purchase may not be accepted, it would not terminate the listing agreement. (162)

12. **D** The answer is each seller must agree to a new listing with the new broker. Because the listing agreement is a contract for the personal services of the original broker, every seller has the right to cancel the listing agreement and not work with the new broker. (162)

13. **A** The answer is exclusive right-to-sell and exclusive agency listings. Under an exclusive right-to-sell and exclusive agency listing, one broker is appointed as the seller's sole agent. Open and option listings do not specifically exclude other brokers from acting as the seller's agent. (160–161)

14. **C** The answer is takes a listing that does not include a date on which the listing expires. If the broker breaches the listing contract or cancels it without cause, the broker may be liable for damages; however, it is not usually grounds for suspension or revocation of the license. Courts discourage the use of automatic extension clauses, and these clauses are even illegal in some states. (163)

15. **C** The answer is the age of the seller. Information needed for the listing agreement includes lot size, possibility of seller financing, and the property taxes. The age of the seller is not needed. (164)

16. **C** The answer is stacked firewood. Firewood is not attached to the real property and is therefore considered personal property. All the other items, even the door key, are normally considered to be part of the real property. (173)

MATH PRACTICE

1. **D** The answer is none of these. The seller paid the brokerage none of these: The sales price of $429,350 × 4% + $1,000 = $18,174.

2. **B** The answer is $6,125. The sales associate's share is $6,125: $175,000 × 5% × 70% = $6,125.

3. **A** The answer is $5,557.50. The sales associate receives $5,557.50: $285,000 × 6.5% x 50% × 60% = $5,557.50.

4. **D** The answer is $220,000. The selling price was $220,000: $16,500 ÷ 7.5% = $220,000.

5. **B** The answer is $20,400. The seller is liable to the broker for $20,400: $340,000 × 6% = $20,400. Because the seller had signed an exclusive right-to-sell listing agreement, the seller is responsible for paying a commission regardless of who finds the buyer.

ACTIVITY: LISTING CONTRACTS

1. open listing

2. exclusive-agency listing

3. exclusive-right-to-sell listing

ACTIVITY: LISTING WORKSHEET

These answers were derived from the floor plan and information included in the narrative. The room dimensions are approximate and were determined by measuring the floor plan with a digital tape measure. Keep in mind that garages are not considered living space; thus, they are not included in the house square footage. The lot size was measured as 96 feet by 79 feet (7,584 sq. ft.) and converted to acres (7,584 × 43,560 = 0.174 acres). The electrical and heating system specifications presume some familiarity with these technical aspects of the floor plan.

Property Address: 128 Winding Way

Owners: K

Style: Ranch

Sq. Ft.: 1,356 ±

Bedrooms: 3

Age: 20

Stories: 1

Basement: none

Garage: 2-car attached

Utilities:

Electric: 200 amp. 3 phase cir brkr

Heat: 3.5 ton heat pump

A/C: 3.5 ton heat pump

Humidifier: ??

Air Filter: ??

Water: 80 gal. elec. h/w

Lot Size: 7,584 sq. feet (approximate) or 0.17 acre

Taxes: $1,875

Softener: ??

Sewer: ??

Exterior:

Roof: terra cotta

Siding: stucco

Deck: yes—11 × 16 + 3 × 8

Patio: yes—around pool

Sunroom: none

Pool: yes

Shed: yes

Fence: yes

Landscaping: yes

Other:

Rooms	Level	Size	Floor Cover	Features	Comments
Living Room	1	20 × 21	carpet	fireplace, closet	carpet worn
Dining Room	1	8 × 10	carpet		
Family Room	–	–	–		
Kitchen	1	7 ×10	ceramic	modernized 2011	
Rec. Room	–	–	–		
Master BR	1	10 × 21	carpet	walk-in closet	
Bedroom 1	1	9 × 10	carpet		
Bedroom 2	1	9 × 10	carpet		
Bedroom 3	–	–	–		
Bath (full)	1	6 × 8	tile		
Bath (¾)	1	4 × 8	tile		
Bath (½)	1	–	–		
Other (Den)	1	11 × 10	carpet		
Utility Room	1	4 × 10	?	has washer and dryer	

UNIT 11

Real Estate Contracts

LEARNING OBJECTIVES

When you have completed this unit, you will be able to

> **describe** the essential elements of a contract;
> **explain** the various means by which a contract may be enforced, terminated, assigned, or replaced; and
> **describe** the primary written agreements and forms used in real estate sales and leasing.

KEY TERMS

amendment
assignment
bilateral contract
breach of contract
consideration
contingencies
contract
counteroffer
disclosure
earnest money
enforceable contract

executed contract
executory contract
express contract
implied contract
land contract
liquidated damages
novation
offer and acceptance
option
owner financing
purchase money mortgage

rescission
statute of frauds
suit for specific performance
"time is of the essence"
unenforceable contract
unilateral contract
valid contract
void contract
voidable contract

MATCHING A

Write the letter of the matching term on the appropriate line.

A. bilateral contract

B. consideration

C. contract

D. executed contract

E. executory contract

F. express contract

G. implied contract

H. mutual assent

I. offeree

J. unilateral contract

1. ____ A voluntary, legally enforceable promise between legally competent parties to perform (or refrain from performing) some legal act

2. ____ A contract in which the parties state their intentions in words

3. ____ A contract established by the acts and conduct of the parties

4. ____ A contract in which both parties promise to perform some act

5. ____ An agreement having one promise

6. ____ A contract that has been completely performed

7. ____ The status of a real estate sales contract prior to closing

8. ____ The person who accepts the offer in a contract

9. ____ Complete agreement about the purpose and terms of a contract

10. ____ Something of legal value offered by one party and accepted by another as an inducement to act or refrain from acting

MATCHING B

Write the letter of the matching term on the appropriate line.

A. void

B. assignment

C. breach

D. contingencies

E. earnest money

F. legal capacity

G. liquidated damages

H. equitable title

I. counteroffer

J. novation

1. ____ A contract that is without legal force or effect because it lacks one or more essential elements

2. ____ The transfer of rights or duties under a contract

3. ____ The substitution of a new contract to replace an earlier one

4. ____ A violation of any of the terms or conditions of a contract without legal excuse

5. ____ A new offer that rejects the original offer

6. ____ A deposit customarily made by a prospective purchaser when making an offer

7. ____ The interest held by a buyer prior to delivery and acceptance of the deed

8. ____ An amount of money that the parties agree will be the complete compensation available in the event of a breach

9. ____ Additional conditions that must be satisfied before a property sales contract is fully enforceable

10. ____ Parties must be of legal age and have enough mental capacity to understand the consequences of their actions in the contract

TRUE OR FALSE

Circle the correct answer.

1. An agreement to be bound by most of the terms proposed in an offer constitutes acceptance.
   A. True
   B. False

2. All contracts must be in writing to be enforceable.
   A. True
   B. False

3. A contract is only valid if it contains a binder.
   A. True
   B. False

4. Consideration is something of legal value offered by one party and accepted by the other as an inducement to act.
   A. True
   B. False

5. In an implied contract, the actual agreement between the parties is inferred from general or vague statements in the written agreement itself.
   A. True
   B. False

6. The difference between a bilateral and a unilateral contract is the number of parties involved.
   A. True
   B. False

7. A sales contract is an executory contract from the time it is signed until closing; at closing, it becomes an executed contract.
   A. True
   B. False

8. A contract that may be rescinded or disaffirmed by one or both of the parties based on some legal principle is void, even though it may appear to be valid.
   A. True
   B. False

9. The person who makes an offer is the offeree; the person who accepts or rejects the offer is the offeror.
   A. True
   B. False

10. The essential elements of a contract are offer and acceptance, consideration, legal purpose, and consent and performance.
    A. True
    B. False

11. An oral agreement for the sale of real estate is unenforceable.
    A. True
    B. False

12. Under a land contract, the buyer obtains both possession and legal title to the property by agreeing to make regular monthly payments to the seller over a number of years.
    A. True
    B. False

13. Assignment is the substitution of a new contract in place of the original one, while novation is a transfer of rights or duties under a contract.
    A. True
    B. False

14. An offer or counteroffer may be revoked at any time prior to its acceptance.
    A. True
    B. False

15. An option is a contract by which the optionee gives the optionor the right to buy or lease property at a fixed price within a specific period of time.
    A. True
    B. False

16. The Uniform Vendor and Purchaser Risk Act provides that the buyer bear any loss for damage to the property that occurs before title passes or the buyer takes possession.
    A. True
    B. False

17. The interest held by a buyer during the time between the signing of a sales contract and the transfer of title is called equitable title.
    A. True
    B. False

18. An example of an addendum to a real estate sales contract is an attached page that provides for seller's contribution to the payment for repairs revealed by the property inspection that will be made after closing by the buyer.
    A. True
    B. False

19. An option is a unilateral contract.
    A. True
    B. False

20. A real estate contract entered into by a minor is void.
    A. True
    B. False

MULTIPLE CHOICE

Circle the correct answer.

1. Which of these is an example of a unilateral contract?
   A. Lease
   B. Agreement of sale
   C. Option
   D. Listing agreement

2. A seller accepted all of the terms that the buyer offered, making only one small change in the amount of the earnest money. At that point, the seller has made
   A. an offer.
   B. a counteroffer.
   C. an acceptance.
   D. an executed contract.

3. After making an offer on a vacation home, but before receiving any response from the seller, the offeror decided against buying the property. The offeror's agent was directed to withdraw the offer. The offeror's action is called
   A. a counteroffer.
   B. a rejection.
   C. a breach of contract.
   D. a revocation.

4. The sales associates in a realty office are told by their broker that a $1,000 bonus will be paid to the top-selling sales associate each quarter. This contract is
   A. an implied bilateral contract.
   B. an express unilateral contract.
   C. an implied unilateral contract.
   D. an express bilateral contract.

5. A buyer makes an offer on a house, and the seller accepts in writing. What is the current status of this relationship?
   A. The buyer and seller do not have a valid contract until the seller delivers title at closing.
   B. The buyer and seller have an express, bilateral executed contract.
   C. The buyer and seller have an express, bilateral executory contract.
   D. The buyer and seller have an implied, unilateral executory contract.

6. A buyer offers to buy a seller's house for the full $215,000 asking price. The offer contains this clause: "Possession of the premises on August 1." The seller is delighted to accept the buyer's offer and signs the contract. First, however, the seller crosses out "August 1" and replaces it with "August 3," because the seller will be out of town until then. The seller begins scheduling movers. What is the status of this agreement?
   A. Because the seller changed the date of possession rather than the sales price, there is a valid contract.
   B. The seller has accepted the buyer's offer. Because the reason for the change is out of the seller's control, the change is of no legal effect once the seller signed the contract.
   C. The seller has rejected the buyer's offer and made a counteroffer, which the buyer is free to accept or reject.
   D. While the seller technically rejected the buyer's offer, the seller's behavior in scheduling movers creates an implied contract between the parties.

7. A contract that is entered into by a person who is under the age of contractual capacity is
   A. unenforceable.
   B. void.
   C. voidable.
   D. valid.

8. A property buyer wants to take over the seller's mortgage. The lender releases the seller from the obligation, substituting the buyer as the party liable for the debt. This new agreement is called
   A. an assignment.
   B. a novation.
   C. a conversion.
   D. a consideration.

9. A buyer and a seller enter into a sales contract for the sale of a home. The seller backs out of the contract at the last minute, and the buyer suffers a financial loss of $1,500 and must rent a home in which to live. Unless the contract provides otherwise, all of these are legal actions that are likely to succeed *EXCEPT*
    A. the buyer may sue the seller for specific performance, forcing the sale of the home to the buyer.
    B. the buyer may sue the seller for damages to recover the $1,500 loss.
    C. the seller is not liable because the buyer should not have incurred the $1,500 cost before the sale.
    D. the buyer may sue the seller for the rent he paid.

10. On March 7, a buyer and a seller execute a contract for the purchase of the seller's property. Closing is set for June 10. On April 15, the property is struck by lightning and destroyed by the resulting fire. If the Uniform Vendor and Purchaser Risk Act has been adopted by the state in which the property is located, which party bears liability for the loss?
    A. Under the act, the buyer and the seller share the loss equally.
    B. Under the act, the seller bears the loss alone.
    C. The act does not apply. The buyer bears the loss alone, by virtue of his equitable title.
    D. Under the act, neither the buyer nor the seller bears the loss. A state fund covers the loss.

11. A buyer makes an offer on a seller's house. Pursuant to this offer, the buyer is obligated to perform only if the buyer is first able to sell a condominium. This is an example of
    A. a mortgage contingency.
    B. an option contingency.
    C. a time-is-of-the-essence contingency.
    D. a property sale contingency.

12. All of these are essential to a valid real estate sales contract *EXCEPT*
    A. offer and acceptance.
    B. consideration.
    C. an earnest money deposit, held in an escrow account.
    D. legally competent parties.

13. A 14-year-old comes into a brokerage office and says, "I want to make an offer on this property. Here is a certified check for 10% of the asking price. Please help me with the paperwork." Why should the broker be concerned?
    A. Because one of the parties is a minor, the contract is illegal.
    B. The earnest money deposit must be at least 20% of the asking price when a minor is involved in the transaction.
    C. The sales contract may be disaffirmed by the minor.
    D. The sales contract will be void because the minor's age is a matter of public record.

14. In case the buyer decides not to buy for no legal reason, the contract may provide that the earnest money be used as
    A. actual damages.
    B. nominal damages.
    C. punitive damages.
    D. liquidated damages.

15. The buyer and seller agreed to a closing date of September 7 and that *time is of the essence*. Which of these is the closest meaning of the phrase?
    A. The date of closing may only be delayed by one day at a time.
    B. If closing is not held on September 7, there is an automatic extension built in.
    C. Closing must be on or before September 7.
    D. If either party gives notice, the date can be moved back.

16. Which of these is *NOT* typically a factor in determining the amount of the earnest money deposit?
    A. Whether it is an amount sufficient to cover the broker fees
    B. Whether it is an amount sufficient to discourage the buyer from defaulting
    C. Whether it is an amount sufficient to compensate the seller for taking the property off the market
    D. Whether it is an amount sufficient to cover any expenses the seller might incur if the buyer defaults

17. If a property owner is forced under threat of violence to sign a contract to sell property for a low price, the contract is voidable because there is lack of
    A. consent.
    B. discharge.
    C. consideration.
    D. offer and acceptance.

18. If a contract seems to be valid, but neither party can sue the other to force performance, the contract is said to be
    A. voided.
    B. breached.
    C. rescinded.
    D. unenforceable.

19. What is minimum consideration in a valid contract?
    A. One dollar
    B. Any item that can be appraised to determine its likely market value
    C. Specified goods or services
    D. Anything the parties agree is good and valuable

20. If a contract does *NOT* contain a time or date for performance, the obligations required by the contract should be performed within
    A. a reasonable time.
    B. one week.
    C. two weeks.
    D. one month.

21. If a seller allows a buyer to back out of a contract, returns the earnest money, and both are back to the positions they held before the contract, the contract has been
    A. cancelled.
    B. rescinded.
    C. assigned.
    D. executed.

22. When is an offer considered to be accepted?
    A. When the broker notifies the buyer that the seller has accepted the offer
    B. When the buyer gives a signed receipt to the broker to show the buyer has received the acceptance
    C. The moment the seller accepts the buyer's offer
    D. One business day after the offer is accepted and signed by the seller

23. The informal document that may be used to begin negotiations between the parties in a complex transaction is
    A. the binder.
    B. the offer.
    C. the contingency.
    D. the letter of intent.

24. The amount of the earnest money in a sales contract should
    A. cover any expenses the buyer might incur if the seller defaults.
    B. discourage the buyer from walking away from the agreement.
    C. pay the broker's commission.
    D. pay for any required inspections.

25. The term *statute of limitations* is *BEST* described as
    A. the time period in which parties to a contract may bring a lawsuit to enforce their rights.
    B. the parties' abilities to demand a "time is of the essence" clause in a sales contract.
    C. the amount of damages that can be claimed in the event of breach.
    D. the broker's right to a commission.

ACTIVITY: SALES CONTRACT

The following document (Agreement for Sale of Real Estate) is the first page of a standard real estate sales contract. Complete the document using information from this narrative.

You represent the buyer. The date is today. The property is 1105 Azalea Street in Poleduck County, City of Pleasant Valley, Virginia 98675. The lot dimensions are 70 feet by 160 feet. The sellers are Paul and Polly Purveyor, who currently live in the house being sold.

The buyer is particularly insistent that the kitchen appliances (a stove, dishwasher, and refrigerator) convey with the property, and that an outdoor gas cooker and swing set stay as well. The earnest money deposit is 15% of the purchase price of $317,500, paid by check, with an additional 10% of the balance due in one business week.

The closing will take place exactly 64 days from today at the office of the buyer's attorney, R. Tassel. The financing will be by conventional, fixed-rate mortgage, in the amount of the balance due. The buyer will not accept an interest rate greater than 7.5%. The commitment date is two weeks from today. The listing broker is F. J. Broker.

Agreement for Sale of Real Estate

BUYER(S): _____

   Address: _____

      City: _____ State: ___ Zip: _____ agrees to purchase, and

SELLER(S): _____

   Address: _____

      City: State: ___ Zip: _____ agrees to sell to Buyer(s)

at the Price of : _____ Dollars ($_____)

the Property commonly described as _____

(City of _____, County of _____ State of _____)

1. PROPERTY DESCRIPTION: "the Property," a complete legal description of which may be attached
    to this contract by either party. The Property has approximate lot dimensions of _____,
    together with all existing improvements and fixtures, if any, to be transferred to the Buyer(s) by Bill of
    Sale at the time of closing, including (but not limited to): hot water heater, furnace, plumbing and
    electrical fixtures, sump pumps, central heating and cooling systems, fixed floor coverings, built-in
    kitchen appliances and cabinets, storm and screen windows and doors, window treatment hardware,
    shelving systems, all planted vegetation, garage door openers and car units, and the following items of
    personal property:

2. EARNEST MONEY: Buyer has paid $_____ by check by note (delete one), and will pay
    within ____ days the further sum of $_____, as earnest money to be applied against
    the purchase price. The earnest money shall be held by the Listing Broker for the mutual benefit of the
    parties. The balance of the purchase price, $_____, shall be paid in full at closing.

3. CLOSING DATE: The closing date shall be _____, 20__, at _____.

4. POSSESSION: Possession shall be at closing.

5. COMMISSION: Seller(s) agree that _____, Listing Broker, brought about this
    sale and agrees to pay a Broker's commission as agreed vin the listing agreement.

6. FINANCING: This contract is subject to the condition that Buyer(s) shall, by _____, 20__,
    obtain a written commitment for a loan secured by a mortgage or deed of trust on the Property in the
    amount of $_____. Financing shall be secured in the form of a mortgage of the
    following type: (delete those items that do not apply) Conventional (fixed or adjustable rate); FHA
    mortgage; VA mortgage; assumption of existing mortgage; financing by Seller(s).

UNIT 11 ANSWERS

MATCHING A

1. **C**

2. **F**

3. **G**

4. **A**

5. **J**

6. **D**

7. **E**

8. **I**

9. **H**

10. **B**

MATCHING B

1. **A**

2. **B**

3. **J**

4. **C**

5. **I**

6. **E**

7. **H**

8. **G**

9. **D**

10. **F**

TRUE OR FALSE

1. **B** The answer is false. An agreement to be bound by *all* of the terms proposed in an offer constitutes *acceptance*. (189–190)

2. **B** The answer is false. While a contract may be written or oral, only certain types of contracts must be in writing to be enforceable. (188)

3. **B** The answer is false. A contract is valid when it meets all the essential elements that make it legally sufficient and legally binding. A binder is often used in commercial transactions to present a buyer's offer. (189–190)

4. **A** The answer is true. Consideration is some interest or benefit accruing to one party, or some loss or responsibility by another party as an inducement to perform or to refrain from performing some act. (190)

5. **B** The answer is false. In an implied contract, the actual agreement between the parties is *demonstrated by their acts and conduct*. (190)

6. **B** The answer is false. The difference between a bilateral contract and a unilateral contract is the number of parties bound to perform; both parties to a bilateral contract are obligated to perform, but in a unilateral contract, the second party is not legally obligated to act. (189)

7. **A** The answer is true. An executory contract exists when one or both parties still have an act to perform; a sales contract is executory from the time it is signed until closing of the transaction. (189)

8. **B** The answer is false. A contract that may be rescinded or disaffirmed by one or both of the parties based on some legal principle is *voidable*, even though it may appear to be valid. (191)

9. **B** The answer is false. The person who makes an offer is the *offeror*; the person who accepts or rejects the offer is the *offeree*. (189)

10. **B** The answer is false. The essential elements of a contract are offer and acceptance, consideration, legal purpose, consent, and legal capacity. Performance is an element of discharging the contract. (189–191)

11. **A** The answer is true. Because the statute of frauds requires that any transfer of real property interests must be in writing, an oral purchase agreement is unenforceable. (188)

12. **B** The answer is false. Under a *land contract*, the buyer obtains possession, but the seller retains legal title until the terms of the contract have been satisfied. (200)

13. **B** The answer is false. *Novation* is the substitution of a new contract in place of the original one, while *assignment* is a transfer of rights or duties under a contract. (193)

14. **A** The answer is true. The offeror may revoke the offer any time before notification of acceptance, but the revocation must be communicated to the offeree by the offeror, either directly or through the parties' agents. (190)

15. **B** The answer is false. An *option* is a contract by which the *optionor* gives the *optionee* the right to buy or lease property at a fixed price within a specific period of time. (200)

16. **B** The answer is false. The Uniform Vendor and Purchaser Risk Act provides that the seller bear any loss for damage to the property that occurs before title passes or the buyer takes possession. (197)

17. **A** The answer is true. After both buyer and seller have executed a sales contract, the buyer acquires an interest in the property, called equitable title. (197)

18. **A** The answer is true. An addendum is any provision added to an existing contract without altering the content of the original; it is essentially a new contract between parties that includes the provisions of the original contract by reference. (200)

19. **A** The answer is true. Because an option is enforceable by the optionee only, it is a unilateral contract. (189)

20. **B** The answer is false. A voidable contract is considered by the courts to be valid if the party who has the option to disaffirm the agreement does not do so within a period of time. A contract entered into by a minor is voidable. (191)

MULTIPLE CHOICE

1. **C** The answer is option. In a unilateral contract, only one party is obligated to perform. The optionor-owner of the property must sell at the agreed-upon price only if the optionee decides to buy. (200)

2. **B** The answer is a counteroffer. Proposing any deviation from the terms of the offer is considered a rejection of the original offer and is called a counteroffer. (196)

3. **D** The answer is a revocation. The person who makes an offer may revoke the offer at any point before being notified that the seller has accepted the offer. (190)

4. **B** The answer is an express unilateral contract. The offer of a bonus to the top-selling sales associate each quarter is an *express contract* because the broker's offer was clearly stated to the sales associates. It is a *unilateral contract* because the broker is obligated to keep the promise made, but the sales associates are not obligated to perform. (189)

5. **C** The answer is the buyer and seller have an express, bilateral executory contract. Because the seller has promised to sell and the buyer has promised to buy, it is clearly a *bilateral contract*. It is *express* because they announced their intentions in writing. The contract is *executory* because the sale has not yet closed. (188–189)

6. **C** The answer is the seller has rejected the buyer's offer and made a counteroffer, which the buyer is free to accept or reject. Even changing the smallest of terms, for whatever reason, constitutes a rejection and counteroffer that the other party is not under obligation to accept. (190)

7. **C** The answer is voidable. The underage party may void the contract, but the older party who entered into the contract with the minor cannot. (191)

8. **B** The answer is a novation. Creating a new contract to discharge the old obligation is called *novation*. (193)

9. **C** The answer is the seller is not liable because the buyer should not have incurred the $1,500 cost before the sale. In this case, the seller breached the contract without legal excuse. The buyer is likely to be successful in a suit against the seller for specific performance, for the $1,500 loss, and for the cost of rent as a hardship. However, many contracts limit the remedies available to parties. (193)

10. **B** The answer is under the act, the seller bears the loss alone. In states that have adopted the Uniform Vendor and Purchaser Act, the seller remains responsible for the property until the day of closing. (197)

11. **D** The answer is a property sale contingency. A property sale contingency protects a buyer who has to sell a property in order to buy the seller's property. (199)

12. **C**   The answer is an earnest money deposit, held in an escrow account. Earnest money is an optional term in a contract, not a requirement. The essential elements of a contract are offer and acceptance, consideration, legally competent parties, consent, and legal capacity. (196–197)

13. **C**   The answer is the sales contract may be disaffirmed by the minor. A minor may void the contract by saying, "I am underage." A minor's guardian may purchase for the minor. (191)

14. **D**   The answer is liquidated damages. Liquidated damages limit the compensation available to the injured party should a breach of contract occur. (197)

15. **C**   The answer is closing must be on or before September 7. Time is of the essence requires that the contract be completed during that time frame; otherwise, the party who fails to perform on time is liable for breach of contract. (192)

16. **A**   The answer is whether it is an amount sufficient to cover the broker fees. Broker fees are not the focus when the parties are working out an agreement concerning the earnest money deposit. (196–197)

17. **A**   The answer is consent. Because a contract must be entered into by consent as a free and voluntary act of each party, a contract made under duress deprives a person of that ability. The contract is voidable by the injured party. (191)

18. **D**   The answer is unenforceable. An unenforceable contract may appear to be valid; however, neither party can sue the other to enforce performance. (192)

19. **D**   The answer is anything the parties agree is good and valuable. The parties must agree that the consideration is good and valuable. The courts do not consider whether the consideration is adequate. (191)

20. **A**   The answer is a reasonable time. Interpretation of what is a reasonable time depends on the situation; however, courts have sometimes declared contracts invalid if they did not contain a time or date for performance. (192)

21. **B**   The answer is rescinded. Rescission allows both parties to return to their original positions before the contract, so any monies exchanged must be returned. (194)

22. **A**   The answer is when the broker notifies the buyer that the seller has accepted the offer. Buyer notification is the key. It is not an accepted offer until the buyer is notified. (196)

23. **D**   The answer is the letter of intent. A letter of intent can be used to indicate the interest of a prospective buyer or lessee and, if the intent is reciprocated by the property owner, to begin negotiations. A contingency is any additional condition that must be satisfied before a sales contract is fully enforceable. A binder is a short version of a sales contract that is used until a more complete version is drafted. (196)

24. **B**   The answer is discourage the buyer from walking away from the agreement. The amount of earnest money should be sufficient that the seller feels reassured that the buyer is committed to the purchase. Earnest money is not used to pay for inspections or the broker's commission. (196–197)

25. **A**   The answer is the time period in which parties to a contract may bring a lawsuit to enforce their rights. Every state limits the time during which parties to a contract may bring a legal action to enforce their rights. Rights not enforced within the applicable time period are lost. (193)

ACTIVITY: SALES CONTRACT

Agreement for Sale of Real Estate

BUYER(S): _Student's Name_

  Address: _Student's Address_

    City: _____ State: ___ Zip: _____ agrees to purchase, and

SELLER(S): _Paul and Polly Purveyor (h/w)_

  Address: _1105 Azalea St._

    City: _Pleasant Valley_ State: _VA_ Zip: _98765_ agrees to sell to Buyer(s)

at the Price of : _Three Hundred Seventeen Thousand Five Hundred_ Dollars ($ _317,500_)

the Property commonly described as _1105 Azalea St._

(City of _Pleasant Valley_ , County of _Poleduck_ State of _Virginia_)

1. PROPERTY DESCRIPTION: "the Property," a complete legal description of which may be attached to this contract by either party. The Property has approximate lot dimensions of _70' by 160'_ , together with all existing improvements and fixtures, if any, to be transferred to the Buyer(s) by Bill of Sale at the time of closing, including (but not limited to): hot water heater, furnace, plumbing and electrical fixtures, sump pumps, central heating and cooling systems, fixed floor coverings, built-in kitchen appliances and cabinets, storm and screen windows and doors, window treatment hardware, shelving systems, all planted vegetation, garage door openers and car units, and the following items of personal property:

   Kitchen stove, dishwasher, refrigerator, outdoor gas cooker and swing set

2. EARNEST MONEY: Buyer has paid $ _47,625.00_ by check by note (delete one), and will pay within _5_ days the further sum of $ _26,987.50_ , as earnest money to be applied against the purchase price. The earnest money shall be held by the Listing Broker for the mutual benefit of the parties. The balance of the purchase price, $ _242,887.50_ , shall be paid in full at closing.

3. CLOSING DATE: The closing date shall be _today + 64 days_ , 20__, at _Law Office of R. Tassel_ .

4. POSSESSION: Possession shall be at closing.

5. COMMISSION: Seller(s) agree that _F. J. Broker_ , Listing Broker, brought about this sale and agrees to pay a Broker's commission as agreed vin the listing agreement.

6. FINANCING: This contract is subject to the condition that Buyer(s) shall, by _today + 2 wks_ , 20__, obtain a written commitment for a loan secured by a mortgage or deed of trust on the Property in the amount of $ _242,887.50_ . Financing shall be secured in the form of a mortgage of the following type: (delete those items that do not apply; Conventional (fixed ~~or adjustable~~ rate); ~~FHA mortgage; VA mortgage; assumption of existing mortgage; financing by Seller(s).~~ *Not to exceed 7.5%.*

UNIT 12

Real Estate Financing

LEARNING OBJECTIVES

When you have completed this unit, you will be able to

> **describe** the factors that contribute to housing affordability, including mortgage terms and ability to pay;
> **describe** the terms, conditions, and use of the promissory note;
> **explain** the elements and use of security instruments, the mortgage and deed of trust, and the roles, rights, and obligations of the parties involved in each;
> **describe** the various types of real estate financing;
> **explain** the distinction between a judicial foreclosure and a non-judicial foreclosure, and the process involved in each; and
> **describe** the various consumer protections related to homeownership.

KEY TERMS

acceleration clause	deficiency judgment	negative amortization
adjustable-rate mortgage (ARM)	discount points	negotiable instrument
alienation clause	equity	note
amortized loan	foreclosure	novation
assumption of mortgage	growing-equity mortgage	PITI (principal, interest, taxes, and insurance)
balloon payment	homeowners insurance	prepayment penalty
beneficiary	hypothecation	promissory note
Comprehensive Loss Underwriting Exchange (CLUE)	index	release deed
	interest	reverse mortgage
	interest-only loan	satisfaction of mortgage
debt to income (DTI)	loan origination fee	short sale
deed in lieu of foreclosure	loan-to-value ratio (LTV)	straight loan
deed of reconveyance	margin	"subject to"
deed of trust	mortgage	trustor
defeasance clause	mortgagee	usury
	mortgagor	

MATCHING A

Write the letter of the matching term on the appropriate line.

A. acceleration clause

B. hypothecation

C. discount points

D. executing

E. deed of trust

F. mortgagor

G. mortgagee

H. usury

I. interest

J. promissory note

1. ___ The borrower in a mortgage loan

2. ___ The lender in a mortgage loan

3. ___ The act of signing a loan instrument

4. ___ A borrower's personal pledge to repay a debt according to agreed-upon terms

5. ___ The pledging of a property as security for payment of a loan without actually surrendering the property itself

6. ___ A financing instrument that conveys bare legal title on behalf of a beneficiary, but no right of possession

7. ___ A charge for the use of money

8. ___ The act of charging interest in excess of the maximum legal rate

9. ___ A charge imposed by lenders to adjust for the difference between a loan's interest rate and the yield an investor demands

10. ___ The part of a financing agreement that gives the lender the right to declare the entire debt due and payable immediately on default

MATCHING B

Write the letter of the matching term on the appropriate line.

A. alienation clause

B. deed in lieu of foreclosure

C. loan origination fee

D. deficiency judgment

E. short sale

F. foreclosure

G. straight loan

H. defeasance clause

I. amortized loan

J. subordination agreement

K. prepayment penalty

L. HUD

M. beneficiary

N. trustee

O. trustor

1. ___ Percentage of the loan amount charged to a borrower for the costs of generating a loan

2. ___ The part of a financing agreement that requires the lender to execute a satisfaction or release when the note has been paid in full

3. ___ A provision in a financing agreement that permits the lender to declare the entire debt due immediately in the event the property is sold

4. ___ A device by which one lender agrees to change the priority of its loan relative to another lender

5. ___ A legal procedure in which property pledged as security is taken from the borrower to satisfy the debt

6. ___ A document by which property is transferred to the lender by mutual agreement rather than by lawsuit

7. ___ A sale in which the sales price is less than the remaining indebtedness

8. ___ A type of loan where each payment partially pays off both principal and interest

9. ___ A procedure for obtaining the unpaid balance of a debt where the foreclosure sale does not generate sufficient funds

10. ___ Loan that requires payments of interest only, with the entire principal due at the end of the loan term

11. ___ Agency that certifies housing counselors to assist borrowers

12. ___ The borrower's legal status on a deed of trust

13. ___ Fee that a borrower pays on any payment made ahead of schedule (if allowed)

14. ___ The lender's legal status on a deed of trust

15. ___ On a deed of trust, a third party who holds the deed as security for the loan

TRUE OR FALSE

Circle the correct answer.

1. A mortgage is classified as an involuntary lien on real estate.
   A. True
   B. False

2. A mortgage is a security instrument in which a mortgagee pledges real property to the mortgagor as security for a debt.
   A. True
   B. False

3. In one form of security instrument, the borrower actually turns over legal title to the secured property, while retaining equitable title.
   A. True
   B. False

4. When a property is mortgaged, the owner must execute both a promissory note and a security instrument.
   A. True
   B. False

5. PITI refers to principal, interest, time, and insurance.
   A. True
   B. False

6. In a typical deed of trust, the mortgagee is the beneficiary, and the borrower is the trustor.
   A. True
   B. False

7. A point is 1% of the purchase price of the property being offered as security for the loan.
   A. True
   B. False

8. In the event of a borrower's default, a subordination clause makes foreclosure easier by giving a lender the right to declare the entire debt due and payable.
   A. True
   B. False

9. In most mortgage documents, the defeasance clause requires the mortgagee to execute a satisfaction when the note has been fully paid, returning to the mortgagor all interest in the real estate.
   A. True
   B. False

10. When a real estate loan secured by a deed of trust has been repaid in full, the beneficiary executes a discharge that releases the property back to the trustor.
    A. True
    B. False

11. A buyer who purchases real property and assumes the seller's debt becomes personally obligated for the repayment of the entire debt.
    A. True
    B. False

12. An adjustable-rate mortgage begins at one rate of interest, then fluctuates up or down during the loan term.
    A. True
    B. False

13. In states that permit strict foreclosure, the court simply awards full legal title to the lender and no sale of the property takes place.
    A. True
    B. False

14. A reverse mortgage allows a homeowner aged 62 or older to borrow money against the equity built up in the home.
    A. True
    B. False

15. Usury is defined as the act of charging interest in excess of the maximum legal rate.
    A. True
    B. False

16. After the redemption period (if applicable), the successful bidder at a foreclosure sale receives a deed that conveys whatever title the borrower had, with no warranties.
    A. True
    B. False

17. Lenders are allowed to charge prepayment penalties on mortgage loans insured or guaranteed by the federal government.
    A. True
    B. False

18. If the lender must obtain insurance on property located in a flood hazard area because the borrower has not, the lender can add the premium cost to the unpaid debt.
    A. True
    B. False

19. An assignment of mortgage occurs when the borrower pays off the loan.
    A. True
    B. False

20. When a mortgage lender finds that a borrower has not made necessary repairs to the property, the lender usually immediately proceeds to foreclosure.
    A. True
    B. False

MULTIPLE CHOICE

Circle the correct answer.

1. A married couple, both 65 years old, have retired. They have almost $800,000 in equity in their home, but they don't have enough cash to travel as they have always dreamed of doing. The couple could consider which of the following financing alternatives?
   A. Novation
   B. An adjustable-rate mortgage
   C. A reverse mortgage
   D. A growing-equity mortgage

2. A document that indicates that a loan has been made is called
   A. a promissory note.
   B. a mortgage deed.
   C. a deed of trust.
   D. a satisfaction.

3. A borrower defaults on a mortgage, and the lender forecloses. The lender's foreclosure suit is filed on March 15, and the sale is to be held on May 10. If the borrower attempts to redeem the property on May 1, which of the following statements applies?
   A. The borrower is exercising the statutory right of redemption.
   B. The borrower is exercising the equitable right of redemption.
   C. The borrower's attempt to redeem the property is too early; by statute, the borrower must wait until after the sale.
   D. The borrower cannot redeem the property after a foreclosure suit is filed.

4. A house is listed for $250,000. It is purchased for $230,000, with a 20% down payment. The balance is financed by a fixed-rate mortgage at 6%. The lender charges four points. If there are no other closing costs involved, how much money does the buyer need at closing?
   A. $7,360
   B. $26,000
   C. $46,000
   D. $53,360

5. One afternoon, a client calls a real estate broker. "My lender just told me that my note and mortgage is a negotiable instrument," says the client. "What does that mean?" Which of these would be the broker's *BEST* response?
   A. "That's great! It means the lender is willing to negotiate on the interest rate."
   B. "Oh no! That means the mortgage can't be assumed by the next person you sell to."
   C. "Don't worry. That means the mortgage can be sold by the lender, but you're not affected."
   D. "Uh-oh! That means we have to go back to the sellers and ask them to pay the points."

6. A deed of trust involves all of these terms *EXCEPT*
   A. lender.
   B. borrower.
   C. trustee.
   D. mortgagor.

7. In a lien theory state, a buyer purchases property from a seller and gives the seller a mortgage as part of the purchase price. Which of these statements is *FALSE*?
   A. The buyer retains equitable title to the property.
   B. If the buyer defaults on the loan, the seller must undergo a formal foreclosure proceeding to recover the security.
   C. The buyer has given legal title to the seller.
   D. The seller has only a lien interest in the property.

8. A basic form homeowners insurance policy provides property coverage against
   A. floods.
   B. fire, lightning, and smoke damage.
   C. damage due to the weight of ice, snow, or sleet.
   D. falling objects.

9. A mortgage company charges borrowers a 1.5% loan origination fee. What will the mortgage company charge as a fee if the asking price of a house was $235,000, the sales price is $210,000, and the buyer is making a down payment of $50,000?
   A. $2,400
   B. $3,150
   C. $3,525
   D. $3,750

10. A mortgage document contains the clause: "In the event of Borrower's default under the terms of this Agreement, Lender may declare the entire unpaid balance of the debt due and payable immediately." This clause is called
    A. a hypothecation clause.
    B. an acceleration clause.
    C. a defeasance clause.
    D. a release clause.

11. This month, a borrower made the last payment on a mortgage loan. The lender must execute
    A. a release deed.
    B. a promissory note.
    C. a possessory note.
    D. a satisfaction of mortgage.

12. A consumer's income, outstanding loans, and other financial factors, will be reflected in the consumer's
    A. interest paid on overdue real estate taxes.
    B. state of residence.
    C. credit score.
    D. withholding taxes.

13. A buyer purchases property from a seller for $45,000 in cash and assumes the seller's outstanding mortgage balance of $98,500. The lender executes a release for the seller. The buyer fails to make any mortgage payments, and the lender forecloses. At the foreclosure sale, the property is sold for $75,000. Based on these facts, who is liable, and for what amount?
    A. The seller is solely liable for $23,500.
    B. The buyer is solely liable for $23,500.
    C. The buyer and the seller are equally liable for $23,500.
    D. The buyer is solely liable for $30,000.

14. The decision whether to buy or rent should involve consideration of
    A. the design and functionality of available properties.
    B. the terms of the security agreement.
    C. housing affordability and current mortgage interest rates.
    D. the availability of a reverse mortgage.

15. A borrower defaulted on a mortgage loan, leaving an unpaid balance of $95,000. After receiving only $85,000 from the sale of the property, the lender filed for
    A. a lis pendens.
    B. a release deed.
    C. a satisfaction.
    D. a deficiency judgment.

16. When a homeowner defaulted on a home loan, the trustee immediately sold the property to recover the debt. The trustee acted under the terms of the security instrument. Based on these facts, which of these statements is *TRUE*?
    A. The exercise of this power of sale clause is an example of strict foreclosure.
    B. The trustee's sale of the property was illegal unless the state permits a so-called friendly foreclosure.
    C. The exercise of this power of sale clause is an example of nonjudicial foreclosure.
    D. The homeowner could have exercised the statutory right of redemption at any time prior to the trustee's sale of the property.

17. The difference between the interest rate that the lender charges and what the investment demands can be made up by charging
    A. discount points.
    B. loan origination fees.
    C. satisfaction fees.
    D. underwriting fees.

18. What is the term that refers to a lender charging an interest rate that is higher than that permitted by law?
    A. Alienation
    B. Usury
    C. Hypothecation
    D. Defeasance

19. Parties to lending agreements are referred to by different terms. Which of these refers to the same party?
    A. Borrower = beneficiary
    B. Borrower = mortgagor
    C. Trustee = borrower
    D. Trustor = mortgagee

20. If the lender wants to call the entire note due and payable if the borrower stops making payments, the security instrument must include
    A. an acceleration clause.
    B. a defeasance clause.
    C. an alienation clause.
    D. a prepayment clause.

21. When a deed of trust is the security instrument, which party usually chooses the trustee?
    A. The borrower
    B. The lender
    C. The devisee
    D. The county government

22. Lenders charge a loan origination fee to
    A. guard against charges of usury.
    B. cover the losses involved if the borrower repays the loan before the end of the loan term.
    C. cover the expenses involved in generating the loan.
    D. guard against losses in the event of a short sale.

23. How does an acceleration clause help lenders?
    A. Without the acceleration clause, lenders would have to sue the borrower for every overdue payment.
    B. Lenders would rather foreclose on property than hold a long-term loan.
    C. It results in a deed in lieu of foreclosure rather than the default process.
    D. It sets out the provisions for the impound account.

24. After a foreclosure sale, what responsibility does the purchaser at the sale have for the mortgage and any junior liens?
    A. The purchaser pays off the mortgage after the sale, but the junior lienholders receive nothing.
    B. The mortgage holder receives funds from the sale, but the purchaser must pay off the junior lienholders to obtain title.
    C. The purchaser must pay off both the mortgage and junior lienholders after the sale.
    D. The purchaser has no responsibility because the purchaser receives the property title without the mortgage and junior liens.

25. What is a major disadvantage to lenders of accepting a deed in lieu of foreclosure?
    A. The lender takes the real estate subject to all junior liens.
    B. The lender gains rights to private mortgage insurance.
    C. The process is lengthy and involves a lawsuit.
    D. It is an adverse element in the borrower's credit history.

MATH PRACTICE

Use this loan table to solve the following five problems.

Annual Interest Rate (%)	Amortized Loans Life of Loan (in Years) (Monthly Payments per $1,000 of Loan Principal)							
	5	**10**	**15**	**20**	**25**	**30**	**35**	**40**
5.00	$18.87	$10.61	$7.91	$6.60	$5.85	$5.37	$5.05	$4.82
5.50	19.10	10.85	8.17	6.88	6.14	5.68	5.37	5.16
6.00	19.33	11.10	8.44	7.16	6.44	6.00	5.70	5.50
6.50	19.57	11.35	8.71	7.46	6.75	6.32	6.04	5.85
7.00	19.80	11.61	8.99	7.75	7.07	6.65	6.39	6.21
7.50	20.04	11.87	9.27	8.06	7.39	6.99	6.74	6.58
8.00	20.28	12.13	9.56	8.36	7.72	7.34	7.10	6.95
8.50	20.52	12.40	9.85	8.68	8.05	7.69	7.47	7.33
9.00	20.76	12.67	10.14	9.00	8.39	8.05	7.84	7.71
9.50	21.00	12.94	10.40	9.32	8.74	8.41	8.22	8.10
10.00	21.25	13.22	10.75	9.65	9.09	8.78	8.60	8.49
10.50	21.49	13.49	11.05	9.98	9.44	9.15	8.98	8.89
11.0	21.74	13.78	11.37	10.32	9.80	9.52	9.37	9.28

1. A man wants to borrow $125,000 for 20 years. He will pay 8.5% interest.

    a. What will be his monthly payments?

    b. What will be the cost of interest over the life of the loan?

2. A woman wants to borrow $200,000 to buy a house. If she must pay 6.5% annual interest and can afford a monthly payment of $1,350 (principal and interest), what is the lowest number of years she can borrow the money?

3. A couple plans to borrow $75,000 to buy a condominium. If they obtain mortgage money at 6% instead of 7.5% for a 30-year loan, how much lower will their monthly principal and interest payments be?

4. A man can afford $1,175 per month for a payment that includes principal, interest, taxes, and insurance. Annual property taxes are $840, and insurance will cost $480 per year. If current interest rates are at 7% and the man wants a 30-year loan, how much can he afford to borrow?

5. A borrower wants a 15-year mortgage instead of the typical 30-year mortgage. He will be borrowing $300,000 at 6.5%.

    a. How much more will this cost each month compared to a 30-year mortgage?

    b. How much will he save in interest payments over the life of the loan?

UNIT 12 ANSWERS

MATCHING A

1. **F**

2. **G**

3. **D**

4. **J**

5. **B**

6. **E**

7. **I**

8. **H**

9. **C**

10. **A**

MATCHING B

1. **C**

2. **H**

3. **A**

4. **J**

5. **F**

6. **B**

7. **E**

8. **I**

9. **D**

10. **G**

11. **L**

12. **O**

13. **K**

14. **M**

15. **N**

TRUE OR FALSE

1. **B** The answer is false. A mortgage is classified as a voluntary lien on real estate. (213)

2. **B** The answer is false. A mortgage is a financing agreement in which a mortgagor pledges real property to the mortgagee as security for a debt. (213)

3. **A** The answer is true. A deed of trust gives actual title to secured property to a trustee for the benefit of the lender. Legal title is returned to the borrower only when the debt is repaid in full (or some other obligation is fulfilled). (214)

4. **A** The answer is true. The borrower signs a promissory note pledging to repay the debt and gives the lender a mortgage, which is security for the property. (210)

5. **B** The answer is false. PITI refers to principal, interest, taxes, and insurance. These are the basic costs of owning a home. (209)

6. **A** The answer is true. There are three parties to a deed of trust: the trustee holds the deed of trust on behalf of the lender, who is called the beneficiary, the holder of the note. The borrower is the trustor. (214)

7. **B** The answer is false. A point is 1% of the amount being borrowed. For borrowers, one discount point equals 1% of the loan amount and is charged as prepaid interest at the closing. (212)

8. **B** The answer is false. In the event of a borrower's default, an acceleration clause makes foreclosure easier by giving a lender the right to declare the entire debt due and payable. (215)

9. **A** The answer is true. By the defeasance clause, the lender is required to execute a satisfaction when the note has been fully paid. The lender is then divested of all interest in the property. (216)

10. **B** The answer is false. After a real estate loan that is secured by a deed of trust has been repaid in full, the trustee executes a release deed or deed of reconveyance that releases the property back to the trustor. (216)

11. **A** The answer is true. Unlike buying subject to the mortgage, a buyer who purchases a property and assumes the seller's debt becomes personally obligated for the payment of the entire debt. (217)

12. **A** The answer is true. The fluctuation is based on a specified economic indicator. Details of how and when the interest rate will change are included in the note. (219)

13. **A** The answer is true. After appropriate notice is made to the delinquent borrower, in some states, the lender may acquire mortgaged property through strict foreclosure. The court awards full legal title to the lender, and no sale takes place. (223)

14. **A** The answer is true. With a reverse mortgage, the homeowner's equity diminishes as the loan amount increases. (222)

15. **A** The answer is true. Usury is the practice of charging interest at a higher rate than the maximum rate allowed by state law. (211)

16. **A** The answer is true. After the redemption period, if the delinquent borrower does not repay the loan, an official, such as a sheriff, executes a deed to the person who paid the debts. The deed conveys whatever title the borrower had prior to the redemption period. (224)

17. **B** The answer is false. Mortgage lenders also cannot charge prepayment penalties on loans that have been sold to a government-sponsored enterprise. (212)

18. **A** The answer is true. If the lender purchases flood insurance on behalf of the borrower, the cost of the insurance may be charged back to the borrower. (216–217)

19. **B** The answer is false. An assignment of mortgage occurs when the lender sells the loan to an investor or other mortgage company. (216)

20. **B** The answer is false. The loan documents may provide for a grace period, such as 30 days, within which the borrower can meet the obligation and cure the default. (215)

MULTIPLE CHOICE

1. **C** The answer is a reverse mortgage. A reverse mortgage allows a homeowner aged 62 or older to borrow money against the equity built up in the home. The money may be used for any purpose. (222)

2. **A** The answer is a promissory note. The evidence that a loan has been made is found in the promissory note. A mortgage or deed of trust provides security for the loan. A satisfaction or release indicates that the loan has been repaid in full. (210)

3. **B** The answer is the borrower is exercising the equitable right of redemption. The borrower has an equity interest in the property until the foreclosure sale is complete; thus, the borrower may exercise the equitable right of redemption. In some states, the borrower may retain a statutory right of redemption for a period of time after the foreclosure sale. (224)

4. **D** The answer is $53,360. The buyer needs $53,360 at closing. Three steps:
   1. Calculate down payment: $230,000 × 20% = $46,000.
   2. Determine points charge: $230,000 × 80% × 4% = $7,3603.
   3. Total the two amounts: $46,000 + $7,360 = $53,360.
   (212)

5. **C** The answer is "Don't worry. That means the mortgage can be sold by the lender, but you're not affected." Negotiable instruments are transferable. A note and mortgage will often be sold on the secondary market. (216)

6. **D** The answer is mortgagor. A mortgagor is the borrower in a mortgage. In a deed of trust, the borrower is the trustor, and the trustee holds legal title in trust for the beneficiary (lender). (213)

7. **C** The answer is the buyer has given legal title to the seller. A borrower who gives a mortgage, even in the seller financing situation described in this question, retains both equitable and legal title to the property serving as security. (213)

8. **B** The answer is fire, lightning, and smoke damage. A basic form policy covers fire, lightning, and smoke damage, among other hazards. A broad-form policy generally covers the hazards of falling objects and damage due to the weight of ice, snow, or sleet. Flood damage is covered under a separate flood insurance policy. (226–227)

9. **A** The answer is $2,400. The buyer's loan origination fee is $2,400: ($210,000 − $50,000) × 1.5% = $2,400. The asking price is not relevant to this problem. (212)

10. **B**   The answer is an acceleration clause. An acceleration clause can be used to make the remaining balance of a loan due if the borrower defaults. Hypothecation is the act of offering the property as security without giving up possession. The defeasance clause in a mortgage defeats the granting clause. A release indicates that the loan has been repaid in full. (215)

11. **D**   The answer is a satisfaction of mortgage. The promissory note shows that a loan was made. The satisfaction indicates that the loan was fully repaid. Satisfaction of mortgage is also sometimes called a release, but not a release deed. (216)

12. **C**   The answer is credit score. A consumer's income, outstanding loans, payment history, and other factors are all reflected in the consumer's credit score. Even the number of credit inquiries can influence the score. (209–210)

13. **B**   The answer is the buyer is solely liable for $23,500. Because the lender released the original borrower, the second borrower is fully responsible for the deficiency. (224)

14. **C**   The answer is housing affordability and current mortgage interest rates. Other considerations include tax consequences, what might happen to home prices in the future, and a person's overall financial situation. (208–209)

15. **D**   The answer is a deficiency judgement. A deficiency results when the foreclosed property does not bring enough money to fully repay the loan; the mortgagor may be entitled to a personal judgment against the borrower for the unpaid balance. Lis pendens gives notice that the property is the subject of legal action. A satisfaction indicates that the loan was fully repaid. (224)

16. **C**   The answer is the exercise of this power of sale clause is an example of nonjudicial foreclosure. This foreclosure and sale were nonjudicial; that is, they did not require a court order. Strict foreclosure and friendly foreclosure do not involve a sale. The statutory right of redemption applies only after the sale. (223)

17. **A**   The answer is discount points. The lender can increase its yield on the investment by charging interest upfront in the form of discount points. Loan origination fees are charged to cover the cost of making the loan. The satisfaction indicates that the loan has been fully repaid. (212)

18. **B**   The answer is usury. To protect consumers from unscrupulous lenders, many states have enacted laws limiting the interest rate that may be charged on loans. (211)

19. **B**   The answer is borrow = mortgagor. The person who makes the payments to repay the loan is called the borrower. The person who gave the property as security is called the mortgagor. Both are the same person. (213)

20. **A**   The answer is an acceleration clause. The acceleration clause permits the lender to declare the entire note due upon default by the borrower. The alienation clause is also called the due on sale clause, permitting the lender to declare the entire note due if the property is sold, and thus preventing a loan assumption. (215)

21. **B**   The answer is the lender. The lender usually also reserves the right to substitute trustees in the event of death or dismissal. (214)

22. **C**   The answer is cover the expenses involved in generating the loan. The processing of a mortgage application is called loan origination. When a home loan is originated, a loan origination fee is charged by most lenders to cover the expenses involved in generating the loan. (211)

23. **A**   The answer is without the acceleration clause, lenders would have to sue the borrower for every overdue payment. A lender's purpose is to make long-term loans, not foreclose. The impound account is set up under a different provision of the loan. (215)

24. **D**   The answer is the purchaser has no responsibility because the purchaser receives the property title without the mortgage and junior liens. The proceeds from the sale are used to pay off the mortgage and junior lienholders. If the proceeds are insufficient, and state law permits, these creditors can seek a deficiency judgment against the original owner for the remaining debt. The purchaser at the sale is not involved unless the purchaser is a mortgage or lienholder. (224)

25. **A**   The answer is the lender takes the real estate subject to all junior liens. The lender loses rights to FHA or private mortgage insurance or VA guarantees. The process is called friendly foreclosure, because a lawsuit is not involved. It is an adverse element for the borrower, but that does not affect the lender. (223)

MATH PRACTICE

1. a. The monthly payment will be $1,085:

    $125,000 ÷ 1,000 × 8.68 = $1,085 monthly

    b. Interest over the life of the loan is $135,400:

    $1,085 × 240 = $260,400; $260,400 − $125,000 = $135,400 interest over the life of the loan

2. Lowest number of years she can borrow the money is 25: $200,000 ÷ 1,000 = 200;

    $1,350 ÷ 200 = 6.75, which is the factor for 6.5% at 25 years

3. The couple's payment will be $74.25 lower each month:

    At 7.5%: 75 × 6.99 = $524.25

    At 6%: 75 × 6.00 = $450.00

    $524.25 − $450 = $74.25 lower each month

4. The maximum loan amount is $160,150:

    $840 ÷ 12 = $70 tax per month

    $480 ÷ 12 = $40 insurance per month

    $1,175 − $70 − $40 = $1,065; $1,065 ÷ 6.65 × 1,000 = $160,150 (maximum loan amount)

5. a. The borrower will have to pay $717 more each month with the 15-year loan:

    15-year: 300 × 8.71 = $2,613

    30-year: 300 × 6.32 = $1,896

    $2,613 − $1,896 = $717

    b. The borrower will save $212,220 in interest over the life of the loan with the 15-year loan:

    15-year: $2,613 × 15 × 12 = $470,340

    30-year: $1,896 × 30 × 12 = $682,560

    In actuality, lenders usually offer a lower interest rate on 15-year loans as opposed to 30-year loans. Therefore, the borrower is likely to have a lower monthly payment than the one projected for the 15-year loan term and will save even more in total interest.

UNIT
13

Government Involvement in Real Estate Financing

LEARNING OBJECTIVES

When you have completed this unit, you will be able to

> **explain** the primary and secondary mortgage marketplaces, the roles of the parties in each, and the impact on the parties through government influence;
> **describe** the difference between conventional, government, and private loan programs available for real estate financing;
> **describe** the various alternative and special-purpose loan programs which can meet a borrower's special needs; and
> **explain** the primary government regulations which govern real estate lending and provide consumer protection against unfair lending practices.

KEY TERMS

blanket loan
buydown
certificate of reasonable value (CRV)
Community Reinvestment Act of 1977 (CRA)
construction loan
conventional loan
Equal Credit Opportunity Act (ECOA)
Fannie Mae
Farmer Mac

Federal Deposit Insurance Corporation (FDIC)
Federal Reserve System (Fed)
FHA-insured loan
Freddie Mac
Ginnie Mae
government-sponsored enterprises (GSEs)
home equity loan
mortgage insurance premium (MIP)
Office of the Comptroller of the Currency (OCC)

open-end loan
package loan
primary mortgage market
private mortgage insurance (PMI)
Real Estate Settlement Procedures Act (RESPA)
Regulation Z
sale-and-leaseback
secondary mortgage market
triggering terms
Truth in Lending Act (TILA)
VA-guaranteed loan

MATCHING A

Write the letter of the matching term on the appropriate line.

A. Federal Reserve

B. loan-to-value ratio (LTV)

C. fiduciary lenders

D. private mortgage insurance

E. Ginnie Mae

F. mortgage brokers

G. secondary mortgage market

H. Farmer Mac

I. primary mortgage market

J. discount rate

1. ___ A national system of banking districts designed to maintain sound credit conditions and a favorable economic climate

2. ___ Creates a secondary market for agricultural mortgage loans

3. ___ Lenders who originate loans by making money available to borrow

4. ___ Thrifts, savings associations, and commercial banks

5. ___ Intermediaries who bring borrowers and lenders together

6. ___ Investors who buy and sell loans after the loan is funded

7. ___ A method of providing a lender with part of a conventional loan balance in the event that a borrower defaults on the loan

8. ___ A governmental agency organized as a nonstock corporation that administers special assistance programs and guarantees mortgage-backed securities using FHA and VA loans

9. ___ The rate charged for loans the Fed makes to banks

10. ___ The ratio of debt to the value of the property

MATCHING B

Write the letter of the matching term on the appropriate line.

A. blanket loan

B. Office of the Comptroller of the Currency (OCC)

C. buydown

D. certificate of eligibility

E. Equal Credit Opportunity Act

F. package loan

G. conventional loan

H. purchase-money mortgage

I. Truth in Lending Act

J. Real Estate Settlement Procedures Act

1. ___ Fiduciary lenders are subject to the standards and regulations established by this office

2. ___ The type of loan viewed as most secure because of its low loan-to-value ratio

3. ___ The document that determines the maximum VA loan guarantee to which a veteran is entitled

4. ___ A form of seller financing whereby the buyer gives the seller a note and mortgage

5. ___ A loan that finances the purchase of both real and personal property

6. ___ A method of financing the purchase of property that temporarily (or permanently) lowers the interest rate through the payment of a lump sum of cash to the lender

7. ___ Lending law prohibiting discrimination based on marital status or sex

8. ___ Type of mortgage used by developers, securing the loan with several parcels

9. ___ Law that is designed to ensure that buyer and seller are both fully informed of all closing costs

10. ___ Law that requires lenders to reveal the true cost of borrowing money

TRUE OR FALSE

Circle the correct answer.

1. The Federal Reserve System is comprised of the lenders who originate loans.
   A. True
   B. False

2. Income from a loan is generated by up-front finance charges collected at closing, plus interest collected during the loan term.
   A. True
   B. False

3. The primary mortgage market includes savings associations, insurance companies, and mortgage bankers.
   A. True
   B. False

4. Fannie Mae is a government agency.
   A. True
   B. False

5. Farmer Mac was established by Congress to create a secondary market for agricultural mortgage and rural utilities loans.
   A. True
   B. False

6. In mortgage loans, the lower the ratio of debt to value, the higher the down payment by the borrower.
   A. True
   B. False

7. Regulation Z was enacted by the Federal Reserve to enforce the Truth in Lending Act (TILA) and requires that credit institutions inform borrowers of the true cost of obtaining credit.
   A. True
   B. False

8. The Helping Families Save their Homes Act amended TILA by requiring that lenders provide refinancing terms to borrowers who need them.
   A. True
   B. False

9. The value portion of a property's loan-to-value ratio (LTV) is the higher of the sale price or the appraised value.
   A. True
   B. False

10. The FHA is not a mortgage lender.
    A. True
    B. False

11. A home equity loan takes first lien priority over the original mortgage loan.
    A. True
    B. False

12. A blanket loan covers more than one parcel or lot and is usually used to finance subdivision developments.
    A. True
    B. False

13. In an open-end loan the interest rate on the initial amount borrowed is fixed, but the rate on future advances is linked to future market rates.
    A. True
    B. False

14. Under the Truth in Lending Act, consumers must be fully informed of all finance charges and of the true interest rate prior to the completion of a transaction.
    A. True
    B. False

15. Under Regulation Z, a residential purchase-money borrower has three business days in which to rescind a transaction by notifying the lender of intent to rescind.
    A. True
    B. False

16. Under the Community Reinvestment Act, the findings of the government agency review of an institution's reinvestment activities are strictly confidential.
    A. True
    B. False

17. Freddie Mac encourages the use of its automated underwriting service by charging lenders a minimal fee per transaction to use it.
    A. True
    B. False

Unit 13

18. A VA appraisal is called a certificate of reasonable value (CRV).
    A. True
    B. False

19. TILA and RESPA disclosures must be made on forms created by the Consumer Financial Protection Bureau.
    A. True
    B. False

20. FHA loans are attractive to lenders, because the loans have insurance against loss due to borrower default.
    A. True
    B. False

21. The VA limits the amount of principal in a VA loan.
    A. True
    B. False

22. The Community Reinvestment Act requires financial institutions to help meet their communities' needs for low-income and moderate-income housing.
    A. True
    B. False

23. When a loan is sold in the secondary mortgage market, the purchasing investor always assumes the servicing of the loan.
    A. True
    B. False

MULTIPLE CHOICE

Circle the correct answer.

1. All of these are roles of the Federal Reserve System *EXCEPT*
   A. help counteract inflationary trends.
   B. create a favorable economic climate.
   C. maintain sound credit conditions.
   D. make direct loans to buyers.

2. A lender who collects payments, processes them, and follows up on loan delinquencies is said to
   A. increase the yield to the lender.
   B. service the loan.
   C. insure loan payments.
   D. underwrite the loans.

3. The primary mortgage market lenders that have most recently branched out into making mortgage loans are
   A. credit unions.
   B. endowment funds.
   C. insurance companies.
   D. savings associations.

4. The Federal Deposit Insurance Corporation (FDIC) does which of these?
   A. Administers Freddie Mac and Ginnie Mae
   B. Administers Freddie Mac only
   C. Insures deposits in insured institutions up to $250,000 per depositor, per account
   D. Services loans

5. One way a borrower can obtain a conventional mortgage loan with a lower down payment than 20% of the purchase price is by
   A. obtaining a package loan.
   B. obtaining a blanket loan.
   C. obtaining private mortgage insurance.
   D. obtaining permission from the FDIC.

6. A package loan includes
   A. real and personal property.
   B. private mortgage insurance.
   C. multiple parcels or lots.
   D. cash for the construction of improvement on real estate.

7. What does private mortgage insurance cover?
   A. Pays the lender if the borrower dies
   B. Reimburses the cosigner if the borrower defaults
   C. Protects the top 20% to 30% of the loan against borrower default
   D. Pays the borrower if the borrower loses the house to a title claim

8. Regulation Z generally applies to
   A. a credit transaction secured by a residence.
   B. business loans.
   C. commercial loans.
   D. agricultural loans of more than $25,000.

9. A construction loan usually is
   A. the only loan a homebuyer will need to obtain.
   B. short-term financing.
   C. issued for the full amount of the expected cost of construction.
   D. maintained until the purchase price has been fully paid.

10. A buydown loan enables a borrower
    A. to lower the interest rate on a mortgage or deed of trust loan.
    B. to pay off a mortgage loan earlier.
    C. to make interest-only payments for the life of the loan.
    D. with poor credit to postpone payment of part of the interest charged until later in the loan term.

11. All of these are lenders in the primary mortgage market *EXCEPT*
    A. endowment funds.
    B. mortgage brokers.
    C. insurance companies.
    D. credit unions.

12. The Homeowner's Protection Act of 1998 (HPA) requires that the lender automatically
    A. lower the interest rate on a mortgage.
    B. terminate the private mortgage insurance payment if the borrower has accrued at least 22% equity in the home.
    C. provide for a home equity line of credit.
    D. allow for refinancing terms if requested by the borrower.

Unit 13

13. A house had a sale price of $240,000. The buyer obtained a loan for $220,000. If the lender charges three points, how much will the buyer pay in points?
    A. $5,335
    B. $6,600
    C. $6,950
    D. $7,540

14. On which type of loan can the borrower prepay without penalty?
    A. Loans sold to Fannie Mae and Freddie Mac
    B. FHA loans
    C. VA loans
    D. All of these

15. The Equal Credit Opportunity Act prohibits discrimination in the lending process based on
    A. race.
    B. religion.
    C. marital status.
    D. all of these.

16. A buyer purchased a home. The asking price for the home was $585,000; the buyer offered $565,000 and the seller accepted. The appraised value of the home is $560,000. The buyer plans to pay $94,600 in cash and take out a mortgage for the remainder. What is the LTV for this property?
    A. 82%
    B. 83%
    C. 84%
    D. 85%

17. A buyer is purchasing property. The seller bought the property on December 20, 1999, with an FHA loan and has lived there ever since. Because of its favorable terms, the buyer would like to assume the seller's mortgage. Is this possible?
    A. Yes, there are no restrictions on the assumption of this mortgage.
    B. Yes, but the buyer will have to undergo the complete buyer qualification process.
    C. Yes, but the buyer will have to undergo a creditworthiness review only.
    D. No, this FHA loan is not assumable.

18. In 1967, a lieutenant in the Air Force served for six months on active duty in Vietnam. In 1998, the veteran was killed in a skiing accident. The veteran's surviving spouse wishes to use the veteran's life insurance proceeds to make a down payment on a condominium and finance the remainder of the purchase with a VA-guaranteed loan. Is the surviving spouse entitled to a VA-guaranteed loan?
    A. Yes, the unremarried spouse of a qualified veteran is entitled to a VA-guaranteed loan.
    B. Yes, whether or not a surviving spouse remarries, the surviving spouse is entitled to the same VA benefits as the veteran was during the veteran's lifetime.
    C. No, the veteran's death was not service-related.
    D. No, the veteran did not meet the time-in-service criteria for qualified veterans.

19. Which of these makes direct loans to qualified borrowers?
    A. VA
    B. FSA
    C. Fannie Mae
    D. FHA

20. A buyer is purchasing a fully furnished condominium unit. In this situation, the buyer would be MOST likely to use
    A. a package loan.
    B. a blanket loan.
    C. a wraparound loan.
    D. a buydown.

21. HUD foreclosure sales of FHA-insured homes include an early bidding period for buyers who
    A. are willing to fix up and resell the property within 24 months.
    B. intend to be owner-occupants.
    C. have not previously been residents of the community.
    D. have resided in the community for at least 36 months before the purchase.

22. The Equal Credit Opportunity Act prohibits lenders from discriminating against credit applicants on the basis of all of these factors EXCEPT
    A. religion.
    B. past credit history.
    C. income from public assistance.
    D. marital status.

23. Lenders that make conventional loans to sell in the secondary mortgage market follow the standardized forms and guidelines issued by Fannie Mae and
    A. the FSA.
    B. the FHA.
    C. Ginnie Mae.
    D. Freddie Mac.

24. Which of these may lawfully be used as part of a loan application evaluation process?
    A. The applicant's religious beliefs
    B. The fact that the borrower is over 40 years old
    C. A credit score
    D. None of these

25. The real estate financing market comprises
    A. the primary and secondary mortgage markets.
    B. Fannie Mae and Ginnie Mae.
    C. the primary and secondary mortgage markets, plus government influences such as the Federal Reserve system.
    D. none of these.

26. A 16-year-old applied for a conventional loan in order to purchase a condominium. The lender denied the application, citing the applicant's age as the reason for the denial. Which of these is *TRUE*?
    A. The lender violated the ECOA because the applicant is too young to be expected to have an employment history.
    B. The lender violated the ECOA because lending decisions cannot be based on age.
    C. The lender lawfully denied the application because the applicant was under 18 and therefore was too young to legally sign a contract.
    D. None of these are true.

27. What helps lenders reduce the risk on a conventional mortgage loan with a high LTV?
    A. Private mortgage insurance
    B. Flood insurance
    C. Sale-and-leaseback arrangement
    D. Home equity

UNIT 13 ANSWERS

MATCHING A

1. **A**

2. **H**

3. **I**

4. **C**

5. **F**

6. **G**

7. **D**

8. **E**

9. **J**

10. **B**

MATCHING B

1. **B**

2. **G**

3. **D**

4. **H**

5. **F**

6. **C**

7. **E**

8. **A**

9. **J**

10. **I**

TRUE OR FALSE

1. **B** The answer is false. The primary mortgage market consists of the lenders who originate loans—those who make loans directly to borrowers. (235)

2. **A** The answer is true. Up-front fees (origination fees and discount points) collected at the time of closing as well as interest collected over the term of the loan generate income. (241)

3. **A** The answer is true. Major lenders in the primary market include savings associations, commercial banks, insurance companies, credit unions, pension funds, endowment funds, and mortgage banking companies. (235)

4. **B** The answer is false. Although Fannie Mae was created as a government agency in 1938, it became a private shareholder-owned corporation in 1968, although still under congressional supervision. (237)

5. **A** The answer is true. Farmer Mac is part of the Farm Credit System and is regulated by the Farm Credit Administration. (238)

6. **A** The answer is true. Mortgage loans can be classified based on their loan-to-value ratio (LTV). The lower the ratio of debt to value, the higher the down payment by the borrower. (238)

7. **A** The answer is true. With proper disclosures, borrowers can compare the costs of various lenders to promote the informed use of credit. (246)

8. **B** The answer is false. The Helping Families Save Their Homes Act amended TILA by requiring that consumers be notified of the sale or transfer of their mortgage loans. (246–247)

9. **B** The answer is false. The value portion of a property's LTV is the lower of the sale price or the appraised value. (238)

10. **A** The answer is true. The FHA insures loans; it does not make loans, and it does not hold loans. (240)

11. **B** The answer is false. A home equity loan has a junior lien priority to a first mortgage lien. (245–246)

12. **A** The answer is true. A blanket loan covers more than one parcel or lot and is usually used to finance subdivision developments. (244)

13. **A**   The answer is true. An open-end loan is often less costly than a home improvement loan; the initial interest rate is fixed, but interest on future advances may be charged at the market rate then in effect. (244)

14. **A**   The answer is true. The Truth in Lending Act, as enforced by Regulation Z, requires that credit institutions inform the borrower of the true cost of obtaining credit. (246)

15. **B**   The answer is false. Under Regulation Z, a borrower other than a residential purchase-money or first mortgage borrower has three business days in which to rescind a transaction by notifying the lender of intent to rescind. (246–247)

16. **B**   The answer is false. Under the Community Reinvestment Act, the findings of the government agency review of an institution's community reinvestment activities must be made public. (248–249)

17. **B**   The answer is false. As of June 1, 2015, Freddie Mac no longer charges lenders a fee to use its automated underwriting service. (249)

18. **A**   The answer is true. The VA's certificate of reasonable value states the property's current market value based on a VA-approved appraisal. (242)

19. **A**   The answer is true. The disclosures required by TILA and RESPA have been combined into two disclosure forms created by the Consumer Financial Protection Bureau. (249)

20. **A**   The answer is true. As with private mortgage insurance, the FHA insures lenders against loss from borrower default. (240–241)

21. **B**   The answer is false. The VA limits the amount of the loan it will guarantee. Lenders determine the amount of the loan and qualification of the borrower. (242)

22. **A**   The answer is true. Under the Community Reinvestment Act of 1977 (CRA), financial institutions are responsible for meeting the deposit and credit needs of the communities in which they are located. (248–249)

23. **B**   The answer is false. The original lender may continue to service the loan and collect payments. The investor is then charged a fee for servicing the loan. (235)

MULTIPLE CHOICE

1. **D**   The answer is make direct loans to buyers. The Federal Reserve helps counteract inflationary trends, creates a favorable economic climate, and maintains sound credit conditions, but it does not make direct loans to consumers. (234)

2. **B**   The answer is service the loan. In addition to the income directly related to loans, some lenders derive income from servicing loans for other mortgage lenders or investors who have purchased the loans. (235)

3. **A**   The answer is credit unions. Credit unions were known for short-term consumer loans but have more recently branched out into originating home mortgage loans. (235)

4. **C**   The answer is insures deposits in insured institutions up to $250,000 per depositor, per account. Deposits in insured institutions are covered up to the specified limit, which is currently $250,000 per depositor, per account. The FDIC does not service loans and does not administer Freddie Mac or Ginnie Mae. (235)

5. **C**   The answer is obtaining private mortgage insurance. Private mortgage insurance provides the lender with funds in the event that the borrower defaults on the loan and the value of the equity fails to cover the outstanding loan balance. This allows the lender to assume more risk so that the LTV can be higher than for other conventional loans. (239)

6. **A**   The answer is real and personal property. Package loans usually include items such as drapes, refrigerator, dishwasher, and other appliances as part of the sales price of the home. A blanket loan covers more than one parcel or lot. A construction loan finances the construction of improvements on real estate. (244)

7. **C**   The answer is protects the top 20% to 30% of the loan against borrower default. Private mortgage insurance, usually required for loans with an LTV of more than 80%, provides security to the lender if the borrower defaults. (239)

8. **A**   The answer is a credit transaction secured by a residence. The truth-in-lending law, implemented by Regulation Z, generally applies to a credit transaction secured by a residence, but it does not apply to commercial, business, or agricultural loans of more than $25,000. (246–247)

9. **B** The answer is short-term financing. A construction loan is generally short-term or interim financing. Funds are issued in draws as construction is completed; after that point, a permanent loan is obtained to repay the construction loan. (245)

10. **A** The answer is to lower the interest rate on a mortgage or deed of trust loan. By paying part of the interest upfront to offset monthly mortgage payments at the beginning of the loan term, the borrower can qualify for a loan with the expectation that the borrower's income will increase, making future, higher payments possible. (245)

11. **B** The answer is mortgage brokers. Mortgage brokers do not loan their own money; they are intermediaries who bring borrowers and lenders together. (236)

12. **B** The answer is terminate the private mortgage insurance payment if the borrower has accrued at least 22% equity in the home. The borrower must also be current on mortgage payments. (239–240)

13. **B** The answer is $6,600. The buyer will pay $6,600: $220,000 × 3% = $6,600. Points are charged on the loan amount, not the sale price. (241)

14. **D** The answer is all of these. Prepayment penalties are fairly unusual in today's market. (240)

15. **D** The answer is all of these. The ECOA prohibits discrimination in granting credit based on race, color, religion, national origin, sex, marital status, age, and receipt of public assistance. (248)

16. **C** The answer is 84%. The LTV on the loan amount is 84%. LTV = loan amount ÷ appraised value or sale price (whichever is lower), thus: $565,000 − $94,600 = $470,400; $470,400 ÷ $560,000 = 84%. (238–239)

17. **B** The answer is yes, but the buyer will have to undergo the complete buyer qualification process. Because the loan was made after December 15, 1989, assumptions are not permitted without complete buyer qualification. (241)

18. **C** The answer is no, the veteran's death was not service-related. The surviving spouse of a veteran whose death is service-related may use the veteran's entitlements. In this situation, the surviving spouse does not qualify. (242–243)

19. **B** The answer is FSA. The Farm Service Agency will guarantee loans made and serviced by private lenders and guaranteed for a specific percentage; the FSA will also make loans directly to the borrower. (243)

20. **A** The answer is a package loan. A loan secured by a fully furnished condominium unit is secured by both real and personal property. A blanket loan is secured by several properties. (244)

21. **B** The answer is intend to be owner-occupants. HUD allows an early bidding period for those who intend to be owner-occupants and properties that remain unsold are made available to investors only after that period has elapsed. (241)

22. **B** The answer is past credit history. Lenders may deny a loan request because of the borrower's previous credit history. Otherwise, lenders may not discriminate on the basis of race, color, religion, national origin, sex, receipt of public assistance, age, or marital status. (248)

23. **D** The answer is Freddie Mac. Freddie Mac and Fannie Mae are the dominant participants in the secondary mortgage market. (237)

24. **C** The answer is a credit score. A credit score is one factor that can be lawfully considered in evaluating a loan application. The Equal Credit Opportunity Act prohibits consideration of age or religion. (248)

25. **C** The answer is the primary and secondary mortgage markets, plus government influences such as the Federal Reserve system. These are the three basic components of the real estate financing market. (234)

26. **C** The answer is the lender lawfully denied the application because the applicant was under 18 and therefore was too young to legally sign a contract. A lender may not consider age unless the applicant is too young to legally sign a contract. (248)

27. **A** The answer is private mortgage insurance. Private mortgage insurance provides lenders with funds in case of borrower default and encourages lenders to make higher LTV loans. (239–240)

UNIT 14

Closing the Real Estate Transaction

LEARNING OBJECTIVES

When you have completed this unit, you will be able to

> **describe** the steps involved to achieve conveyance of clear and marketable title, including compliance with all applicable laws;
> **describe** closing procedures and the respective roles of all parties;
> **explain** the Real Estate Settlement Procedures Act (RESPA) and the Mortgage Disclosure Improvement Act (MDIA);
> **identify** all buyer and seller charges and credits contained in a closing statement; and
> **explain** the financial entries and mathematical calculations contained in a closing statement.

KEY TERMS

accrued items	escrow account	prorations
affiliated business arrangement (ABA)	escrow closing	Real Estate Settlement Procedures Act (RESPA)
closing	impound account	survey
Closing Disclosure	Loan Estimate	TILA-RESPA Integrated Disclosure Rule (TRID)
closing statement	Mortgage Disclosure Improvement Act (MDIA)	
credit	mortgage servicing transfer statement prepaid items	
debit		

MATCHING

Write the letter of the matching term on the appropriate line.

A. accrued items

B. federally related loans

C. banking year

D. closing

E. credit

F. debit

G. escrow

H. kickback

I. prepaid items

J. proration

1. ___ The fulfillment of a real estate sales contract

2. ___ A method of closing in which a disinterested third party acts as the agent of both buyer and seller to coordinate the closing activities

3. ___ The type of loan in a real estate settlement governed by RESPA

4. ___ A charge that a party owes and must pay at closing

5. ___ An amount in a party's favor that has already been paid, that is being reimbursed, or that will be paid in the future

6. ___ The division of financial responsibility for various items between the buyer and seller

7. ___ Expenses to be divided between the parties that are owed by the seller but later will be paid by the buyer

8. ___ Expenses that have been paid by and are credited to the seller

9. ___ A 360-day period used in calculating prorations

10. ___ An unearned fee, paid as part of a real estate transaction, that is prohibited by RESPA

TRUE OR FALSE

Circle the correct answer.

1. At closing, the seller delivers marketable title to the property.
   A. True
   B. False

2. Shortly before the closing, the buyer will usually conduct a final inspection of the property, often called a spot survey.
   A. True
   B. False

3. While the particulars of closing in escrow vary from state to state, the escrow agent is always a licensed attorney.
   A. True
   B. False

4. When closing in escrow, the seller will deposit proof of a new hazard insurance policy with the escrow agent.
   A. True
   B. False

5. Under the TILA-RESPA Integrated Disclosure rule, the timeliness of certain disclosures affects the date of closings.
   A. True
   B. False

6. RESPA applies to all federally related first mortgage loans for purchase of one- to four-unit residential real estate except for those administered by HUD.
   A. True
   B. False

7. Real estate professionals are exempt from RESPA's rules governing affiliated business arrangements and referrals.
   A. True
   B. False

8. *Your Home Loan Toolkit*, which provides information on closing, must be provided by the creditor to all mortgage applicants, if the loan is regulated by TRID.
   A. True
   B. False

9. The Loan Estimate form must be provided to the consumer within three business days after a loan application is submitted.
   A. True
   B. False

10. RESPA's rules prohibit paying or receiving kickbacks.
    A. True
    B. False

MULTIPLE CHOICE

Circle the correct answer.

1. A sale is closing on August 31. Real estate taxes, calculated on a calendar year basis, have not been paid for the current year. The tax is estimated to be $1,800. What amount of proration will be credited to the buyer (paid by the seller)?
   A. $1,100
   B. $1,200
   C. $1,485
   D. $1,500

2. A seller would be responsible for providing all of these items *EXCEPT*
   A. documents necessary to clear any clouds on the title.
   B. affidavits of title.
   C. the deed.
   D. preparation of mortgage and note.

3. What form must be provided to a loan applicant within three business days of application?
   A. Closing Disclosure
   B. Settlement Transfer
   C. Loan Estimate
   D. Mortgage Servicing

4. If the owner sells a fully-occupied rental property, how will the tenants' security deposits be treated at closing?
   A. Credit seller, debit buyer
   B. Debit both seller and buyer
   C. Credit buyer, debit seller
   D. None of these

5. If the interest rate on a loan increases more than 0.125% from that stated in the Closing Disclosure, what must the lender do?
   A. The lender must consult the seller to determine whether or not the seller will approve of the issuance of a new Closing Disclosure and additional three-day waiting period before closing can occur.
   B. The lender must provide a new Closing Disclosure and obtain a waiver from the buyer of the three-day waiting period so that closing can occur on schedule.
   C. The lender must provide a new Closing Disclosure and obtain a waiver from the seller of the three-day waiting period so that closing can occur on schedule.
   D. The lender must provide a new Closing Disclosure with a revised APR and wait an additional three business days before closing the loan.

6. Since 2002, a real estate broker has had an understanding with two of the five mortgage lenders in town. The broker recommends only those two lenders to clients and does not tell clients about any other lenders. In return, the recommended lenders pay for the vacations the broker offers sales associates as rewards for high performance. Based on these facts, which of these statements is *TRUE*?
   A. The broker is not doing anything illegal.
   B. Because this arrangement has been in existence for more than 10 years, it is exempt from RESPA.
   C. This is a permissible controlled business arrangement under RESPA because the broker is not paid a fee for the recommendations.
   D. The broker's arrangement with the lenders is an illegal kickback under RESPA.

7. All of these items are usually prorated at closing *EXCEPT*
    A. prepaid general real estate taxes.
    B. unpaid general real estate taxes.
    C. appraisal fees.
    D. rents collected in advance.

8. How is earnest money treated if the buyer does not default and shows up for closing?
    A. Credit seller
    B. Debit buyer
    C. Credit buyer
    D. Debit seller

UNIT 14 ANSWERS

MATCHING

1. **D**

2. **G**

3. **B**

4. **F**

5. **E**

6. **J**

7. **A**

8. **I**

9. **C**

10. **H**

TRUE OR FALSE

1. **A**   The answer is true. The seller delivers the deed to the property and the buyer accepts it. (260)

2. **B**   The answer is false. Shortly before the closing, the buyer will usually conduct a final inspection of the property, often called a walkthrough. (256)

3. **B**   The answer is false. While the particulars of closing in escrow vary from state to state, the escrow agent may be an attorney, title company, trust company, escrow company, or a lender's escrow department. (262)

4. **B**   The answer is false. When closing in escrow, the buyer will deposit proof of new hazard insurance with the escrow agent. (262)

5. **A**   The answer is true. Under the TILA-RESPA Integrated Disclosure rule, the timeliness of certain disclosures affects the date of closings; if the annual percentage rate increases by more than a certain amount, then creditors must provide a new Closing Disclosure with a revised annual percentage rate, and then wait an additional three business days before closing the loan. (265)

6. **B**   The answer is false. RESPA applies to all such loans, including those administered by HUD. (263)

7. **B**   The answer is false. Real estate professionals are not exempt from RESPA's rules governing controlled business arrangements and referrals. Real estate professionals must clearly inform the consumer about the relationship among the service providers, that participation is not required, that other providers are available, and the ownership interest or franchise relationship. (264)

8. **A**   The answer is true. The Consumer Financial Protection Bureau requires that *Your Home Loan Toolkit* be provided to mortgage loan applicants. (274)

9. **A**   The answer is true. The Loan Estimate form must be provided to the loan applicant by the lender within three business days after a loan application is submitted. (265)

10. **A**   The answer is true. RESPA prohibits the payment of kickbacks, or unearned fees, in any real estate settlement service; it prohibits referral fees when no services are actually rendered. (274)

MULTIPLE CHOICE

1. **B**   The answer is $1,200. The seller pays $1,200: $1,800 ÷ 12 months × 8 months = $1,200. (280)

2. **D**   The answer is preparation of mortgage and note. Documentation for the new loan—preparation of note and mortgage—is the responsibility of the buyer. The seller is responsible for documents necessary to clear any clouds on the title, affidavits of title and the deed. (262)

3. **C**   The answer is Loan Estimate. TRID requires this form to be delivered to a loan applicant within three business days of loan application. (265)

4. **C**   The answer is credit buyer, debit seller. The seller must pay the security deposits to the buyer who will, as the new owner, be responsible for returning the money to the tenants at the end of their lease terms. (276)

5. **D**   The answer is that the lender must provide a new Closing Disclosure with a revised APR and wait an addition three business days before closing the loan. This is a requirement of the Mortgage Disclosure Improvement Act that has been incorporated into the CFPB disclosure requirements. (274)

6. **D**   The answer is the broker's arrangement with the lenders is an illegal kickback under RESPA. By not telling clients about the other lenders in town, the broker is limiting their ability to get the best possible financing. That, added to the fact that the lender pays for the sales associates' vacations, makes the broker's behavior look very suspicious. (274)

7. **C**   The answer is appraisal fees. Appraisal fees and credit report fees are paid before closing by the buyer; they are not prorated. (277)

8. **C**   The answer is credit buyer. The earnest money is brought to closing and credited to the buyer. (276)

UNIT 15

Real Estate Taxes and Other Liens

LEARNING OBJECTIVES

When you have completed this unit, you will be able to

> **describe** the characteristics of statutory and equitable liens;
> **describe** general taxes and special assessment taxes; and
> **explain** real property liens, including judgments and taxes, as well as the protection and limitations they offer the respective parties.

KEY TERMS

ad valorem tax
assessment equalization
   factor
equitable lien
equitable right of redemption
estate tax
general lien
general real estate tax
inheritance tax

involuntary lien
judgment
junior lien
lien
mechanic's lien
mill
mortgage lien
special assessment
specific lien

statutory lien
statutory right of redemption
subordination agreement
tax lien
tax sale
vendor's lien
voluntary lien
writ of attachment

MATCHING A

Write the letter of the matching term on the appropriate line.

A. ad valorem	**1.** ___ A charge or claim against a person's property, to enforce the payment of money
B. equitable lien	**2.** ___ A lien that is created intentionally by the property owner's action
C. subordination	**3.** ___ A lien created by law
D. statutory lien	**4.** ___ A lien created by a court judgment
E. lien	**5.** ___ A lien that affects all the real and personal property owned by a debtor
F. priority	**6.** ___ A lien that is secured by and only affects certain property of the debtor
G. specific lien	**7.** ___ The order in which claims against property will be satisfied
H. general lien	**8.** ___ A written agreement between lienholders to change the priority of a lien
I. taxes	**9.** ___ Charges imposed by state and local governments to fund their functions and services
J. voluntary lien	**10.** ___ A type of tax based on the assessment of a property's value

MATCHING B

Write the letter of the matching term on the appropriate line.

A. assessment	**1.** ___ The official process of valuing real estate for tax purposes
B. money judgment	**2.** ___ A device to achieve uniformity in statewide assessments
C. equalization factor	**3.** ___ ¹⁄₁,₀₀₀ of a dollar, or $0.001
D. equitable right of redemption	**4.** ___ The right of a delinquent taxpayer to recover property before a tax sale
E. lis pendens	**5.** ___ The right of a delinquent taxpayer to recover property after a tax sale
F. attachment	**6.** ___ Taxes levied on specific properties that benefit from public improvement
G. mechanic's lien	**7.** ___ A specific, involuntary lien that gives security to persons or companies who perform labor, or who furnish material to improve real property
H. mill	**8.** ___ A court decree that establishes the amount owed by a debtor and provides for money to be awarded
I. special assessments	**9.** ___ A notice of a possible future lien based on a lawsuit
J. statutory right of redemption	**10.** ___ A writ that permits a court to retain custody of a debtor's property until the creditor's lawsuit is concluded

TRUE OR FALSE

Circle the correct answer.

1. A voluntary lien may be classified as either statutory or equitable.
   A. True
   B. False

2. A charge or claim against a person's property by a creditor, which is made to enforce the payment of money, is called a lien.
   A. True
   B. False

3. All encumbrances are liens.
   A. True
   B. False

4. Both federal estate taxes and state inheritance taxes are general, statutory, and involuntary liens.
   A. True
   B. False

5. Taking out a mortgage loan is an example of creating an equitable lien.
   A. True
   B. False

6. Once in place, a lien runs with the land and will bind all successive owners.
   A. True
   B. False

7. A special assessment is always a general and statutory lien.
   A. True
   B. False

8. A court's decree that establishes the amount owed by a debtor is enforced by the creditor obtaining a lis pendens directing the sheriff to seize and sell the debtor's property.
   A. True
   B. False

9. Mechanics' liens take priority over tax or special assessment liens.
   A. True
   B. False

10. Ad valorem taxes apply to the difference between the assessed value of a property and the value added by resale or improvement.
    A. True
    B. False

11. All liens are encumbrances.
    A. True
    B. False

12. The presence of a lien on real property does not prevent the owner from conveying title to another party.
    A. True
    B. False

13. A taxing body determines the appropriate tax rate by dividing the total monies needed for the coming fiscal year by the total assessments of all taxable real estate located within the taxing body's jurisdiction.
    A. True
    B. False

14. A delinquent taxpayer may redeem property at any time prior to a tax sale by exercising a statutory right of redemption.
    A. True
    B. False

15. A mechanic's lien is a specific, involuntary lien.
    A. True
    B. False

MULTIPLE CHOICE

Circle the correct answer.

1. Generally, in a court-ordered sale, which of these is paid first?
   A. First mortgage
   B. Mechanics' liens
   C. Child support liens
   D. Real estate taxes

2. Which of these is an example of a specific, voluntary lien?
   A. Decedent's debts
   B. Internal Revenue Service liens
   C. Mortgage lien
   D. Corporate franchise liens

3. The millage breakout for ad valorem taxes is library: 0.5; school: 1; school debt service: 0.5; community college: 1; vocational school: 0.5; and all others: 5. If a property is assessed at $165,000, how much is the tax bill?
   A. $1,200.25
   B. $1,402.50
   C. $1,405.75
   D. $1,800.50

4. All of these are liens against real property *EXCEPT*
   A. a mortgage.
   B. real estate taxes.
   C. lis pendens.
   D. home improvement loan of a deceased property owner.

5. Which of these characteristics apply to a real estate tax lien?
   A. Specific, involuntary lien
   B. Specific, voluntary lien
   C. General, involuntary lien
   D. General, voluntary lien

6. Which of these would permit a law enforcement officer to seize and sell a debtor's property?
   A. Lis pendens
   B. Satisfaction of judgment
   C. Writ of execution
   D. Writ of attachment

7. Which of these is a general, statutory, and involuntary lien on both real and personal property?
   A. Federal tax lien
   B. Mechanic's lien
   C. Special assessment
   D. Consumer loan lien

8. In February, a homeowner contracted with a general contractor to have a basement storage space converted to a sauna, but never paid for the work. The homeowner stopped making mortgage payments in June. The owner is two years delinquent in property taxes to the county. The state gives mechanics' liens priority. If all of these creditors obtain judgments against the owner in November, what will be the priority of their liens (first to last)?
   A. Contractor → mortgage company → county
   B. County → mortgage company → contractor
   C. Contractor → county → mortgage company
   D. County → contractor → mortgage company

9. A town wants to construct new concrete curbs in a residential neighborhood. How will the town most likely raise the money necessary for the improvement?
   A. Ad valorem tax
   B. Special assessment
   C. Equalized assessment
   D. Utility lien

10. All of these liens must be recorded to be effective *EXCEPT*
    A. money judgment.
    B. mechanic's lien.
    C. real estate tax lien.
    D. voluntary lien.

11. The market value of an undeveloped parcel is $40,000. Its assessed value is 40% of market value, and properties in its county are subject to an equalization factor of 1.50. If the tax rate is $4 per $100, what is the amount of the tax owed on the property?
    A. $480
    B. $960
    C. $1,080
    D. $1,800

12. To give notice of a potential claim against property and to establish priority, a creditor may file
    A. a lis pendens.
    B. an attachment.
    C. a general lien.
    D. a specific lien.

13. A homeowner considered having a new garage built and talked about the project with a contractor. In April, while the homeowner was on vacation, the contractor began building the garage according to the man's specifications. Work was complete by the end of May. In June, the homeowner returned from vacation and refused to pay for the garage. The contractor decided to file a mechanic's lien in July. Is the contractor entitled to a lien?
    A. Yes, because the garage was constructed according to the homeowner's specifications.
    B. Yes, because the garage is not a part of an owner-occupied residence.
    C. No, because notice of the lien should have been filed in May, when the work was completed.
    D. No, because there was no express or implied contract between the homeowner and the contractor.

FILL-IN-THE-BLANK

Select the word or words that best complete these statements:

assessed value

certificate of sale

golf course

hospital

Local Improvement
District (LID)

mechanic's lien

satisfaction of judgment

subordination agreement

tax levy

tax lien

title search

voluntary lien

writ of attachment

1. To reveal any recorded liens, a property buyer should require a(n) _____ before closing a real estate transaction.

2. A county assessor usually bases a property's _____ on the sale prices of comparable properties.

3. Usually, a vote of the taxing district's governing body is needed to impose a(n) _____.

4. In many states, when a purchaser at a tax sale receives the _____, the purchaser gains the right to take possession of the property.

5. A lien that is created intentionally by the property owner's action, such as taking out a mortgage loan, is called a(an) _____.

6. The priority of a(n) _____ may be established as of the date construction began or materials were first furnished.

7. A court order against the property of another person that directs the sheriff to take control of a property is called a(n) _____.

8. When real property is sold to pay off a debt, the debtor should get a legal document called a(n) _____.

9. An example of a property that is exempt from taxation is a(n) _____.

10. When a large-scale improvement project, such as sewer construction, is planned, it may be funded by creating a(an) _____.

ACTIVITY: LIEN CHARACTERISTICS

Identify the characteristics of liens by placing check marks in the appropriate columns.

Type of Lien	General	Specific	Voluntary	Involuntary	Equitable	Statutory
Mechanic's Lien						
Mortgage						
Bail Bond						
Municipal Utility Lien						
Federal Estate Tax Lien						
Corporate Franchise Tax						
State Inheritance Tax						
Judgment						
Real Property Tax						

UNIT 15 ANSWERS

MATCHING A

1. E

2. J

3. D

4. B

5. H

6. G

7. F

8. C

9. I

10. A

MATCHING B

1. A

2. C

3. H

4. D

5. J

6. I

7. G

8. B

9. E

10. F

TRUE OR FALSE

1. **B** The answer is false. An *involuntary* lien may be classified as either statutory or equitable. Voluntary liens are never statutory. (288)

2. **A** The answer is true. A lien is a charge or claim against a person's property made to enforce the payment of money; a lien represents an interest only in ownership; it does not constitute actual ownership of the property. (288)

3. **B** The answer is false. Although all liens are encumbrances, not all encumbrances are liens. An encumbrance is any charge or claim that attaches to real property and lessens its value or impairs its use, but does not prevent the transfer of the property. (288)

4. **A** The answer is true. General liens affect all property owned by the debtor. State and federal taxes are imposed involuntarily by statute. (288)

5. **B** The answer is false. A voluntary lien is created intentionally by the property owner's action, such as when someone takes out a mortgage loan. (288)

6. **A** The answer is true. A lien binds all successive owners until the lien is paid or settled and title is cleared by the filing of a release of lien by the lien holder. (289)

7. **B** The answer is false. A special assessment is always a specific and statutory lien. (293)

8. **B** The answer is false. A court's decree that establishes the amount owed by a debtor is enforced by the creditor obtaining a *writ of execution* directing the sheriff to seize and sell the debtor's property. (295)

9. **B** The answer is false. Real estate taxes and special assessments generally take priority over all other liens, regardless of the order in which the liens are recorded. (289)

10. **B** The answer is false. *Ad valorem* taxes are based on the value of the property being taxed and are specific, involuntary, statutory liens. (290)

11. **A** The answer is true. A lien is a charge or claim against a person's property made to enforce the payment of money; a lien represents only an interest in ownership; it does not constitute actual ownership of the property. (288)

12. **A**   The answer is true. Although the existence of a lien does not necessarily prevent a property owner from transferring title to someone else, once in place, the lien runs with the land and will bind all successive owners until the underlying debt is paid and the lien is cleared. (289)

13. **A**   The answer is true. After determining the budget, the taxing body authorizes the expenditure of funds. The tax rate is determined by dividing the total monies needed for the coming fiscal year by the total assessments of all real estate located within the taxing body's jurisdiction. (291–292)

14. **B**   The answer is false. A delinquent taxpayer may redeem property any time prior to a tax sale by exercising an *equitable* right of redemption. (293)

15. **A**   The answer is true. Specific liens are secured by specific property and affect only that particular property; examples include mechanics' liens, vendors' liens, mortgages, and real estate tax liens. (288)

MULTIPLE CHOICE

1. **D**   The answer is real estate taxes. Real estate taxes do not have to be recorded to be effective, and they are usually given priority over all other liens. (290)

2. **C**   The answer is mortgage lien. A mortgage lien is a specific, voluntary lien. (294)

3. **B**   The answer is $1,402.50. The tax bill is $1,402.50: 0.5 + 1 + 0.5 + 1 + 0.5 + 5 = 8.5 mills or $0.0085 per dollar of valuation. $165,000 × 0.0085 = $1,402.50. (292)

4. **C**   The answer is lis pendens. A lis pendens is only the notice of a possible future lien. If it becomes a lien, its priority is established by the date and time that the lis pendens was originally filed. (295)

5. **A**   The answer is specific, involuntary lien. A real estate tax is levied on an individual property; few would argue that individuals choose to have the tax levied, hence, an involuntary lien. (290)

6. **C**   The answer is writ of execution. A *writ of execution* directs the sheriff to seize and sell as much of the debtor's property as necessary to pay both the debt and the expenses of the sale. (295)

7. **A**   The answer is federal tax lien. An Internal Revenue Service lien is a general lien against the real and personal property owned by the delinquent taxpayer. (296)

8. **D**   The answer is county → contractor → mortgage company. The priority is taxes, mechanic's lien, and then first mortgage. Although the mortgage was filed first, property taxes always have first priority, and the state has given second priority to mechanic's liens. (289, 294)

9. **B**   The answer is special assessment. The town will most likely levy a special assessment against the benefiting properties to pay for the new concrete curbs. (293)

10. **C**   The answer is real estate tax lien. Real estate tax liens do not have to be recorded to be effective, and they always take precedence over all other liens. This is why many lenders collect $\frac{1}{12}$ of the taxes each month, so that the lender can pay the taxes when due. Unpaid taxes take priority over mortgage liens. (290)

11. **B**   The answer is $960. The tax owned on the property is $960: $40,000 × 40% × 1.5 ÷ 100 × 4 = $960. (292)

12. **A**   The answer is a lis pendens. A *lis pendens* is a notice of a possible future lien. If it becomes an actual lien, the effective date of the lien will be the date and time that the lis pendens was filed. (295)

13. **D**   The answer is no, because there was no express or implied contract between the homeowner and the contractor. Because the contractor was in no way given authority to act, the contractor has no right to file a mechanic's lien. (294)

FILL-IN-THE BLANK

1. To reveal any recorded liens, a property buyer should require a *title search* before closing the real estate transaction.

2. A county assessor usually bases a property's *assessed value* on the sales prices of comparable properties.

3. Usually, a vote of the taxing district's governing body is needed to impose a *tax levy*.

4. In many states, when a purchaser at a tax sale receives the *certificate of sale*, the purchaser gains the right to take possession of the property.

5. A lien that is created intentionally by the property owner's action, such as taking out a mortgage loan, is called a *voluntary lien*.

6. The priority of a *mechanic's lien* may be established as of the date construction began or materials were first furnished.

7. A court order against the property of another person that directs the sheriff to take control of a property is called a *writ of attachment.*

8. When real property is sold to pay off a debt, the debtor should get a legal document called a satisfaction of *judgment.*

9. An example of a property that is exempt from taxation is a *hospital.*

10. When a large-scale improvement project, such as sewer construction, is planned, it may be funded by creating a *Local Improvement District (LID).*

ACTIVITY: LIEN CHARACTERISTICS

Type of Lien	General	Specific	Voluntary	Involuntary	Equitable	Statutory
Mechanic's Lien		✓		✓		✓
Mortgage		✓	✓		✓	
Bail Bond		✓	✓			✓
Municipal Utility Lien		✓		✓	✓	
Federal Estate Tax Lien	✓			✓		✓
Corporate Franchise Tax	✓			✓		✓
State Inheritance Tax	✓			✓		✓
Judgment	✓			✓	✓	
Real Property Tax		✓		✓		✓

UNIT
16

Real Estate Appraisal

LEARNING OBJECTIVES

When you have completed this unit, you will be able to

> **explain** appraisal concepts and the process employed by the appraiser;
> **differentiate** between value and price; and
> **describe** the three approaches to value.

KEY TERMS

accrued depreciation
anticipation
appraisal
Appraiser Independence
   Requirements (AIR)
assemblage
broker's price opinion (BPO)
capitalization rate
change
competition *
conformity
contribution
cost approach
depreciation

economic life
external obsolescence
functional obsolescence
gross income multiplier (GIM)
gross rent multiplier (GRM)
highest and best use
income approach
law of diminishing returns
law of increasing returns
market data approach
market value
net operating income (NOI)
physical deterioration
plottage

progression
property inspection waiver
   (PIW)
reconciliation
regression
sales comparison approach
sales price
substitution
supply and demand
*Uniform Standards of
   Professional Appraisal
   Practice (USPAP)*
value

MATCHING A

Write the letter of the matching term on the appropriate line.

A. anticipation

B. appraisal

C. appraiser

D. assemblage

E. change

F. conformity

G. contribution

H. highest and best use

I. income approach

J. market value

1. ___ An opinion of value based on supportable evidence and approved methods

2. ___ An independent professional who is trained to provide an unbiased estimate of value

3. ___ A way to estimate value based on the present worth of the rights to future income

4. ___ The most probable price that a property should bring in a fair sale

5. ___ The principle that value is created by the expectation that certain events will occur

6. ___ The principle that no physical or economic condition remains constant

7. ___ The principle that value is created when a property is in harmony with its surroundings

8. ___ The principle that the value of any part of a property is measured by its effect on the value of the whole property

9. ___ The most profitable single use to which property may legally, physically, and financially be put

10. ___ The process of merging two separately owned lots under one owner

MATCHING B

Write the letter of the matching term on the appropriate line.

A. cost approach

B. depreciation

C. economic life

D. sales comparison

E. regression

F. external obsolescence

G. physical deterioration

H. plottage

I. supply and demand

J. substitution

1. ___ The principle that merging or consolidating adjacent lots into a single one will produce a higher total value than the sum of the two sites valued separately

2. ___ The principle that the worth of a better-quality property is adversely affected by the presence of a nearby lesser-quality property

3. ___ The principle that the maximum value of a property tends to be set by how much it would cost to purchase an equally desirable property

4. ___ The economic principle that the value of a property depends on the number of similar properties available in the marketplace

5. ___ The approach that estimates value by comparing the subject property with recently sold similar properties

6. ___ An estimate of value made by determining the value of the land as if it were vacant, adding the current cost of constructing improvements, and deducting accrued depreciation

7. ___ A curable item in need of repair

8. ___ Depreciation caused by negative factors not on the subject property

9. ___ A loss in value due to any cause

10. ___ The period during which a property is expected to remain useful for its original intended purpose

TRUE OR FALSE

Circle the correct answer.

1. Title XI of FIRREA requires that all residential property be appraised by a federally licensed or certified appraiser.
   A. True
   B. False

2. A comparative market analysis should never be represented as an appraisal.
   A. True
   B. False

3. The market value of a property is what it actually sells for in an open market transaction.
   A. True
   B. False

4. Cost and market value are the same.
   A. True
   B. False

5. The value of a property may be affected by events that have not yet occurred.
   A. True
   B. False

6. The law of diminishing returns applies when, no matter how much money is spent on a property, its value will not keep pace with the expenditures.
   A. True
   B. False

7. According to the economic principle of plottage, combining two adjacent lots into a large one may produce a higher total land value than the sum of the value of the two sites if owned separately.
   A. True
   B. False

8. The economic principle of contribution holds that the maximum value of a property tends to be set by the cost of purchasing a similarly desirable property.
   A. True
   B. False

9. In the sales comparison approach to value, the value of a feature that is present in the subject property but is not present in a comparable property is subtracted from the sale price of the comparable.
   A. True
   B. False

10. Physical deterioration and external obsolescence are both considered in the cost approach to value.
    A. True
    B. False

11. Depreciation may be curable or incurable, depending on whether the expense required to correct it contributes to the property's value.
    A. True
    B. False

12. External obsolescence is always incurable.
    A. True
    B. False

13. The income approach to value is based on the future value of the rights to present income.
    A. True
    B. False

14. If a buyer is interested in purchasing a one- to four-unit residential rental property, the gross rent multiplier (GRM) based on monthly rental income could be used for a rough approximation of value.
    A. True
    B. False

15. Reconciliation involves averaging the results derived from the three approaches to value.
    A. True
    B. False

16. The first step in using the income approach to value is to add the debt service to the annual operating expenses.
    A. True
    B. False

17. The art of analyzing and weighing the findings from the three approaches to value in an appraisal is called reconciliation.
    A. True
    B. False

18. If a property improvement results in a higher value, the law of increasing returns applies.
    A. True
    B. False

19. To use the sales comparison approach, an appraiser must find a minimum of four properties comparable to the property being appraised.
    A. True
    B. False

20. An estimate of the rate of return (yield) that an investor would expect for investing in a piece of property is called the anticipation rate.
    A. True
    B. False

MULTIPLE CHOICE

Circle the correct answer.

1. A property is listed for sale at $235,000. A buyer's offer of $220,000 is rejected by the seller. Six months later, the seller reduces the price to $225,000. Another buyer offers $210,000, and the seller accepts because the seller has found another house to buy and needs to close quickly. The property is subsequently appraised at $215,000. Which of these figures *MOST* accurately represents the property's market value?
    A. $210,000
    B. $215,000
    C. $225,000
    D. $235,000

2. Which appraisal approach would be *BEST* to appraise a 25-year-old owner-occupied house in a 30- year-old neighborhood?
    A. Sales comparison
    B. Income approach
    C. Cost approach
    D. GRM

3. When appraising a new, vacant home, an appraiser will likely use
    A. the sales comparison approach.
    B. the income approach.
    C. the cost approach.
    D. the GRM.

4. Assuming that all of the transactions are federally related, which of these properties would *NOT* have to be appraised by a state licensed or certified appraiser?
    A. The commercial property valued at $350,000
    B. The condominium unit with a sale price of $67,850
    C. The residential property valued at $262,500
    D. The commercial property valued over $1 million in a refinance

5. An appraiser's role is to
    A. set the market price.
    B. average value.
    C. determine value.
    D. provide an opinion of value.

6. The principle that maximum value is realized when land use is in harmony with surrounding uses is
    A. contribution.
    B. conformity.
    C. highest and best use.
    D. competition.

7. A business plans to build a large warehouse store in an area of smaller stores, so the business purchases five neighboring lots from their five owners. What is the term for this activity?
    A. Substitution
    B. Plottage
    C. Progression
    D. Assemblage

8. W buys a small house in a highly desirable neighborhood consisting of large homes and pays $390,000. X buys a nearly identical house in a neighborhood of similarly sized homes and pays $290,000. What economic principle *BEST* describes the reason why W paid more than X?
    A. Plottage
    B. Substitution
    C. Regression
    D. Progression

9. It would cost approximately $350,000 to build a house and its various improvements on a parcel of property. If the property was vacant, undeveloped land, it would be worth about $100,000. At present, the property's physical deterioration equals about $60,000. If an appraiser were to apply the cost approach, what would be an estimate of the value of this property?
    A. $250,000
    B. $390,000
    C. $450,000
    D. $480,000

10. A property use that is physically possible, legally permitted, economically feasible, and maximally productive is
    A. the property's competitive use.
    B. highest and best use.
    C. anticipated use.
    D. nonconforming use.

11. Air pollution from increased automobile traffic near a building with ornate exterior decoration has dissolved much of the intricate detail work. The cost of restoring the front of the building is roughly five times the building's present value. These facts describe
    A. curable external obsolescence.
    B. incurable functional obsolescence.
    C. incurable physical deterioration.
    D. curable external deterioration.

12. Which of these reports would a sales associate *MOST* likely research and deliver to a prospective seller?
    A. Comparative market analysis
    B. Appraisal
    C. Letter of intent
    D. Cost benefit analysis

13. What is the GRM for a residential duplex (two-unit building) with a selling price of $234,000 if the monthly rent for each unit is $925?
    A. 1.054
    B. 10.54
    C. 126.5
    D. 252.9

14. Which of these approaches is given the *greatest* weight in reconciling the appraised value of a two-bedroom, owner-occupied home?
    A. Income approach
    B. Sales comparison approach
    C. Cost approach
    D. Market value approach

15. The characteristics of value include
    A. demand, utility, scarcity, and transferability.
    B. demand, utility, price, and transferability.
    C. popularity, location, price, and transferability.
    D. demand, scarcity, price, and popularity.

16. A house has been on the market for several months because most buyers do not want to walk through the master bedroom from the garage to reach the kitchen. This floor plan is an example of
    A. regression.
    B. economic obsolescence.
    C. functional obsolescence.
    D. physical deterioration.

17. An owner is considering installing a below-ground swimming pool, which will cost many thousands of dollars to build. Before hiring a contractor, the owner should consider the concept of
    A. change.
    B. competition with the neighbors.
    C. conformity within the neighborhood.
    D. contribution.

18. Which of these formulas is incorrect for the income approach?
    A. Income ÷ value = rate
    B. Income ÷ rate = value
    C. Value ÷ rate = income
    D. Value × rate = income

19. A house sits on the corner of a busy intersection. Two of the corners are occupied by gas stations, and directly across from the house is a fast food restaurant. The house's owners have been told that the property would be worth more if the lot were vacant. This is an example of
    A. progression.
    B. highest and best use.
    C. regression.
    D. conservation.

20. A two-unit apartment building is being appraised. In this neighborhood, the accepted gross rent multiplier is 144. The annual income generated by the building is $16,800 (both units rented). The monthly expenses are $300. Based on the income approach, what is the estimated market value of the apartment building?
    A. $201,600
    B. $224,800
    C. $232,500
    D. $258,600

21. An apartment building has $65,000 in potential gross annual income. The vacancy rate is estimated at 5%, total operating expenses are $29,000, and the capitalization rate is 9%. Using the income approach, what is the value of the building?
    A. $324,773
    B. $363,889
    C. $372,895
    D. $392,367

22. Which of these concepts applies to every appraisal?
    A. Diminishing returns
    B. Plottage
    C. Highest and best use
    D. Assemblage

23. The property being appraised is called
    A. the lot.
    B. the parcel.
    C. the subject property.
    D. the comparable property.

24. An empty lot is located in a neighborhood of single-family homes. It is the only empty lot in this well-maintained neighborhood. A busy street with many stores is located three blocks away. An industrial area is about two miles away. What is the probable highest and best use of this lot?
    A. A store
    B. A factory
    C. A parking lot
    D. A single-family home

25. What is the process for creating a broker's price opinion (BPO)?
    A. The broker drives by the property, takes a picture, and fills out the BPO form.
    B. The broker engages a certified appraiser to perform an appraisal.
    C. The broker prepares a report compiled from research of comparable properties.
    D. The attorney engages a broker to perform a comparative market analysis.

26. Which of these is *NOT* an essential assumption in determining market value?
    A. The buyer and seller must be unrelated.
    B. The payment must be in cash or its equivalent.
    C. The buyer and seller must be acting without excessive pressure.
    D. The property must be on the market for at least three months.

27. The principle of value that is the interaction of supply and demand is called
    A. anticipation.
    B. competition.
    C. conformity.
    D. contribution.

28. All of these reflect basic principles of value *EXCEPT*
    A. anticipation and conformity.
    B. competition and plottage.
    C. change.
    D. financing concessions.

29. New roofing is an example of curing
    A. physical deterioration.
    B. functional obsolescence.
    C. external obsolescence.
    D. straight-line depreciation.

ACTIVITY: PENNYTREE LANE APPRAISALS

Complete these appraisal problems based on the five homes on the 1200 block of Pennytree Lane depicted in the photos.

| 1230 | 1231 | 1232 | 1233 | 1234 |

1.   1230 Pennytree Lane was just sold. Which house is the best comparable property?_____

2.   The principle of regression is best illustrated by which property? _____

3.   The principle of progression is best illustrated by which property? _____

4.   Pennytree Lane is near an increasingly fashionable and upscale part of town. Incomes in the area are rising rapidly. If 1233 is a newly constructed home, it is an example of which principle of value?

_____

5.   When a garage was added to 1231 and 1233 was built, what likely happened to the values of 1230 and 1232? Why? _____

6.   House number 1233 violates which principle of value? _____

7.   When the kitchen in 1232 was remodeled, which principle of value describes its effect?

_____

UNIT 16 ANSWERS

MATCHING A

1. **B**
2. **C**
3. **I**
4. **J**
5. **A**
6. **E**
7. **F**
8. **G**
9. **H**
10. **D**

MATCHING B

1. **H**
2. **E**
3. **J**
4. **I**
5. **D**
6. **A**
7. **G**
8. **F**
9. **B**
10. **C**

TRUE OR FALSE

1. **B** The answer is false. Title XI of FIRREA requires that residential property valued at $250,000 or more in a federally related transaction be appraised by a state licensed or certified appraiser. (302)

2. **A** The answer is true. Real estate professionals prepare comparative market analyses (CMAs) for their sellers and buyers. The CMA is not an appraisal but rather a tool to assist the clients in determining an appropriate asking or offering price. (303)

3. **B** The answer is false. The market price of a property is what it actually sells for in an open market transaction. (312)

4. **B** The answer is false. Cost and market value may be, but are not necessarily, the same. When the improvements on a property are new, cost and value are likely to be equal, provided the improvements are sought in the marketplace. (312)

5. **A** The answer is true. According to the concept of anticipation, value is created by the expectation that certain events will occur; this concept is the foundation on which the income approach to value is based. (313)

6. **A** The answer is true. The law of diminishing returns applies when, no matter how much money is spent on a property, its value will not keep pace with the expenditures. For example, adding restaurant-quality appliances and elaborate woodwork to a modest home are costs that the owner probably would not be able to recover. (314)

7. **A** The answer is true. Plottage is the principle that the individual value of two adjacent properties may be greater if they are combined than if each is sold separately. (314)

8. **B** The answer is false. The economic principle of *substitution* holds that the maximum value of a property tends to be set by the cost of purchasing a similarly desirable property. Under the principle of contribution, the value of any part of a property is measured by its effect on the value of the whole parcel. (315)

9. **B** The answer is false. In the sales approach to value, the value of a feature that is present in the subject property but not present in a comparable property is *added* to the sales price of the comparable. Remember, CBS is "comp better, subtract" and CPA, "comp poorer, add." (316)

10. **A**   The answer is true. In the cost approach to appraising, depreciation from all causes (physical deterioration, functional obsolescence, and external obsolescence) is subtracted from the current construction cost of buildings and improvements. (317)

11. **A**   The answer is true. In real estate, depreciation is the loss in value for any reason; land never depreciates. Depreciation is the result of a negative condition that affects real property. (318)

12. **A**   The answer is true. If caused by negative factors not on the subject property, such as environmental, social, or economic forces, the depreciation is always considered incurable because the cure is beyond the efforts of the owner. (318–319)

13. **B**   The answer is false. The income approach to value is based on the present value of the rights to future income. (319)

14. **A**   The answer is true. If the buyer is interested in purchasing five or more units, a gross income multiplier (GIM) based on annual income could be used. (321)

15. **B**   The answer is false. *Reconciliation* involves a detailed and professional analysis and application of the three approaches to value, not simply an average of the different values. (321)

16. **B**   The answer is false. Debt services (mortgage payments) is not considered an expense, so it is not included in annual operating expenses. (319)

17. **A**   The answer is true. Reconciliation is the act of analyzing and effectively weighing the findings from three appraisal approaches. (321)

18. **A**   The answer is true. As long as money spent on improvements produces an increase in income or value, the law of increasing returns applies. (314)

19. **B**   The answer is false. The circumstances of the market at the time will indicate the number of property sales that are required to serve as comparables to the property being appraised. Most appraisals for residential properties include a minimum of three comparable sales that are reflective of the subject property. (316–317)

20. **B**   The answer is false. An estimate of the rate of return (yield) that an investor would expect for investing in a piece of property is called the *capitalization* rate or *cap rate*. (319)

MULTIPLE CHOICE

1. **B**   The answer is $215,000. The property's market price is $210,000, while its appraised value (and most probable market value) is $215,000. The seller accepted the lower price because of the pressure to close on the new house. (312)

2. **A**   The answer is sales comparison. The most appropriate method to appraise an existing home in an established neighborhood is the sales comparison approach. (315–316)

3. **C**   The answer is the cost approach. A newly constructed house may be appraised using the cost approach. (317)

4. **B**   The answer is the condominium unit with a sale price of $67,850. Appraisals of residential property and commercial property valued at $250,000 (raised to $500,000 in 2018) or less in federally related transactions are exempt and need not be performed by licensed or certified appraisers. (302)

5. **D**   The answer is set the market price. An *appraiser* is an independent professional trained to provide an unbiased opinion of value using approved methods. (302)

6. **B**   The answer is conformity. The principle of conformity indicates that maximum value is created when a property is in harmony with its surroundings. Contribution is the principle that evaluates the cost of adding an improvement against the value of the property as a whole. Competition is the interaction of supply and demand, while highest and best use is the most profitable single use to which the property may be put. (313)

7. **D**   The answer is assemblage. The process of merging separately owned lots under one owner is called assemblage. Plottage holds that merging these lots together into a single larger one may produce a greater total land value than the sum of the individual lots valued separately. (314)

8. **D**   The answer is progression. W's house benefits from being a smaller one alongside larger, more prestigious ones (i.e., progression). X's house is appropriately valued for its neighborhood. (314)

9. **B**   The answer is $390,000. In the cost approach, the appraiser subtracts depreciation from the current cost of the improvements and then adds on the value of the land as if it were vacant: $350,000 – $60,000 + $100,000 = $390,000. (317)

10. **B** The answer is highest and best use. A property is at its highest and best use when its use is physically possible, legally permitted, economically or financially feasible, and its most profitable or maximally productive use. (313)

11. **C** The answer is incurable physical deterioration. Air pollution has damaged the original design, and the cost of correcting the defect is not financially feasible. This is an example of incurable physical deterioration. (318)

12. **A** The answer is comparative market analysis. A real estate sales associate often prepares a comparative market analysis (CMA), a comparison of the prices of recently sold homes that are similar to a listing seller's home in terms of location, style, and amenities. The CMA helps the owner set an appropriate asking price for the property. (303)

13. **C** The answer is 126.5. Because gross rent multiplier (GRM) for one-unit and two-unit residential properties is based on gross monthly rent, GRM = sales price ÷ gross rent: $234,000 ÷ (2 × $925) = 126.5 GRM. (321)

14. **B** The answer is sales comparison approach. Most owner-occupied residences are best appraised by comparing them to similar properties—that is, by using the sales comparison approach. (315–316)

15. **A** The answer is demand, utility, scarcity, and transferability. Remember the acronym DUST. (312)

16. **C** The answer is functional obsolescence. There is nothing physically wrong with the house, but the design is awkward (functionally obsolescent). Perhaps buyers would be more interested if another room could be used as the master bedroom and the room adjacent to the garage could be used as a home office or hobby room. (318)

17. **D** The answer is contribution. Before embarking on installing the pool, the owner should consider its overall contribution to the value of the property, especially compared to neighboring properties. Sometimes an improvement does not add value equal to its cost. (313)

18. **C** The answer is value ÷ rate = income. As the capitalization rate goes down, the value increases. (320)

19. **B** The answer is highest and best use. Under the principle of highest and best use, the single most profitable use for this property is not a single-family residence; zoning may indicate that a commercial use is feasible and, in the circumstances, probably preferable. (313)

20. **A** The answer is $201,600. The monthly rental income is $1,400 ($16,800 ÷ 12 = $1,400). Rental income × GRM = estimated market value: $1,400 × 144 = $201,600. The monthly expenses are not included in the calculation. (321)

21. **B** The answer is $324,773. Gross income – vacancy and rent losses – operating expenses = net operating income: $65,000 × 5% = $3,250; $65,000 – $3,250 – $29,000 = $32,750. Net operating income ÷ capitalization rate = value: $32,750 ÷ 9% = $363,889. (320)

22. **C** The answer is highest and best use. The principal of highest and best use is the most profitable single use to which a property can be put, and is considered in every appraisal. (313)

23. **C** The answer is the subject property. The subject property is the one being appraised. Comparable properties are properties similar to the subject property. Each comparable property is analyzed for differences and similarities between it and the subject property. (315–316)

24. **D** The answer is a single-family home. The highest and best use is the most profitable or the most likely to be in demand soon. In this neighborhood, the demand is most likely to be for another single-family home. A parking lot is not needed. A store or factory would not be in conformity with the area and might not even be allowed. (313)

25. **A** The answer is the broker drives by the property, takes a picture, and fills out the BPO form. The broker's price opinion (BPO) is a less-expensive alternative way of valuating properties, often used by lenders deciding whether to issue a home equity line or to refinance, when the lender holds the purchase mortgage and an appraisal was made for that purpose. (304)

26. **D** The answer is the property must be on the market for at least three months. Market value is the most probable price that a property should bring on the open market. The property must be on the market for a reasonable time, but no specific time period must be met. (312)

27. **B**   The answer is competition. Anticipation is the expectation that certain events will occur. Conformity states that value is created when a property is in harmony with its surroundings. Contribution means that the value of any part of a property is measured by its effect on the value of the entire property. (313)

28. **D**   The answer is financing concessions. The basic principles of value include the concepts of anticipation, change, competition, conformity, contribution, highest and best use, increasing and diminishing returns, plottage, regression and progression, substitution, and supply and demand. Financing concessions do not reflect the basic principles of property value. (312)

29. **A**   The answer is physical deterioration. Replacing the roofing is an example of curing physical deterioration. External obsolescence is always incurable. Functional obsolescence is a loss in value from the market's response to the item. (318)

ACTIVITY: PENNYTREE LANE APPRAISALS

1. The best comparable appears to be 1232 because it is in the same style and condition as the subject property.

2. Regression is illustrated by 1233 because its value is lowered because of the lesser quality of neighboring properties.

3. Progression is illustrated by 1234 because its value is increased because of the larger, fancier quality of neighboring properties.

4. The new home at 1233 exemplifies the principle of anticipation.

5. The values of 1230 and 1232 increased due to progression.

6. The house at 1233 violates the principle of conformity.

7. Remodeling the kitchen at 1232 illustrates the principle of contribution.

Leases

LEARNING OBJECTIVES

When you have completed this unit, you will be able to

> **explain** the essential elements of leasehold interests;
> **describe** the essential terms of a lease agreement;
> **distinguish** the various types of leases; and
> **explain** the means by which the lease may be terminated and discharged and the remedies available to the parties for its breach.

KEY TERMS

actual eviction
assignment
constructive eviction
estate (tenancy) at sufferance
estate (tenancy) at will
estate (tenancy) for years
estate (tenancy) from period
  to period
gross lease
ground lease

holdover tenancy
lease
lease purchase
leasehold estate
lessee
lessor
month-to-month tenancy
net lease
nondisturbance clause
percentage lease

purchase option
renewal option
rent
reversionary right
right of first refusal
sale-and-leaseback
security deposit
sublease

MATCHING

Write the letter of the matching term on the appropriate line.

A. actual eviction

B. constructive eviction

C. tenancy at will

D. option

E. periodic tenancy

F. reversionary right

G. sublease

H. lease

I. tenancy for years

J. tenancy at sufferance

1. ___ A contract between a real estate owner and a tenant

2. ___ A landlord's right to possession of the premises after the expiration of the lease term

3. ___ A leasehold estate that has a specific beginning and a definite end

4. ___ The estate created when a landlord and tenant enter into a lease agreement that automatically renews

5. ___ A leasehold estate with an indefinite term that may be terminated by the death of either the landlord or tenant

6. ___ The leasehold estate created when a tenant, who was in lawful possession of real property, continues in possession without the landlord's consent

7. ___ The transfer of some of a tenant's interest, but no tenant obligations

8. ___ A lessee's privilege of renewing a lease

9. ___ The legal process by which a landlord regains possession of leased premises following a tenant's breach

10. ___ The action by which a tenant may properly abandon premises that have become unusable due to the landlord's conscious neglect

TRUE OR FALSE

Circle the correct answer.

1. In a lease agreement, the landlord is the lessee and the tenant is the lessor.
   A. True
   B. False

2. Unlike a freehold estate, a leasehold estate is considered personal property.
   A. True
   B. False

3. The primary difference between a tenancy at will and a tenancy at sufferance is the landlord's consent.
   A. True
   B. False

4. Although an extension of a tenancy for years requires a new contract, the lease may be terminated prior to the expiration date by either party at any time.
   A. True
   B. False

5. Periodic tenancies are characterized by continuity because they are automatically renewable.
   A. True
   B. False

6. The elements of a valid lease are (1) offer and acceptance, (2) capacity of the parties, (3) consideration, and (4) legal objective.
   A. True
   B. False

7. The covenant of quiet enjoyment is a guarantee by the landlord that the tenant is entitled to a quiet building without interference from noisy neighbors.
   A. True
   B. False

8. A tenant who is leasing only a part of a building is not required to continue paying rent if the lease premises are destroyed.
   A. True
   B. False

9. When a tenant transfers all leasehold interests to another person, the tenant has assigned the lease.
   A. True
   B. False

10. Under a gross lease agreement, the landlord pays all of the operating expenses of the property, while the tenant pays only a fixed rental.
    A. True
    B. False

11. Ground leases are generally short-term net leases.
    A. True
    B. False

12. The death of either party terminates a tenancy at will.
    A. True
    B. False

13. To be entitled to constructive eviction, the tenant must show only that the premises have become unusable for the purpose stated in the lease.
    A. True
    B. False

14. The Fair Housing Amendments Act of 1988 requires that, in leased housing, the same criteria must be applied to tenants with children as are applied to adults.
    A. True
    B. False

15. All leases must require a security deposit as part of the consideration.
    A. True
    B. False

MULTIPLE CHOICE

Circle the correct answer.

1. A tenant pays for his own utilities and makes one payment each month to the landlord who pays the taxes, insurance on the building, and maintenance. What type of lease arrangement is this?
   A. Net
   B. Gross
   C. Percentage
   D. Graduated

2. Some tenants want to buy the house they are renting. However, they do not have enough money for the down payment. The landlord agreed to put part of the tenants' rent toward the purchase price. The landlord and tenants have agreed to
   A. a lease purchase.
   B. a sale leaseback.
   C. a ground lease.
   D. an option.

3. The expiration date of a one-year lease is September 30. On July 1, the house is sold to a family that wants to live in the rental property. Assuming the lease does not include a sale clause, how soon can they move in?
   A. July 1, present year
   B. July 1, next year
   C. October 1, present year
   D. December 31, present year

4. A tenant rents an apartment under a one-year written lease. The expiration date of the lease is May 1. How much notice must the landlord give the tenant to recover possession when the lease expires?
   A. One week
   B. 30 days
   C. 60 days
   D. None

5. Two years ago, a landowner rented a parcel of property to a tenant farmer. The agreement stated only that the tenant agreed to pay the landowner $500 per month. What type of tenancy does the tenant have?
   A. Holdover
   B. At sufferance
   C. For years
   D. Periodic

6. A tenant rents an apartment under a two-year written lease. Three months after signing the lease, the tenant is transferred to another country for a year. During this period, the tenant leases the apartment to a friend. The friend mails monthly rent checks to the tenant, who continues to make monthly rental payments to the landlord. In this situation, the tenant's friend has
   A. a lease.
   B. a tenancy at will.
   C. a sublease.
   D. a periodic tenancy.

7. Vandals break into a building and destroy the central air-conditioning system. A tenant's apartment becomes uncomfortably warm. The next day, the tenant sues the landlord for constructive eviction. In this situation, will the tenant win?
   A. Yes, if the tenant's lease promises that the apartment will be air conditioned.
   B. Yes, to claim constructive eviction, it is not necessary that the condition be the result of the landlord's personal actions.
   C. No, to claim constructive eviction, the tenant must prove that the premises are uninhabitable.
   D. No, the premises are not unusable, the condition was not due to the landlord's conscious neglect, and the tenant has not abandoned the apartment.

8. In August, a tenant signs a one-year lease in an apartment complex. Rent payments are due on the 15th of each month. On December 12, the apartment complex is sold to a new owner. On March 14, the building is destroyed in a fire. Which of these statements accurately describes the tenant's obligations?

   A. The tenant is not required to continue paying rent after March 14 because the premises have been destroyed.

   B. The tenant is not required to continue paying rent after December 12 because the sale voids the preexisting lease.

   C. The tenant is required to continue paying rent for the full lease term because a tenancy for years cannot be terminated by the destruction of the premises.

   D. The tenant is required to continue paying rent, but the residential lease is converted by law into a ground lease.

9. Tenant A signs a lease to rent an apartment, with the lease running from October 1 until November 1 of the following year. Tenant B signs a two-year lease to rent an apartment in a new building that will be ready for occupancy in 15 months. Which of these leases must be in writing to satisfy the statute of frauds?

   A. Tenant A's only

   B. Tenant B's only

   C. Both tenant A's and tenant B's

   D. Neither tenant A's nor tenant B's

10. A tenant signed a one-year lease with a landlord on April 10. On the following March 1, the landlord asked the tenant whether the lease would be renewed. The tenant did not respond but was still in the apartment on April 11. What can the landlord do?

    A. The landlord must initiate eviction proceedings within the first one-month rental period.

    B. The landlord cannot evict the tenant; because the tenant remained in possession of the premises, the lease has been automatically renewed for an additional year.

    C. If the tenant offers a rent check, the landlord must accept it and the tenant is entitled to a renewal of the one-year lease.

    D. The landlord may either evict the holdover tenant or accept a rent check, creating a holdover or periodic tenancy.

11. If a tenant remains in possession of leased property after the expiration of the lease term, without paying rent and without the landlord's consent, what is the tenant's status?

    A. Tenant at will

    B. Trespasser

    C. Periodic tenant

    D. Freehold tenant

12. A prospective tenants wants to rent an apartment. Because of a physical disability, it would be necessary for the tenant to have all the doorknobs replaced with lever-type handles. In this case, which of these statements is *TRUE*?

    A. The Fair Housing Act requires that the man make the accommodation for the tenant at the landlord's expense; no additional rent may be charged for the tenant's modified unit.

    B. The landlord is legally obligated to permit the modifications to be made at the tenant's expense.

    C. Because the modifications demanded by the tenant are not reasonable, the landlord is not legally required to permit them.

    D. Because the proposed modifications would interfere with a future tenant's use of the premises, the landlord may refuse to permit them.

13. A business owner operates a small store in a shopping center. Under the terms of the lease, the landlord pays all operating expenses. The tenant pays a base rent of $1,000 per month, plus 15% of monthly gross profits over $10,000. The tenant has

    A. a gross lease.

    B. a percentage lease.

    C. a net lease.

    D. a variable lease.

14. When a landowner leases unimproved land to a tenant, who agrees to erect a building on the land, the lease is usually called

    A. a lease purchase.

    B. a gross lease.

    C. a ground lease.

    D. an improvement lease.

15. A tenant rented a house. During the lease term, the tenant moved out of the state without telling the landlord. The tenant assigned the lease to a friend, who failed to make any rental payments. In this situation, which of these statements is *TRUE*?
    A. The tenant has no obligation to the landlord because the lease was assigned, not sublet.
    B. The friend has no obligation to the landlord because the friend's lease agreement is with the tenant.
    C. The tenant is still liable to the landlord for the outstanding rent because the landlord did not release the tenant when the lease was assigned to the friend.
    D. The tenant is still liable to the landlord because the tenant's arrangement with the friend, as described, is a sublease, not an assignment.

16. A security deposit held by a landlord
    A. compensates the landlord in the event of rent default or premises damage.
    B. functions as the last month's rent on the lease.
    C. acts as an investment option for the tenant.
    D. does all of these.

17. Who owns the building that is erected on land that has a ground lease?
    A. Testator
    B. Lessor
    C. Lessee
    D. Trustee

18. What *must* a landlord do before commencing a lawsuit for actual eviction?
    A. Notify the sheriff
    B. Contract with a company to forcibly remove the tenant and possessions
    C. Obtain a judgment from the court
    D. Serve notice on the tenant

19. A landlord comes to a tenant's apartment on a daily basis "to make sure everything is okay" or to "make repairs." The apartment, however, is not in need of any repairs. The landlord generally enters the apartment using a spare key. Which of these is *TRUE*?
    A. The landlord has the right to enter the property.
    B. The landlord may only enter a tenant's apartment if the tenant is behind on paying rent.
    C. The landlord is violating the covenant of quiet enjoyment.
    D. The landlord is creating a tenancy at sufferance.

20. A lease that provides for specified rent increases at set future dates is called
    A. an adjustable lease.
    B. a graduated lease.
    C. a percentage lease.
    D. an interval lease.

FILL-IN-THE-BLANK

Select the word or words that best complete these statements:

actual eviction

actual notice

consideration

estate at sufferance

estate at will

estate for years

security deposit

gross

lessee

lessor

nondisturbance

reversionary right

right of first refusal

sale and leaseback

sublease

net

Uniform Residential
Landlord and Tenant Act

1. A type of leasehold estate that gives the right of possession with the landlord's consent for an unspecified term is called a(n) _____.

2. Although rent is the usual _____ given for the right to occupy leased premises, labor could also serve this function.

3. Recording a lease is usually considered unnecessary because anyone who inspects the property receives _____.

4. If the lease allows the tenant the opportunity to buy the property before the owner accepts an offer from another party, the tenant has the _____.

5. If the tenant pays basic rent plus all or most property charges, the tenant has a(n) _____ lease.

6. In a lease agreement, the tenant is called the _____.

7. A leasehold estate that continues for a definite period of time is the _____.

8. A mortgage clause that states the lender agrees not to terminate the tenancies of rent-paying tenants in the event the lender forecloses on the building is the _____ clause.

9. The arrangement when an owner of property sells the property and then obtains a lease from the new owner is called _____.

10. A model law that addresses obligations in leases, such as the landlord's right of entry, premises maintenance, and protection of the tenants from retaliation by the landlord in the event of complaints is the _____.

ACTIVITY: TYPES OF COMMERCIAL LEASES

Based on the following information, write the type of lease and current month's rental beneath the description of each tenant.

A few years ago, a developer purchased a historic downtown block in the exclusive suburban community of West Flightpath. The developer combined the storefronts into a shopping mall. Currently, the mall is completely leased to three tenants.

Acrylic Acres pays a base rent of $1,500 per month and 15% of the shopping mall's property charges, limited to utilities and taxes. Blue Buttons Boutique pays a base rent of $2,000 per month and no property charges. Custom Custards pays a base rent of $1,850 per month and no property charges, but pays 12% of its monthly gross sales over $4,000 to the landlord.

Acrylic Acres earned $10,000 in gross profits and netted $4,850. Blue Buttons Boutique grossed $6,500 and earned a net profit of $3,000. Custom Custards had gross sales of $9,542, with profits after expenses of $7,370 for the month.

This month, the shopping mall had to pay $6,790 in utility bills and $495 in regular repairs and maintenance. The month's prorated share of local property taxes was $2,560, and the prorated insurance fee was $900.

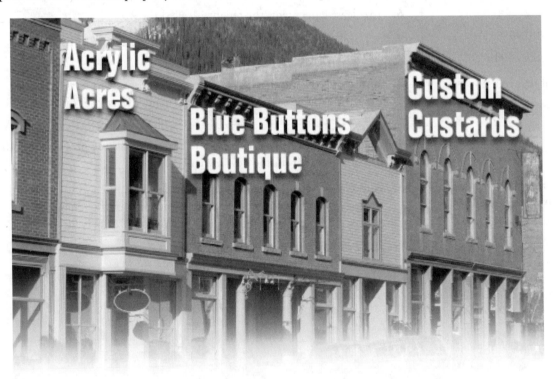

Lease Type: _____   Lease Type: _____   Lease Type: _____

Rent: _____   Rent: _____   Rent: _____

UNIT 17 ANSWERS

MATCHING

1. H
2. F
3. I
4. E
5. C
6. J
7. G
8. D
9. A
10. B

TRUE OR FALSE

1. **B** The answer is false. In a lease agreement, the landlord is the lessor and the tenant is the lessee. (328)

2. **A** The answer is true. A tenant's right to possess real estate for the term of the lease is called a leasehold, less-than- freehold estate and is generally considered personal property. A lease for a term of 49 years or more is treated as a real property interest in some states, which means that the leasehold interest can be used as a security loan. (328)

3. **A** The answer is true. An estate at will is an indefinite term, and possession is with the landlord's consent, while an estate at sufferance is the result of the tenant's previously lawful possession continued without the landlord's consent. (330)

4. **B** The answer is false. Although an extension of a tenancy for years requires a new contract, the lease may be terminated prior to the expiration date only if both parties agree, or if one party has breached the agreement. (329)

5. **A** The answer is true. A periodic tenancy is characterized by continuity because it is automatically renewable under the original terms of the agreement until one of the parties gives notice to terminate. (329)

6. **A** The answer is true. As a contract between the lessor and the lessee, a valid lease must have the same requirements as any other contract: offer and acceptance, capacity of the parties, consideration, and legal objective. (331)

7. **B** The answer is false. The covenant of quiet enjoyment is a guarantee by the landlord that the tenant is entitled to possession of the premises without interference from the landlord. (331)

8. **A** The answer is true. Generally, tenants who are leasing only part of a building, such as offices or commercial space, are not required to continue to pay rent after the leased premises are destroyed. (333)

9. **A** The answer is true. When a tenant transfers all leasehold interests to another person, the lease has been assigned; when a tenant transfers less than all the leasehold interests by leasing them to a new tenant, the original tenant has subleased the property. (333)

10. **A** The answer is true. Under a gross lease agreement, the landlord pays all the operating expenses of the property, while the tenant pays only a fixed rental. (335)

11. **B** The answer is false. Ground leases are generally long-term net leases and are often recorded. (336)

12. **A** The answer is true. An estate at will is a tenancy of indefinite duration and is automatically terminated by the death of either party. (330)

13. **B** The answer is false. To be entitled to constructive eviction, the tenant must show only that the premises have become unusable for the purpose stated in the lease due to the landlord's conscious neglect. (338)

14. **A** The answer is true. All persons must have access to housing of their choice without any differentiation in the terms and conditions because of their race, color, religion, national origin, sex, disability, or familial status. (338–339)

15. **B**   The answer is false. Consideration in a lease consists of the landlord promising possession and the tenant promising rents. A requirement for a security deposit may be a part of the agreement, to be made available for unpaid rent and/or damages to the property. (331)

MULTIPLE CHOICE

1. **B**   The answer is gross. The one-lump sum every month to the landlord is a gross lease. In a net lease, the tenant is responsible for paying all or most of the property charges. Percentage leases are generally used by retail establishments and are based on gross sales. (335)

2. **A**   The answer is a lease purchase. The tenant typically pays a higher *rent* with a portion of the rent being applied to the subsequent purchase of the property. It differs from a sale leaseback, in which the owner of the property wants to obtain equity from the building. The owner sells the building and agrees to rent it back. (336)

3. **C**   The answer is October 1, present year. The tenants have the right to possess the property until the end of their lease. The new owners will have to wait to move in. (334)

4. **D**   The answer is none. This lease will be terminated May 1—an estate for years. State law will probably require that a residential landlord provide at least a 30-day notice to a tenant that the lease will not be extended or renewed at the end of the lease term. (329)

5. **D**   The answer is periodic. Any lease that automatically renews itself is a periodic tenancy. It will continue until either party gives proper notice requesting a change. (329)

6. **C**   The answer is a sublease. The friend holds a sublease because the tenant has given up possession for some of the lease term. Giving up all of the remaining rights would be an assignment. In either situation, the original tenant is still responsible for the rent payment. (333)

7. **D**   The answer is no, the premises are not unusable, the condition was not due to the landlord's conscious neglect, and the tenant has not abandoned the apartment. Constructive eviction is a result of the landlord not providing essential services, making the premises unsafe or uninhabitable, conditions that are not met in this situation. (338)

8. **A**   The answer is the tenant is not required to continue paying rent after March 14 because the premises have been destroyed. Typically, if a residential rental unit is destroyed, the lease is terminated. This is not the case with agricultural land or ground leases. (333)

9. **C**   The answer is both tenant A's and tenant B's. Both leases are covered by the statute of frauds and must be in writing because they will both terminate more than one year from the date of execution. (331)

10. **D**   The original lease was an estate for years and no notice was required to terminate. If the tenant does not pay rent, it will become a tenancy at sufferance. If the tenant pays rent and the landlord accepts it, it will be a holdover or periodic tenancy, which could be changed into an estate for years if they enter into yet another year-long lease. (329)

11. **B**   The landlord can treat the tenant as a trespasser and proceed with eviction and damages action; however, the landlord must comply with notice to quit requirements. (330)

12. **B**   The answer is the landlord is legally obligated to permit the modifications to be made at the tenant's expense. These modifications would appear to be within the scope of *reasonable* modifications. They also would not interfere with a future tenant's use of the property. (332–333)

13. **B**   The answer is a percentage lease. Many retail shopping centers use percentage leases. Part of the tenant's success is due to location. Landlords will help with promotional events to draw in customers knowing that the more successful the tenant, the more rent for the landlord. (335)

14. **C**   A tenant who intends to construct a building on leased land generally does so under a ground lease, often for up to 50 years. The tenant will often record the lease to serve constructive notice of their long-term interest. (336)

15. **C**   The answer is the tenant is still liable to the landlord for the outstanding rent because the landlord did not release the tenant when the lease was assigned to the friend. While rights to possession may be assigned or sublet, the obligation to pay rent may not be assigned to another party unless the landlord agrees to the plan. (333)

16. **A**   The answer is compensates the landlord in the event of rent default or premises damage. Security deposits are often used if the tenant defaults on payment of

rent or destroys the premises; they cannot usually be applied to the final month's rental. That would be an advance rental, and the landlord must treat it as income for tax purposes. (333)

17. **C** The answer is lessee. Ground leases typically involve separate ownership of the land and the buildings, so the lessor owns the land and the lessee owns the building. (336)

18. **D** The answer is serve notice on the tenant. To regain possession through a legal process called actual eviction, the landlord must serve notice on the tenant before commencing the lawsuit. (337–338)

19. **C** The answer is the landlord is violating the covenant of quiet enjoyment. A lessor is bound by the covenant of quiet enjoyment—the promise that the lessee can occupy the premises without interference from the owner or anyone else. A tenancy at sufferance refers to a tenant's previously lawful possession that has continued without the landlord's consent. (331)

20. **B** The answer is a graduated lease. A form of variable lease is the graduated lease that provides for specified rent increases at set future dates. (336)

FILL-IN-THE BLANK

1. A type of leasehold estate that gives the right of possession with the landlord's consent for an unspecified term is called an *estate at will*.

2. Although rent is the usual *consideration* given for the right to occupy leased premises, labor could also serve this function.

3. Recording a lease is usually considered unnecessary because anyone who inspects the property receives *actual notice*.

4. If the lease allows the tenant the opportunity to buy the property before the owner accepts an offer from another party, the tenant has the *right of first refusal*.

5. If the tenant pays basic rent plus all or most property charges, the tenant has a *net* lease.

6. In a lease agreement, the tenant is called the *lessee*.

7. A leasehold estate that continues for a definite period of time is the *estate for years*.

8. A mortgage clause that states the lender agrees not to terminate the tenancies of rent-paying tenants in the event the lender forecloses on the building is the *nondisturbance* clause.

9. The arrangement when an owner of property sells the property and then obtains a lease from the new owner is called *sale-and-leaseback*.

10. A model law that addresses obligations in leases, such as the landlord's right of entry, premises mainte-nance, and protection of the tenants from retaliation by the landlord in the event of complaints is the *Uniform Residential Landlord and Tenant Act*.

ACTIVITY: TYPES OF COMMERCIAL LEASES

Acrylic Acres has a net lease with $2,902.50 rent for the current month calculated as follows:

$6,790 utilities + $2,560 taxes × 15% = $1,402.50

Base rent = $\underline{1,500.00}$

Total rent = $2,902.50

Blue Buttons Boutique has a gross lease with $2,000 rent for the current month. With a gross lease, no calculations are required. The tenant pays the rent; the landlord takes care of all expenses.

Custom Custards has a percentage lease with $2,515 rent for the current month calculated as follows:

$9,542 gross sales – $4,000 forgiven sales = $5,542.00

$5,542.00 qualifying sales × 12% = 665.04

Base rent = $\underline{1,850.00}$

Total rent = $2,515.04

Fair Housing

LEARNING OBJECTIVES

When you have completed this unit, you will be able to

> **explain** the significance of the Civil Rights Act of 1866 to equal opportunity in housing;
> **describe** the various federal laws which protect Americans from unfair housing practices;
> **describe** blockbusting, steering, redlining, and other abusive housing practices;
> **list** the various recourses available to the aggrieved person who believes illegal discrimination has occurred including acts of real estate professionals; and
> **describe** the importance to real estate professionals and the public of understanding and complying with fair housing laws.

KEY TERMS

administrative law judge (ALJ)	Department of Housing and Urban Development (HUD)	redlining
Americans with Disabilities Act (ADA)	Fair Housing Act	steering
blockbusting	Fair Housing Amendments Act	Title VIII of the Civil Rights Act of 1968
Civil Rights Act of 1866	Housing for Older Persons Act (HOPA)	
conciliation		

MATCHING

Write the letter of the matching term on the appropriate line.

A. familial status

B. Housing for Older Persons Act (HOPA)

C. Civil Rights Act of 1968

D. disability

E. blockbusting

F. Fair Housing Act

G. ADA

H. HUD

I. steering

J. *Jones v. Mayer*

1. ___ A law that prohibits discrimination in housing based on race, color, religion, and national origin

2. ___ The Civil Rights Act of 1968, the Housing and Community Development Act of 1974, and the Fair Housing Amendments Act of 1988, collectively

3. ___ The agency that administers the federal fair housing laws

4. ___ The presence of one or more persons who are under the age of 18, living with a parent or adult guardian

5. ___ A physical or mental impairment

6. ___ A U.S. Supreme Court decision that prohibits all racial discrimination in housing

7. ___ Law repealing requirement that housing for those 55 and older have special facilities for seniors

8. ___ A law that requires accessibility to employment, goods, and services for individuals with disabilities

9. ___ Encouraging the sale or renting of property by claiming a protected class of people are moving into the area and will have a negative impact on property values

10. ___ Encouraging home seekers to limit their search to particular neighborhoods based on noneconomic factors such as race or religion

TRUE OR FALSE

Circle the correct answer.

1. The purpose of the civil rights laws that affect the real estate industry is to make everyone equal.
    A. True
    B. False

2. Failing to comply with state and federal fair housing laws may subject a real estate professional to both fines and disciplinary action.
    A. True
    B. False

3. The Civil Rights Act of 1968 applies only to race.
    A. True
    B. False

4. Under HUD regulations, a dwelling is limited to single-family houses, condominiums, and cooperatives.
    A. True
    B. False

5. The fair housing laws protect persons with AIDS.
    A. True
    B. False

6. There are no exemptions under the federal Fair Housing Act.
    A. True
    B. False

7. The Fair Housing Act is administered by the county in which the property is located.
    A. True
    B. False

8. The *ADA Accessibility Guidelines* contain ADA's specific requirements for curb ramps, elevators, and other measures to make spaces accessible for people with disabilities.
    A. True
    B. False

9. Redlining is the act of encouraging people to sell or rent their homes on the basis that the entry of members of a protected class into the neighborhood will reduce property values.
    A. True
    B. False

10. Channeling home seekers to particular neighborhoods based on noneconomic factors is an illegal practice called steering.
    A. True
    B. False

11. There are no exceptions to HUD's rules regarding statements of preference or limitations in advertising regarding race.
    A. True
    B. False

12. While not valid considerations for the underlying real estate transaction, these factors may be considered by an appraiser in evaluating a property: race, color, religion, national origin, sex, disability, and familial status.
    A. True
    B. False

13. Individuals who believe they are the victim of illegal discrimination in a real estate transaction may file a complaint with HUD within three years of the alleged act.
    A. True
    B. False

14. Failure to prominently display the Equal Housing Opportunity poster can be considered evidence of discriminatory practices.
    A. True
    B. False

15. A real estate professional is obligated to provide ethnic-diversity information to homebuyers.
    A. True
    B. False

16. If a tenant has a visual disability and needs an assistance animal, the landlord can require a higher security deposit than for other tenants.
    A. True
    B. False

17. A church violates the Fair Housing Act if it owns and operates rental housing only for its member employees and others who belong to the religion.
    A. True
    B. False

18. One reason that real estate professionals need to be concerned about meeting requirements of the ADA is because their offices are public spaces.
    A. True
    B. False

19. If a real estate professional says to a potential seller that the neighborhood is "changing" and "isn't what it used to be," that message may be considered blockbusting.
    A. True
    B. False

20. The Fair Housing Act prohibits landlords from asking potential tenants for citizenship or immigration documents during the screening process.
    A. True
    B. False

MULTIPLE CHOICE

Circle the correct answer.

1. Which of these laws extended housing discrimination protections to families with children and persons with disabilities?
   A. Civil Rights Act of 1866
   B. Fair Housing Amendments Act of 1988
   C. Housing and Community Development Act of 1974
   D. Civil Rights Act of 1968

2. The Fair Housing Act is administered by
   A. the Office of Equal Opportunity.
   B. the Department of Housing and Urban Development.
   C. the Department of Justice.
   D. the federal court system.

3. The Fair Housing Act does *NOT* prohibit discrimination on the basis of
   A. familial status.
   B. national origin.
   C. religious preference.
   D. sexual preference.

4. Which of these are exempt from the federal Fair Housing Act?
   A. Owner-occupied buildings with no more than four units
   B. Buildings subject to the *ADA Accessibility Guidelines*
   C. Buildings that are not publicly advertised as being for sale or for rent
   D. None of these

5. Real estate professionals may have a legal obligation to comply with the ADA because they
   A. often have clients with disabilities.
   B. frequently own their own homes.
   C. may be employers.
   D. may need to require reasonable accommodation in a home they have listed.

6. A real estate broker sends a bright yellow flyer to all the homeowners in a neighborhood. The flyer contains a reprinted article from a local newspaper describing the future relocation plans of various employers in the region and this statement, printed in bold red letters: "Warning! The failure to sell your property within the next six months could cost you a bundle!" At the bottom of the page was printed the broker's name, photo, office address, and phone number. Based on these facts, the broker
   A. is guilty of steering.
   B. is guilty of blockbusting.
   C. has committed no offense.
   D. has violated the HUD advertising guidelines.

7. A newspaper advertisement states, "One-bedroom apartment immediately available. Good neighborhood. Only able-bodied individuals should apply." Which of these is *TRUE*?
   A. The ad is not permitted under HUD's advertising guidelines because it discriminates on the basis of disability.
   B. The ad is acceptable under HUD's advertising guidelines.
   C. The ad is not permitted under HUD's advertising guidelines due to the remark, "Good neighborhood."
   D. Newspapers are inherently discriminatory because not everyone can afford to buy them.

8. Under what conditions can someone refuse to rent to an African-American on the basis of race?
   A. Never
   B. If the owner is also living in one of the apartments of a small apartment building
   C. If the owner is handling the leasing without the aid of a real estate professional
   D. If the owner is a small investor and is selling one of the three houses

9. Under the Fair Housing Act, what is HUD's first action on receiving a complaint of illegal discrimination?
   A. Investigates for reasonable cause to bring a charge
   B. Holds an administrative hearing
   C. Issues an injunction against the offender
   D. Files a civil action in federal district court

10. The Fair Housing Amendments Act of 1988 included
    A. a repeal of the facilities and services requirements designed to help older persons with physical and social needs.
    B. the addition of sex to the list of protected classes.
    C. more severe penalties for violations and additional damages.
    D. the addition of religion to the list of protected classes.

11. Under the Civil Rights Act of 1968, what is the time limit to file a housing discrimination complaint with HUD?
    A. 100 days
    B. 1 year
    C. 2 years
    D. The same as the statute of limitations for torts committed in the state in which the alleged discriminatory act occurred

12. Complaints of discriminatory housing practices filed with HUD will be referred to a local enforcement agency if
    A. the federal law is substantially more inclusive than the state or municipal law.
    B. HUD determines that an administrative law judge should decide the case.
    C. the state or municipal law is substantially equivalent to the federal law.
    D. the complaint involves a real estate professional who is the victim of a threat or act of violence because the professional has complied with the fair housing laws.

13. In a dispute before HUD, the term *conciliation* is *BEST* defined as
    A. the equivalent of paying a fine.
    B. the informal resolution of a dispute by obtaining assurances that the person responding to the complaint will remedy the violation.
    C. the referral of the matter to a local agency.
    D. the formal process under which the aggrieved party files a civil action in federal court.

14. All of these people are considered members of protected classes *EXCEPT*
    A. a member of Alcoholics Anonymous.
    B. a visually disabled person with a seeing-eye dog.
    C. a person diagnosed with AIDS.
    D. a person convicted of the manufacture or distribution of illegal drugs.

15. A homeowner decides to rent a spare bedroom in her single-family house to a tenant for $500 per month. When a 24-year-old man asks to see the room, the homeowner refuses, telling him that she will only rent to women over the age of 50. The prospective tenant threatens to sue for a violation of the Fair Housing Act on the basis of age. Should the homeowner be concerned?
    A. Yes, because the amount of rent being charged is immaterial for purposes of the Fair Housing Act.
    B. Yes, because while the homeowner is permitted to exclude individuals on the basis of age or sex, she cannot exclude on the basis of both.
    C. No, because the rental of rooms in an owner-occupied single-family home is exempt from the Fair Housing Act.
    D. No, because there was no real estate professional involved in this transaction, the homeowner is free to discriminate on the basis of any of the normally protected classes.

16. A seller tells a real estate professional "don't show my house to anybody not born in the United States." In this circumstance, the professional
    A. must show the house to anyone who wants to see it.
    B. must decline to take the listing with this requirement.
    C. may take the listing and ignore the instruction.
    D. may take the listing and hope that no foreign-born persons ask to see the property.

17. A neighborhood has a large population of recent immigrants from Asian countries. When a couple that had just arrived from South Korea came to a broker to look for a home to buy, he suggested they look at listings only in this neighborhood. The broker violated the Fair Housing Act because his actions constitute
    A. stereotyping.
    B. blockbusting.
    C. redlining.
    D. steering.

18. A woman met with a landlord to view a two bedroom apartment. She has two children and is also pregnant. The landlord told her that the rules of the building allow only two children per two-bedroom apartment, so he cannot rent to her. Is this a violation of the Fair Housing Act?
    A. No, rental standards can include a restriction on the number of occupants in an apartment.
    B. No, the Fair Housing Act allows property owners to limit the number of children in a development.
    C. Yes, indicating a preference for a certain number of children as occupants is illegal discrimination on the basis of familial status.
    D. Yes, until the third child is born, the woman meets the standards for the number of children in the family.

19. A landlord rented an apartment to a person with a wheelchair. The landlord allowed the tenant to install bath rails and replace the bathroom sink vanity with a pedestal sink with lever faucet handles; however, the landlord required the tenant to sign a restoration agreement that the accommodations would be restored to their former condition at the end of the lease. In addition, the landlord required the tenant to pay sufficient funds (over a period of time) into an escrow account to cover the bathroom restoration. Has the landlord violated the Fair Housing Act?
    A. No, the landlord can require a restoration agreement and the escrow account.
    B. No, the landlord does not have to allow the tenant to make any of these modifications.
    C. Yes, the landlord cannot require restoration of the modifications.
    D. Yes, the landlord cannot require the escrow account.

20. An occupancy requirement is exempt from familial status protection under the Fair Housing Act if the housing is intended to be occupied by
    A. at least one person in each unit who is 50 years of age or older.
    B. persons 62 years of age or older.
    C. persons 55 years of age or older.
    D. at least one person age 60 or older in 80% of the units.

21. For fair housing purposes, what is the definition of the term *disability*?
    A. An impairment of mobility that prevents a person from using stairs
    B. A physical impairment that requires a caregiver's assistance
    C. An impairment that prevents a person from holding a job
    D. An impairment that substantially limits one or more of an individual's major life activities

22. A landlord refuses to rent a vacant apartment to a couple with two small children because he is concerned the children will disturb the sick and elderly woman in the apartment next door. Which of these is most likely *TRUE*?
    A. Because the landlord has good intentions, there is no violation of the Fair Housing Act.
    B. If the sick and elderly woman is over the age of 80, there is no violation of the Fair Housing Act.
    C. The refusal constitutes a violation of the Fair Housing Act if the family and the elderly woman have different national origins.
    D. The refusal constitutes a violation of the Fair Housing Act because it discriminates on the basis of familial status.

23. The provisions of the ADA apply to any employer with at least
    A. 5 or more employees.
    B. 10 or more employees.
    C. 12 or more employees.
    D. 15 or more employees.

24. What is one negative result of redlining?
    A. Appraisers have a difficult time evaluating properties in the area.
    B. It is often a contributor to the deterioration of older neighborhoods.
    C. The effects test must be applied to determine whether to file a lawsuit.
    D. Real estate professionals are not able to advertise in local newspapers.

25. The resolution of a fair housing complaint by obtaining assurance that the respondent will remedy the violation is called
    A. conciliation.
    B. administrative proceedings.
    C. civil action.
    D. a judgment.

UNIT 18 ANSWERS

MATCHING

1. **C**

2. **F**

3. **H**

4. **A**

5. **D**

6. **J**

7. **B**

8. **G**

9. **E**

10. **I**

TRUE OR FALSE

1. **B** The answer is false. The purpose of the civil rights laws that affect real estate is to create a marketplace in which all persons of similar financial means have a similar range of housing choices. (346)

2. **A** The answer is true. Real estate professionals must comply with fair housing laws and cannot allow discriminatory attitudes of property owners or property seekers to affect compliance with fair housing laws. (346)

3. **B** The answer is false. The Civil Rights Act of 1968 applies to housing discrimination based on race, color, religion, and national origin. (347)

4. **B** The answer is false. Under HUD regulations, a *dwelling* includes single-family houses, condominiums, cooperatives, mobile homes, and vacant land on which any of these structures will be built. (348)

5. **A** The answer is true. A person with AIDS is protected by the fair housing laws as being a person with a disability, which is defined as a physical or mental impairment. (350)

6. **B** The answer is false. The Civil Rights Act of 1866, as interpreted by *Jones v. Mayer*, does not allow any exemptions involving race. Under the federal Fair Housing Act of 1968, some exemptions exist for small investors and certain organizations. (347)

7. **B** The answer is false. The Fair Housing Act is administered by the Department of Housing and Urban Development (HUD), a federal agency. (348)

8. **A** The answer is true. The *ADA Accessibility Guidelines* contain these specifications. (352–353)

9. **B** The answer is false. *Blockbusting* is the act of encouraging people to sell or rent their homes on the basis that the entry of members of a protected class into the neighborhood will reduce property values. (353)

10. **A** The answer is true. Steering is the illegal channeling of prospective home buyers to particular neighborhoods, or by discouraging potential buyers who are members of a protected class from considering certain areas. (354)

11. **A** The answer is true. Advertisements of property for sale or rent may not include language indicating a preference or limitation. (354)

12. **B** The answer is false. Race, color, religion, national origin, sex, disability, and familial status may not be considered in any formal or informal appraisal or evaluation of a property. (355)

13. **B** The answer is false. Individuals who believe they are the victim of illegal discrimination in a real estate transaction may file a complaint with HUD within one year of the alleged act. (356)

14. **A** The answer is true. Failure to display the Equal Housing Opportunity poster can be considered prima facie evidence of discriminatory practices. (348)

15. **B** The answer is false. Pursuant to the 2001 case *Hannah v. Sibcy Cline Realtors*, a real estate professional is not obligated to provide ethnic-diversity information about a neighborhood to a homebuyer. (347)

16. **B** The answer is false. A landlord cannot increase the customary security deposit only for tenants with disabilities. (350)

17. **B** The answer is false. A religious organization may restrict occupancy of dwelling units that it owns to members of the organization. However, membership in the religion must not be restricted on the basis of race, color, or national origin. (351)

18. **A** The answer is true. The Americans with Disabilities Act (ADA) is important because real estate brokers are often employers, and their offices are public spaces. (352)

19. **A** The answer is true. Blockbusting is the act of encouraging people to sell or rent their homes by claiming that the entry of a protected class of people into the neighborhood will have a negative impact on property values. (353)

20. **B** The answer is false. However, HUD provides a specific procedure for collecting and verifying citizenship papers. (356)

MULTIPLE CHOICE

1. **B** The answer is Fair Housing Amendments Act of 1988. The Fair Housing Amendments Act of 1988 added disability and familial status. The Housing and Community Development Act of 1974 added sex to the list of protected classes, which is found in Title VIII of the Civil Rights Act of 1968. The Civil Rights Act of 1866 prohibits discrimination based on race. (347)

2. **B** The answer is the Department of Housing and Urban Development. The Department of Housing and Urban Development (HUD) handles fair housing complaints on the national level. Most states have enacted substantially similar laws, so often it is the state agency that is involved. (356)

3. **D** The answer is sexual preference. Sexual preference is not a protected class under the federal law, but it has been added to many city and state fair housing laws. (347–348)

4. **A** The answer is owner-occupied buildings with no more than four units. Other exemptions include single-family housing sold or rented without the use of a real estate professional and housing operated by organizations and private clubs that limit occupancy to members. (351)

5. **C** The answer is may be employers. Many real estate professionals are brokers who own an office, and the real estate office should be accessible to the public, including a person with a disability. (352)

6. **C** The answer is has committed no offense. Although perhaps in poor taste, the broker is simply distributing a published newspaper article to which anyone has access. He is also not making any statements about a protected class of people moving into the neighborhood. (353)

7. **A** The answer is the ad is not permitted under HUD's advertising guidelines because it discriminates on the basis of disability. The ad discriminates against prospective tenants who are disabled. The remark, "Good neighborhood," is acceptable pursuant to HUD advertising guidelines. (354)

8. **A** The answer is never. Under the Civil Rights Act of 1866, as reinforced by the *Jones v. Mayer* Supreme Court decision, there are no exemptions that permit someone to discriminate in housing simply because of someone's race. (346–347)

9. **A** The answer is investigates for reasonable cause to bring a charge. Within 100 days of the filing of the complaint, HUD either determines that reasonable cause exists to bring a charge of illegal discrimination or dismisses the complaint. (356)

10. **C** The answer is more severe penalties for violations and additional damages. The Fair Housing Amendments Act of 1988 expanded federal civil rights protections to familial status and disability. The Act also changed the penalties for violating the law by making them more severe and by adding additional damages. (347)

11. **B** The answer is 1 year. Persons who wish to file a complaint with HUD under Title VIII of the Civil Rights Act of 1968 must do so within one year of the alleged violation. (356)

12. **C** The answer is the state or municipal law is substantially equivalent to the federal law. If a state or local law is substantially equivalent to the federal law, a complaint filed with HUD is referred to the local enforcement agency. (357)

13. **B** The answer is the informal resolution of a dispute by obtaining assurances that the person responding to the complaint will remedy the violation. HUD can attempt to resolve the dispute informally through conciliation. Conciliation is the resolution of a complaint by obtaining assurance that the person against whom the complaint was filed will remedy any violation that may have occurred. (356)

14. **D**   The answer is a person convicted of the manufacture or distribution of illegal drugs. Persons convicted of manufacturing or distributing illegal drugs do not enjoy any protections under the Fair Housing Act, although disability is a protected class. Individuals who are participating in addiction recovery programs are in a protected class of disability. (350)

15. **C**   The answer is no, because the rental of rooms in an owner-occupied single-family home is exempt from the Fair Housing Act. The woman is exempt from the law because she will be renting a single room in her home. (351)

16. **B**   The answer is must decline to take the listing with this requirement. An instruction to not show the home to someone who was not born in the United States violates the Fair Housing Act. The real estate professional should not take the listing with this requirement. He cannot simply ignore the instruction or pretend it does not exist. (347, 354)

17. **D**   The answer is steering. Channeling home seekers toward or away from particular neighborhoods based on national origin, or any of the other protected classifications, is called steering. (354)

18. **C**   The answer is yes, indicating a preference for a certain number of children as occupants is illegal discrimination on the basis of familial status. Occupancy standards must be based on objective factors, such as sanitation or safety, not number of children. (348, 350)

19. **A**   The answer is no, the landlord can require a restoration agreement and the escrow account. The landlord must permit these reasonable modifications; however, the landlord can require the restoration agreement and escrow account. (350)

20. **B**   The answer is persons 62 years of age or older. Housing is exempt from the familial status protections if it is intended for occupancy only by persons 62 years of age, or for occupancy in 80% of its units by at least one person 55 years of age or older. Strict rules for ongoing verification and reporting are imposed on this second alternative. (351–352)

21. **D**   The answer is an impairment that substantially limits one or more of an individual's major life activities. The definition of the term *disability* is very broad and focuses on impairments that prevent or restrict a person from performing tasks that are of central importance to most people's lives. (350)

22. **D**   The answer is the refusal constitutes a violation of the Fair Housing Act because it discriminates on the basis of familial status. Although the landlord's intent is to make things easier for the sick and elderly tenant, the refusal violates the Fair Housing Act by discriminating on the basis of familial status. (348)

23. **D**   The answer is 15 or more employees. Employers must make reasonable accommodations that enable an individual with a disability to perform essential job functions. (352)

24. **B**   The answer is it is often a contributor to the deterioration of older neighborhoods. Redlining is a prohibited practice by lenders and insurance companies. It frequently leads to the deterioration of older neighborhoods because loans are not made based on racial grounds as opposed to any real objection to an applicant's creditworthiness. (355)

25. **A**   The answer is conciliation. *Conciliation* attempts to resolve the complaint without further legal action, such as an administrative proceeding. However, a conciliation agreement can be enforced through civil action. (356)

UNIT
19

Property Management

LEARNING OBJECTIVES

When you have completed this unit, you will be able to

> **describe** the various property management assignments available in the property management field and the role of the property manager in each;
> **explain** the essential elements of the property management agreement;
> **list** the primary responsibilities of the property manager;
> **describe** the various federal laws, which the property manager must know and follow in the performance of management; and
> **describe** the implementation of risk management procedures to insure the safety and security of a managed property's tenants as well as to protect the landlord from liability and loss.

KEY TERMS

budget comparison statement	multiperil policies	risk management
cash flow report	operating budget	routine maintenance
corrective maintenance	preventive maintenance	surety bonds
management agreement	profit and loss statement	tenant improvements
management plan	property manager	workers' compensation acts

MATCHING

Write the letter of the matching term on the appropriate line.

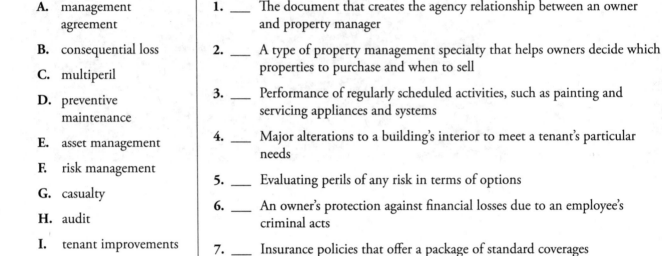

A. management agreement

B. consequential loss

C. multiperil

D. preventive maintenance

E. asset management

F. risk management

G. casualty

H. audit

I. tenant improvements

J. surety bond

1. ___ The document that creates the agency relationship between an owner and property manager

2. ___ A type of property management specialty that helps owners decide which properties to purchase and when to sell

3. ___ Performance of regularly scheduled activities, such as painting and servicing appliances and systems

4. ___ Major alterations to a building's interior to meet a tenant's particular needs

5. ___ Evaluating perils of any risk in terms of options

6. ___ An owner's protection against financial losses due to an employee's criminal acts

7. ___ Insurance policies that offer a package of standard coverages

8. ___ Insurance policies that provide coverage against theft, burglary, and vandalism; specific, not all-inclusive

9. ___ Insurance that covers the revenue a business loses due to a disaster

10. ___ An investigation to determine the need for insurance and types of insurance required

TRUE OR FALSE

Circle the correct answer.

1. One of the key responsibilities of a property manager is to preserve or increase the value of the property.
   A. True
   B. False

2. The management agreement creates a general agency relationship between an owner and the property manager.
   A. True
   B. False

3. Unlike real estate brokers' commissions, property management fees may be standardized by professional organizations.
   A. True
   B. False

4. Rental rates are influenced primarily by supply and demand.
   A. True
   B. False

5. An example of a readily achievable modification under the Americans with Disabilities Act (ADA) is installing a ramp at a building entrance.
   A. True
   B. False

6. The manager of a residential building should carefully consider a prospective tenant's compatibility with existing tenants.
   A. True
   B. False

7. A high tenant turnover rate results in higher profits for the owner.
   A. True
   B. False

8. The three types of maintenance necessary to keep a property in good condition are preventive, rehabilitation, and tenant relations.
   A. True
   B. False

9. Corrective maintenance helps prevent problems and expenses before they arise.
   A. True
   B. False

10. Tenant improvements are major alterations to the interior of commercial or industrial property to accommodate the tenant.
    A. True
    B. False

11. Under Title I of the ADA, all existing barriers must be removed from both residential and commercial properties.
    A. True
    B. False

12. The ADA requirements for new construction are stricter than those for buildings existing before the law was implemented.
    A. True
    B. False

13. The four alternative risk management techniques are transfer, control, avoid, and retain.
    A. True
    B. False

14. In a commercial property, the risk of a shopper suffering a slip-and-fall injury would be covered by casualty insurance.
    A. True
    B. False

15. A depreciated value policy insures a building for what it would cost to rebuild it.
    A. True
    B. False

16. A cash flow report is the most important financial report because it provides a picture of the current financial status of a property.
    A. True
    B. False

17. Property managers have a responsibility to properly manage hazardous environmental problems, such as asbestos.
    A. True
    B. False

18. Courts have always held that tenants, rather than property owners and their agents, are responsible for protecting against physical harm inflicted by intruders.
    A. True
    B. False

19. A critical maintenance objective is to protect the physical condition of the property over the long term.
    A. True
    B. False

20. Examples of variable expenses of property management are employee wages and utilities.
    A. True
    B. False

MULTIPLE CHOICE

Circle the correct answer.

1. A property manager's first responsibility to the owner should be to
   A. keep the building's occupancy rate at 100%.
   B. report all day-to-day financial and operating decisions to the owner on a regular basis.
   C. realize the highest return possible consistent with the owner's instructions.
   D. ensure that the rental rates are below market average.

2. The property manager's relationship with the owner is most similar to that of
   A. a tenant with a landlord.
   B. a cashier with the owner of a store.
   C. a stockholder with the board of directors of a corporation.
   D. a sales associate with the employing broker.

3. All of these should be included in a written management agreement *EXCEPT*
   A. a list of the manager's duties and responsibilities.
   B. a statement of the owner's purpose.
   C. a statement identifying the manager's creditors.
   D. an allocation of costs.

4. If an apartment rents for $750 per month and the manager receives a 12% commission on all new tenants, how much will the manager receive when renting an apartment, assuming that this commission is calculated in the usual way?
   A. $90
   B. $750
   C. $1,080
   D. $1,800

5. What is the annual rent per square foot for a 30 ft × 40 ft property that rents for $2,950 per month?
   A. $1.20
   B. $2.46
   C. $24.65
   D. $29.50

6. Of these, a high vacancy rate *MOST* likely indicates
   A. rental rates are too low.
   B. the property is attractive.
   C. building management is effective and responsive.
   D. an undesirable property.

7. Which of these is an example of corrective maintenance?
   A. Seasonal recharge of refrigerant in an air conditioning unit
   B. Picking up litter in common areas
   C. Repairing a leaking water heater
   D. Moving a partition wall to make a larger office

8. How can tenants insure their personal belongings in apartments they rent?
   A. Pay an extra fee so they are added to their landlord's commercial insurance
   B. Obtain a surety bond
   C. Obtain HO-4 or renter's insurance
   D. Obtain errors and omissions (E&O) insurance

9. Under the ADA, existing barriers *MUST* be removed
   A. in all public buildings by the end of 2020.
   B. only on request from a person with a disability.
   C. even though reasonable alternative accommodation is more practical.
   D. when removal may be accomplished in a readily achievable manner.

10. A company was moving from one part of the city to another. During the move, a truck carrying computer equipment worth more than $250,000 was trapped in a flooded underpass, and the equipment was destroyed. Fortunately, the company was insured under several policies. The policy that would most likely cover the computer equipment during the move from one facility to another is
    A. a consequential loss, use, and occupancy policy.
    B. a casualty policy.
    C. a contents and personal property policy.
    D. a liability policy.

11. All of these are principal responsibilities of the property manager *EXCEPT*
    A. forcibly removing tenants for nonpayment of rent.
    B. generating income for the owners.
    C. preserving and/or increasing the value of the property.
    D. achieving the objectives of the owners.

12. What is the purpose of an operating budget for a property manager?
    A. It documents the month's actual income and expenses.
    B. It is a guide for the property's financial performance in the future.
    C. It presents the current cash flows in a standardized format.
    D. It lists the assets, liabilities, and equity of the investment property.

13. What type of plan does a property manager implement to manage renters who do *NOT* pay their rent in a timely way?
    A. Eviction plan
    B. Collection plan
    C. Foreclosure plan
    D. Cash flow plan

14. One way that property managers meet the goals of ECOA is by
    A. disqualifying tenant applicants on the basis of receiving welfare payments.
    B. not evaluating certain tenant applicants through the use of credit reports.
    C. establishing that certain buildings do not allow children as residents.
    D. making sure to use the same lease application for every applicant.

15. According to the Fair Housing Act, what is *steering*?
    A. Channeling of protected class members to certain buildings or neighborhoods
    B. Encouraging people to rent or sell by claiming that certain protected classes of people will have a negative impact on property values
    C. An appropriate method to manage risks associated with rental property ownership
    D. A method of providing reasonable accommodation for people with disabilities

ACTIVITY: TYPES OF MAINTENANCE

In the following floor plan illustration, identify each maintenance item listed as preventive, corrective, or routine. Mark the approximate location of each item on the floor plan.

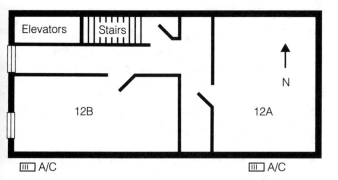

1.   Wash wall mirror across from elevators _____

2.   Fix air conditioner in 12B; blows hot _____

3.   Repaint exterior brick on west side _____

4.   Replace torn carpet on stair landing _____

5.   Repair cracked window, hallway-south _____

6.   Annual elevator inspection and repair _____

7.   Clean off cobweb above doorway to Apartment 12A _____

UNIT 19 ANSWERS

MATCHING

1. **A**

2. **E**

3. **D**

4. **I**

5. **F**

6. **J**

7. **C**

8. **G**

9. **B**

10. **H**

TRUE OR FALSE

1. **A** The answer is true. The role of the property manager is to achieve the objectives of the property owners, generate income for the owners, and preserve and/or increase the value of the investment property. (366)

2. **A** The answer is true. The management agreement creates an agency relationship between the owner and the property manager; the manager is generally considered a general agent empowered to make many decisions on behalf of the owner. (369)

3. **B** The answer is false. Like real estate brokers' commissions, property management fees may not be standardized by local professional organizations but must be negotiated between the parties. (370)

4. **A** The answer is true. Because rental rates are influenced primarily by supply and demand, the property manager should be aware of the advantages and disadvantages of competing space. (372)

5. **A** The answer is true. Existing barriers must be removed when this can be accomplished in a readily achievable manner with little difficulty and at low cost. One example is ramping or removing an obstacle from an otherwise accessible entrance. (378)

6. **B** The answer is false. The manager of a *commercial* building should carefully consider a prospective tenant's compatibility with existing tenants, such as traffic counts, noise, and so on. (374)

7. **B** The answer is false. A high tenant turnover rate results in lower profits for the owner. (375)

8. **B** The answer is false. The three types of maintenance necessary to keep a property in good condition are preventive, corrective, and routine. (376)

9. **B** The answer is false. Preventive maintenance helps prevent problems and expenses before they arise. Corrective maintenance involves the actual repairs that keep the building's equipment, utilities, and amenities functioning. (376)

10. **A** The answer is true. Tenant improvements, or build-outs, are construction alterations to the interior of the building to meet a tenant's particular space needs. (376)

11. **B** The answer is false. Under Title III of the ADA, existing barriers must be removed from commercial properties when this can be accomplished in a readily achievable manner. (378)

12. **A** The answer is true. New construction and remodeled commercial properties must meet higher standards of accessibility and usability because it costs less to incorporate accessible features in the design than to retrofit. (379)

13. **A** The answer is true. Risk management involves answering the question: What happens if something goes wrong? The four alternative risk management techniques include avoidance, control, transfer, and retention. (380)

14. **B** The answer is false. In a commercial property, insurance against the risk of a shopper suffering a slip-and-fall injury would be covered by *liability* insurance. (381)

15. **B** The answer is false. A building insured for what it would cost to rebuild it is a current replacement cost policy. (382)

16. **A** The answer is true. A cash flow report is a monthly statement that details the financial status of the property; as such, it is the most important financial report because it provides a picture of the current financial status of the property. (372)

17. **A** The answer is true. The property manager is not expected to be an expert in all of the disciplines necessary to operate a property, but is expected to be knowledgeable in many diverse subjects, including environmental concerns, such as asbestos, radon, indoor air quality, and so on. (377)

18. **B** The answer is false. Court decisions have held owners and their agents responsible for physical harm that was inflicted on tenants by intruders. (380)

19. **A** The answer is true. One of the most important functions of a property manager is the supervision of property maintenance, balancing the services provided with their costs—that is, to satisfy tenants' needs while minimizing operating expenses. (376)

20. **B** The answer is false. Employee wages and utilities are fixed expenses. Variable expenses may be recurring or nonrecurring and can include capital improvements, building repairs, and landscaping. (371)

MULTIPLE CHOICE

1. **C** The answer is realize the highest return possible consistent with the owner's instructions. The role of the property manager is to achieve the objectives of the property owners, generate income for the owners, and preserve and/or increase the value of the investment property. (366)

2. **D** The answer is a sales associate with the employing broker. A property manager is hired as a general agent with broad authority for a specific activity and for a long time. A sales associate is usually a general agent for the employing broker. (369)

3. **C** The answer is a statement identifying the manager's creditors. A management agreement establishes owner and manager responsibilities, determining who pays for what, all in keeping with the owner's purpose. It does not include a statement identifying the manager's creditors. (369)

4. **C** The answer is $1,080. The manager will receive $1,080: $750 per month × 12 months × 12% = $1,080. (370)

5. **D** The answer is $29.50. The annual rent is $29.50 per square foot: 30 × 40 = 1,200 square feet; $2,950 × 12 = $35,400; $35,400 ÷ 1,200 = $29.50. (374–375)

6. **D** The answer is an undesirable property. An elevated level of vacancy may indicate poor management, a defective or undesirable property, or rental rates that are too high for the market or the property. (373)

7. **C** The answer is repairing a leaking water heater. Repairing a leaking water heater is an example of corrective maintenance, which is fixing what is broken. Seasonal servicing is preventive; picking up litter is routine; moving a partition wall is construction. (376)

8. **C** The answer is obtain HO-4 or renter's insurance. A surety bond covers an owner against financial losses resulting from an employee's criminal acts or negligence. (381)

9. **D** The answer is when removal may be accomplished in a readily achievable manner. Existing barriers must be removed when this can be accomplished in a readily achievable manner with little difficulty and at low cost. One example is ramping or removing an obstacle from an otherwise accessible entrance. (379)

10. **C** The answer is a contents and personal property policy. Contents and personal property insurance covers building contents and personal property during periods when they are not actually located on the business premises. Consequential loss is also called loss of rent or business interruption; casualty covers theft, vandalism, machinery damage; liability covers injuries sustained on the premises. (381)

11. **A** The answer is forcibly removing tenants for nonpayment of rent. The property manager may start eviction proceedings but does not carry out the proceedings, which must be carried out by an officer of the court. (337)

12. **B** The answer is it is a guide for the property's financial performance in the future. The budget is a forward-looking plan that guides and provides expectations. The cash flow report is a monthly statement that details the financial status of the property. The profit and loss statement documents the actual income and expenses. (371)

13. **B** The answer is collection plan. Property managers must implement methods to collect rent before resorting to legal action that is costly and time-consuming. (375)

14. **D** The answer is making sure to use the same lease application for every applicant. Equality is the key. It is acceptable to use credit reports; however, managers need to require them for all applicants. ECOA prohibits discrimination on the basis of receipt of public assistance, such as welfare. (379)

15. **A** The answer is channeling of protected class members to certain buildings or neighborhoods. *Steering* is prohibited under the Fair Housing Act. *Blockbusting* is encouraging people to rent or sell by claiming that the entry of certain protected classes of people in an area will have a negative impact on property values. (379)

ACTIVITY: TYPES OF MAINTENANCE

Types of Maintenance

1. Routine
2. Corrective
3. Preventive
4. Corrective
5. Corrective
6. Preventive
7. Routine

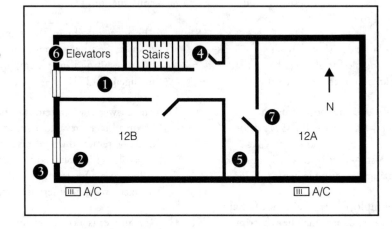

UNIT 20

Land-Use Controls and Property Development

LEARNING OBJECTIVES

When you have completed this unit, you will be able to

> **explain** the concept of police power and the provisions under which it protects the public's health, safety, and welfare;
> **explain** zoning ordinances, permits, and property use;
> **define** building codes as they relate to the requirements and restrictions placed on construction standards;
> **explain** the issues and regulations involved in subdivisions;
> **explain** non-governmental (private) land-use restrictions: covenants, conditions, and restrictions (CC&Rs); and
> **describe** the various laws and agencies which regulate land sales.

KEY TERMS

buffer zone	density zoning	plat map
building code	developer	restrictive covenants
certificate of occupancy	enabling acts	subdivider
comprehensive plan	Interstate Land Sales Full	subdivision
conditional-use permit	Disclosure Act (ILSA)	variance
covenants, conditions, and	nonconforming use	zoning ordinances
restrictions (CC&Rs)	planned unit development	
deed restrictions	(PUD)	

MATCHING A

Write the letter of the matching term on the appropriate line.

A. buffer zones

B. bulk zoning

C. comprehensive plan

D. conditional-use permit

E. enabling acts

F. certificate of occupancy

G. nonconforming use

H. aesthetic zoning

I. variance

J. zoning ordinances

1. ___ The device by which local governments establish development goals

2. ___ Document issued by a building inspector after a newly constructed building is found satisfactory

3. ___ Local laws that implement a comprehensive plan and regulate the control of land and structures within districts

4. ___ The legal means by which states confer zoning powers on local government

5. ___ Areas such as parks used to screen residential from nonresidential areas

6. ___ A special type of zoning used to control density by imposing restrictions, such as setbacks or limiting new construction

7. ___ Specifying certain types of architecture for new buildings

8. ___ A lot or improvement that is not in harmony with current zoning because it existed prior to the enactment or amendment of the zoning

9. ___ The device by which a daycare center might be permitted to operate in a residential neighborhood

10. ___ A form of permitted use, despite being prohibited by zoning, that is granted to an owner because of unique hardship caused by the regulation

MATCHING B

Write the letter of the matching term on the appropriate line.

A. building codes

B. Interstate Land Sales Full Disclosure Act

C. Planned Unit Development (PUD)

D. density zoning

E. developer

F. subdivider

G. building permit

H. plat

I. incentive zoning

J. restrictive covenants

1. ___ An item that a property owner must obtain from municipal officials before constructing a new building

2. ___ A person who buys undeveloped acreage and divides it into smaller lots for sale to others

3. ___ An individual who constructs improvements and sells them

4. ___ A detailed map that illustrates the geographic boundaries of individual lots in a subdivision

5. ___ Ordinances that restrict the average maximum number of houses per acre

6. ___ Standards for building style, setbacks, and use that are included in a deed for property in a subdivision

7. ___ Ordinances that specify construction and safety standards for construction

8. ___ A development where land is set aside for mixed-use purposes, such as residential, commercial, and public areas

9. ___ Law that requires developers to file statements with HUD before the developer can market unimproved lots interstate

10. ___ Ensuring that certain uses are incorporated into developments

TRUE OR FALSE

Circle the correct answer.

1. Zoning ordinances create the broad, general framework for a community; the comprehensive plan defines the details and implements the ordinances.
    A. True
    B. False

2. Bulk zoning ensures that certain types of uses are incorporated into developments.
    A. True
    B. False

3. No uniform planning and land development legislation affects the entire country.
    A. True
    B. False

4. One negative aspect of subdivision development is the potential for increased tax burdens.
    A. True
    B. False

5. A conditional-use permit allows a landowner to use property in a way that is not ordinarily permitted by zoning, due to unusual hardship or deprivation of reasonable use by the regulation.
    A. True
    B. False

6. Zoning permits are usually required before building permits can be issued.
    A. True
    B. False

7. A subdivider is a person who buys undeveloped acreage and divides it into smaller lots for sale to individuals or developers.
    A. True
    B. False

8. A plan is a detailed map that illustrates the geographic boundaries of individual lots in a subdivision.
    A. True
    B. False

9. Laches is the legal principle that allows for zoning variances.
    A. True
    B. False

10. The average number of residential units per acre in a development is called the development's gross density.
    A. True
    B. False

11. A restrictive covenant is considered a reasonable, legal restraint if it protects property values or restricts the free transfer of property.
    A. True
    B. False

12. The Interstate Land Sales Full Disclosure Act requires developers of any property to file a disclosure statement with HUD.
    A. True
    B. False

13. If a local zoning ordinance requires a 30-foot setback for any structure on the property, and a restrictive covenant for the subdivision calls for a 40-foot setback, the 30-foot setback takes precedence because it is less restrictive.
    A. True
    B. False

14. One of the basic elements of the comprehensive plan of a municipality can be energy conservation to reduce energy consumption and to promote the use of renewable energy sources.
    A. True
    B. False

15. Through powers conferred by state enabling acts, local governments exercise their authority based on the state's obligation to protect public health, safety, and welfare.
    A. True
    B. False

MULTIPLE CHOICE

Circle the correct answer.

1. A subdivision built in 1980 included covenants, conditions, and restrictions (CC&Rs) in the deeds for all properties. One covenant bans "all outdoor structures designed for the storage of equipment or as habitations for any animals." In 2008, a resident built a tool shed and a doghouse. The neighbors took no action for six years, but in 2014 they decide the shed and doghouse should be destroyed. Do the neighbors have any recourse?
   A. Yes, they can go to court and sue for monetary damages for violating the covenant.
   B. Yes, they can go to court and be awarded injunctive relief.
   C. No, under the doctrine of laches, the neighbors probably lost the right to enforce the restriction due to their delay in asserting it.
   D. No, covenants such as this are usually considered to be unenforceable restrictions on the free transfer of property.

2. A state delegates zoning powers to a municipality through
   A. the Interstate Land Sales Full Disclosure Act.
   B. eminent domain.
   C. a comprehensive plan.
   D. an enabling act.

3. All of these could be included in a zoning ordinance *EXCEPT*
   A. objectives for future development of the area.
   B. permissible height and style of new construction.
   C. style and appearance of structures.
   D. the maximum allowable ratio of land area to structural area.

4. A plat map is *BEST* described as
   A. a detailed map that illustrates aesthetic preferences.
   B. a detailed map that illustrates the geographic boundaries of individual lots.
   C. a detailed map that illustrates where a variance might be allowed.
   D. none of these.

5. A city passed a zoning ordinance that prohibits all commercial structures over 30 feet high. A company wants to build an office building that will be 45 feet high. In order to obtain permission for the building, the company may apply for
   A. a nonconforming use permit.
   B. a zoning permit.
   C. a conditional-use permit.
   D. a variance or zoning change.

6. A homeowner would like to operate a business in the home, but is in an area zoned for residential use only. What should the homeowner do?
   A. Request that the zoning board declare the home to be a nonconforming use
   B. Ask a court to grant an injunction against the zoning board
   C. Seek a conditional-use permit from the zoning board, if it is defined as allowable
   D. Apply to the zoning board for a variance

7. A builder goes all over the country buying large tracts of vacant land, splitting them into smaller parcels, and building identical communities of single-family ranch-style homes surrounding a central shopping center. The builder sells the homes to residents and leases space in the shopping center to merchants. The builder is
   A. a developer only.
   B. a subdivider only.
   C. both a developer and a subdivider.
   D. an assembler.

8. Which of these *BEST* defines density zoning?
   A. The mandatory use of clustering
   B. The average number of units in a development
   C. A restriction on the average number of houses per acre
   D. A restriction on the average number of acres per parcel

9. Before granting a zoning variance, a zoning board of appeals must
    A. hold a public hearing so that neighbors may voice their opinions.
    B. conduct a door-to-door opinion survey of property owners adjacent to the proposed use.
    C. check whether the landowner has been granted previous variances.
    D. determine whether the proposed use will result in higher property taxes.

10. All of these are common tests of a valid zoning ordinance *EXCEPT*
    A. clear and specific provisions.
    B. anticipation of future housing needs.
    C. a nondiscriminatory effect.
    D. all property owners being affected in a similar manner.

11. A company owns a 2,000-acre tract of undeveloped woodland surrounding a scenic lake. The tract has been divided into 106 individual lots, ranging in size from 15 acres to 100 acres. Telemarketers are hired to sell the lots to residents of the state and the three states with which it shares a common border. Based on these facts, how does the Interstate Land Sales Full Disclosure Act apply to the project?
    A. The company must file a disclosure statement with HUD.
    B. Because the project is not fraudulent, it is exempt from the requirements of the law.
    C. This development project is exempt from the law because of the lot size exemption.
    D. The project is exempt from the law because it is not being marketed outside a contiguous multistate region.

12. Zoning ordinances affect all of these *EXCEPT*
    A. lot sizes.
    B. building heights.
    C. style and appearance of buildings.
    D. racial composition of neighborhood.

13. A developer has included a playground and running trails between the commercial properties facing a busy street and the houses further back in the subdivision. The recreational area is considered
    A. aesthetic zoning.
    B. a buffer zone.
    C. a taking.
    D. a nonconforming use.

14. When an area was rezoned as residential, a store was grandfathered in and allowed to continue business. This is an example of
    A. a variance.
    B. a nonconforming use.
    C. a conditional-use permit.
    D. an amendment.

15. A new structure has been completed to the satisfaction of the inspecting city engineer. What documentation *MUST* be issued before anyone can move in?
    A. Appraisal report
    B. Certificate of occupancy
    C. Certificate of reasonable value
    D. Conditional-use permit

FILL-IN-THE-BLANK

Select the word or words that best complete these statements:

aesthetic zoning
ordinances

bulk zoning ordinances

conditional-use permit
(CUP)

covenants, conditions,
and restrictions (CC&Rs)

environmental impact
report

dedication

gross density

incentive zoning
ordinances

Interstate Land Sales Full
Disclosure Act

plat zoning

subdivision

variance

zones

zoning classifications

1. Land is partitioned according to its use into _____.

2. Zoning laws that specify certain types of architecture for all new construction are called _____.

3. Along with an application for subdivision approval, a developer often must submit a(n) _____ to explain what effect the proposed development will have on the surrounding area.

4. Private rules established by a developer for all parcels within the defined subdivision are called _____.

5. The federal government passed the _____ to help prevent fraudulent marketing schemes when land is sold without being seen by purchasers.

6. A _____ permits a prohibited land use to avoid undue hardship.

7. A developer must keep the average number of units in the development at or below the maximum number per acre, which is also called the _____.

8. A _____ allows a nonconforming but related land use.

9. Taking previously undeveloped acreage and splitting it into smaller lots for sale is called _____.

10. Zoning laws that control overcrowding by requiring setbacks or limiting building heights are called _____.

ACTIVITY: CITY ZONING

Answer the following questions based on this city zoning map.

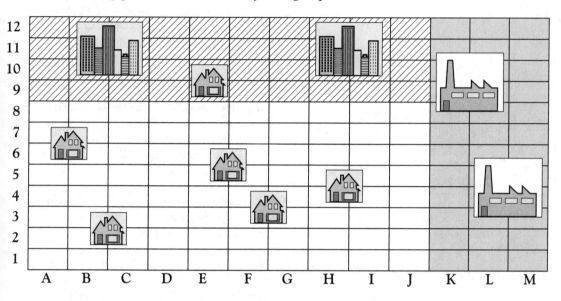

1. What would be necessary before a daycare center could be legally operated in area D5?

2. Where do you think it would be most beneficial for the city to locate a new park as a buffer zone? Why?

3. The city rezones blocks G8 and H8 as a historic district with restrictions on the type of architecture for new buildings. What type of zoning is this?

4. The house at E9 was built prior to the city's zoning ordinance. Why is it permitted to continue being a residence?

5. The city has asked you where to place a new retail and professional services zone, which will take up to six square units on the map. Where would you locate this new zone, and why?

UNIT 20 ANSWERS

MATCHING A

1. **C**

2. **F**

3. **J**

4. **E**

5. **A**

6. **B**

7. **H**

8. **G**

9. **D**

10. **I**

MATCHING B

1. **G**

2. **F**

3. **E**

4. **H**

5. **D**

6. **J**

7. **A**

8. **C**

9. **B**

10. **I**

TRUE OR FALSE

1. **B** The answer is false. A comprehensive plan creates the broad, general framework for a community; zoning ordinances define the details and implement the plan. (388–389)

2. **B** The answer is false. Incentive zoning ensures that certain types of uses are incorporated into developments. (390)

3. **A** The answer is true. Laws governing subdividing and land planning are controlled by state and local governing bodies where the land is located. (393)

4. **A** The answer is true. To protect local taxpayers, many local governments strictly regulate subdivision development and may impose impact fees. (393)

5. **B** The answer is false. A variance provides relief if zoning regulations deprive an owner of the reasonable use of the property. (392)

6. **A** The answer is true. Typically, a zoning permit is required before building permits are issued; the building permit allows municipal officials to be aware of new construction or alterations and can verify compliance with building codes and zoning ordinances. (391)

7. **A** The answer is true. A subdivider is a person who buys undeveloped acreage and divides it into smaller lots. A developer improves the land, constructs homes or other buildings on the lots, and then sells them. (393)

8. **B** The answer is false. A detailed map that illustrates the geographic boundaries of individual lots in a subdivision is called a plat. (394)

9. **B** The answer is false. Laches is the legal principle that a right may be lost through undue delay or failure to assert it. (396)

10. **A** The answer is true. Density zoning ordinances restrict the average maximum number of houses per acre that may be built within a particular subdivision. (395)

11. **B** The answer is false. A restrictive covenant is considered a reasonable, legal restraint if it protects property values and does not restrict the free transfer of property. Restrictive covenants may not be used for illegal purposes, such as for the exclusion of members of certain races, nationalities, or religions. (395)

12. **B** The answer is false. The Interstate Land Sales Full Disclosure Act requires developers of unimproved property offered in interstate commerce by telephone or through the mail to file a disclosure statement with HUD, with certain exceptions. (396)

13. **B** The answer is false. Because the more restrictive requirement takes precedence, the 40-foot setback would be required. Private land-use controls may be more restrictive of an owner's use than the local zoning ordinances. The rule is that the more restrictive of the two takes precedence. (396)

14. **A** The answer is true. A comprehensive plan includes plans for orderly growth, including energy conservation to reduce energy consumption and to promote the use of renewable energy sources. (388–389)

15. **A** The answer is true. Although no nationwide or statewide zoning ordinances exist, the state's enabling acts confer zoning powers to local governments. (388)

MULTIPLE CHOICE

1. **C** The answer is no, under the doctrine of laches, the neighbors probably lost the right to enforce the restriction due to their delay in asserting it. If the neighbors were concerned, they needed to act promptly to enforce the restriction. (396)

2. **D** The answer is an enabling act. Enabling acts permit the state to delegate authority to local officials to enact rules to protect the public's health and safety. (388)

3. **A** The answer is objective for future development of the area. A zoning ordinance might include restrictions for permissible height and style of new construction, style, and appearance of structures, and the maximum allowable ratio of land area to structural area, while objectives for future development of the area might be found in a comprehensive plan. (390)

4. **B** The answer is a detailed map that illustrates the geographic boundaries of individual lots. The plat map shows the lots, blocks, sections, streets, public easements, and monuments in the prospective subdivision. (394)

5. **D** The answer is a variance or zoning change. Because the building does not yet exist, it does not qualify as a nonconforming use; a conditional- use permit is issued for a special use that meets certain standards. A variance, if granted, will permit the company

to use the property in a manner that is otherwise prohibited by the existing zoning. (392)

6. **C** The seek a conditional-use permit from the zoning board, if it is defined as allowable. A conditional-use permit might be granted in this situation if the intended use would not greatly impact the residential nature of the neighborhood. (392)

7. **C** The answer is both a developer and a subdivider. Subdividers buy undeveloped acreage and divide it into smaller lots. A developer improves the land, constructs homes or other buildings, and sells them. Developing is usually more complex than subdividing. (394)

8. **C** The answer is a restriction on the average number of houses per acre. Density zoning ordinances restrict the average maximum number of houses per acre that may be built within a particular subdivision. (395)

9. **A** The answer is hold a public hearing where neighbors may voice their opinions. Both variances and conditional-use permits can only be issued after public hearings. (392)

10. **B** The answer is anticipation pf the future housing needs. The comprehensive plan would seek to anticipate future housing needs. (388)

11. **A** The answer is the company must file a disclosure statement with HUD. The company must file the disclosure statement; the project is being marketed over state lines, it consists of more than 25 lots, and some lots are smaller than 25 acres. (396–397)

12. **D** The answer is racial composition of neighborhood. Zoning may not be used to influence the racial composition of a neighborhood; it must apply in a nondiscriminatory way. (391)

13. **B** The answer is a buffer zone. A buffer zone is a strip of land, such as a park, separating land dedicated to one use (commercial) from land dedicated to another use (residential). (390)

14. **B** The answer is a nonconforming use. Because the store had been there legally before the zoning ordinance, it is permitted to continue operating, usually until its use changes or the building is destroyed. (391)

15. **B** The answer is certificate of occupancy. Once the completed building has been inspected and found to comply with the building codes, the municipal inspector issues a certificate of occupancy or occupancy permit. (393)

FILL-IN-THE-BLANK

1.   Land is partitioned according to its use into zones.

2.   Zoning laws that specify certain types of architecture for all new construction are called aesthetic zoning ordinances.

3.   Along with an application for subdivision approval, a developer often must submit an environmental impact report to explain what effect the proposed development will have on the surrounding area.

4.   Private rules set up by a developer for all parcels within the defined subdivision are called covenants, conditions, and restrictions (CC&Rs).

5.   The federal government passed the Interstate Land Sales Full Disclosure Act to help prevent fraudulent marketing schemes when land is sold without being seen by purchasers.

6.   A variance permits a prohibited land use to avoid undue hardship.

7.   A developer must keep the average number of units in the development at or below the maximum number per acre, which is also called the gross density.

8.   A conditional-use permit (CUP) allows a nonconforming but related land use.

9.   Taking previously undeveloped acreage and splitting it into smaller lots for sale is called subdivision.

10.   Zoning laws that control overcrowding by requiring setbacks or limiting building heights are called bulk zoning ordinances.

ACTIVITY: CITY ZONING

1.   The daycare center needs a conditional-use permit to legally operate in D5.

2.   The most beneficial spot would be J1 through J8; a park would serve the residential neighborhoods and provide a buffer between the residential and industrial zones.

3.   Rezoning as a historic district is aesthetic zoning.

4.   The house is a nonconforming use. It was most likely grandfathered in.

5.   One possible location would be the square bounded by J6, I6, I8, and J8. This location would provide retail services near the residential neighborhood and professional services near the commercial zone, and it would not be disruptive to the industrial zone. Other possibilities include A8 through F8, or six units between J1 and J8 as a buffer. It would probably not be wise to place the new zone in the center of the residential area (due to traffic and noise) or in the industrial zone (it could present hazards to shoppers).

UNIT 21

Environmental Issues and the Real Estate Transaction

LEARNING OBJECTIVES

When you have completed this unit, you will be able to

> **identify** the basic environmental hazards the real estate professional should be aware of for the protection of client interests as well as the personal risk of liability for nondisclosure;

> **describe** groundwater, water table, and the provisions of the Safe Drinking Water Act;

> **describe** the issues involved with underground storage tanks, and the associated legal requirements facing the property owner;

> **explain** the regulation involved in the creation and operation of waste disposal sites and in the control of brownfields;

> **list** the various federal laws which protect the public from uncontrolled hazardous waste, and the liability issues facing those who violate any of these laws; and

> **explain** the responsibilities and duties of real estate professionals regarding environmental issues.

KEY TERMS

asbestos
brownfields
carbon monoxide (CO)
chlorofluorocarbons (CFCs)
Comprehensive Environmental Response, Compensation, and Liability Act (CERCLA)
encapsulation
environmental impact statement (EIS)

environmental site assessment (ESA)
formaldehyde
groundwater
hydraulic fracturing (fracking)
lead
Lead-Based Paint Hazard Reduction Act (LBPHRA)
mold
polychlorinated biphenyls (PCBs)
radon

Small Business Liability Relief and Brownfields Revitalization Act
Superfund Amendments and Reauthorization Act (SARA)
underground storage tanks (USTs)
urea-formaldehyde foam insulation (UFFI)
water table
wetlands

MATCHING

Write the letter of the matching term on the appropriate line.

A. urea formaldehyde

B. hydraulic fracturing

C. encapsulation

D. capping

E. landfill

F. Superfund

G. radon

H. lead

I. asbestos

J. water table

1. ___ A highly friable mineral commonly used as insulation prior to being banned from use in construction in 1978

2. ___ The process of sealing off disintegrating asbestos and chipped or peeling lead-based paint without removing it

3. ___ A material once used in paint that can cause serious brain and nervous system damage

4. ___ A radioactive gas produced by the natural decay of other radioactive substances

5. ___ Chemical used in foam insulation and certain wood products that can release harmful gases

6. ___ The process used to extract natural gas from the layers of rock in which it is embedded

7. ___ The natural level at which the ground is saturated

8. ___ A site for the burial of waste

9. ___ The process of covering a solid waste site with topsoil and plants

10. ___ Money set aside by the Comprehensive Environmental Response, Compensation, and Liability Act to pay for the cleanup of uncontrolled hazardous waste sites and spills

TRUE OR FALSE

Circle the correct answer.

1. The Environmental Protection Agency estimates that approximately 4 million commercial and public buildings contain asbestos insulation.
   A. True
   B. False

2. Asbestos removal is a relatively simple, inexpensive process that can be performed by a layperson.
   A. True
   B. False

3. Under the 1996 final regulations published by the Environmental Protection Agency, owners of homes built prior to 1978 are required to test their properties for the presence of lead-based paint.
   A. True
   B. False

4. Radon is a naturally occurring substance that is suspected of being a cause of lung cancer.
   A. True
   B. False

5. Urea-formaldehyde foam insulation can release harmful gases.
   A. True
   B. False

6. Asbestos-based products have been proven harmless.
   A. True
   B. False

7. Groundwater is water that lies on the earth's surface.
   A. True
   B. False

8. Federal regulations on underground storage tanks do not apply to tanks used to collect storm water or wastewater.
   A. True
   B. False

9. The process of laying two to four feet of soil over the top of a landfill site and then planting foliage to prevent erosion is called layering.
   A. True
   B. False

10. The Superfund Amendments and Reauthorization Act created an "innocent owner" immunity status.
    A. True
    B. False

11. Asbestos is most harmful when it is disturbed or exposed.
    A. True
    B. False

12. Radon gas mitigation consists of installing a minimum of R16-rated insulation in walls and attic spaces.
    A. True
    B. False

13. In homes, the most-likely sources of formaldehyde emissions are pressed wood products, such as particleboard.
    A. True
    B. False

14. Homeowners with private wells have little worry about contamination because well water is drawn from far beneath the ground.
    A. True
    B. False

15. Possible causes of mold problems can be roof leaks, unvented combustion appliances, and gutters that direct water to the building.
    A. True
    B. False

16. Strict liability under the Superfund means that the owner is responsible to the injured party without excuse.
    A. True
    B. False

17. Today, real estate professionals can feel secure that seller-supplied disclosure forms result in accurate and complete disclosure of environmental issues.
    A. True
    B. False

18. Federal requirements for disclosure of mold contamination in homes are contained in the Home Mold Disclosure Act.
    A. True
    B. False

19. Because CFCs are nontoxic and nonflammable, they are easily and safely disposed of by homeowners.
    A. True
    B. False

20. To protect against liability due to mold contamination, real estate professionals should ask sellers about leaks, flooding, and prior damage.
    A. True
    B. False

MULTIPLE CHOICE

Circle the correct answer.

1. Individuals have suffered all of these health problems due to exposure to formaldehyde *EXCEPT*
   A. asthma.
   B. eye irritations.
   C. mold infections.
   D. a burning sensation in the throat.

2. Lead is commonly found in all of these *EXCEPT*
   A. soldered water pipes.
   B. alkyd oil-based paint.
   C. soil around industrial sites.
   D. insulating material.

3. A seller accepts an offer on her home, which was built in 1892. Which of these statements about lead-based paint is *FALSE*?
   A. The seller must attach a lead-based paint disclosure statement to the sales contract.
   B. If the seller is aware of any lead-based paint on the premises, she must disclose that fact to the buyer.
   C. If the buyer requests a lead-based paint inspection, the seller has ten days in which to obtain one at her own expense.
   D. The buyer is entitled to receive a pamphlet that describes the hazards posed by lead-based paint.

4. Where in the United States does radon occur?
   A. Mostly in the western states
   B. Mostly in the warm southern and southwestern regions
   C. In every state in the United States
   D. Only in large urban areas

5. Which of these has been proven to pose a health hazard?
   A. Asbestos
   B. Lead-based paint
   C. Radon
   D. All of these

6. H stores toxic chemical waste in a large steel tank that has only 15% of its volume underground. J lives in the wilderness and has a gas pump connected to a 1,500-gallon tank of gasoline buried ten feet underground near the garage. L keeps three large tanks filled with formaldehyde and battery acid in the basement. Which of these property owners are covered by federal regulations regarding USTs?
   A. H and L
   B. H and J
   C. L only
   D. J only

7. Which of these is responsible for administering the Superfund?
   A. EPA
   B. PRP
   C. CERCLA
   D. HUD

8. Which of these would disqualify someone from claiming innocent landowner immunity under the Superfund Amendments and Reauthorization Act (SARA)?
   A. The pollution was caused by a third party.
   B. The owner exercised due care when the property was purchased.
   C. The owner had only constructive knowledge of the damage.
   D. The owner took reasonable precautions in the exercise of ownership rights.

9. If a potentially responsible party (PRP) refuses to pay the expenses of cleaning up a toxic site, the EPA may
   A. bring a criminal action and have the PRP jailed for up to 10 years.
   B. bring a civil action and be awarded three times the actual cost of the cleanup.
   C. bring an administrative action and be awarded the actual cost of the cleanup, plus court costs.
   D. have no legal recourse.

10. Sealing off asbestos instead of removing it is called
    A. encapsulation.
    B. capping.
    C. irresponsible remediation.
    D. extended liability.

11. Lead-based paint is found in about 75% of all private housing built before
    A. 1978.
    B. 1985.
    C. 1992.
    D. 1996.

12. Which of these is the byproduct of fuel combustion that may result in death if such equipment is not properly vented?
    A. Radon
    B. Lead
    C. Urea-formaldehyde foam insulation
    D. Carbon monoxide

13. At least how much of a tank must be underground for it to be considered an underground storage tank?
    A. 10%
    B. 15%
    C. 25%
    D. 35%

14. How can property owners help avoid carbon monoxide exposure?
    A. Have fuel-burning heating systems checked and maintained annually
    B. Have their basements tested for carbon monoxide seeping in from the soil
    C. Encapsulate sources of carbon monoxide emissions
    D. Install attic vents

15. Which of these is a source of polychlorinated biphenyls (PCBs)?
    A. Plywood and particle board
    B. Small home appliances, such as hair dryers or food processors
    C. Caulking compounds
    D. Computers

16. Why is mold a serious environmental problem in buildings?
    A. It causes stains and a fuzzy growth on walls.
    B. It destroys material it grows on and causes health problems for occupants.
    C. It has an unpleasant odor.
    D. It produces spores that can spoil food.

17. What is the purpose of the Brownfields Law enacted in 2002?
    A. It restores wilderness and agricultural areas damaged by toxic waste.
    B. It is specifically dedicated to cleaning up PCB spills and dumps.
    C. It establishes incinerators to destroy UFFI, DDT, and other persistent chemicals.
    D. It distributes funds to clean up polluted industrial sites so they can be restored to productive use.

18. What causes mold problems in buildings?
    A. Insects
    B. Chronic moisture problems
    C. Fiberglass building materials
    D. Air pollution